My Darkest Years

My Darkest Years

*Memoirs of a Survivor
of Auschwitz, Warsaw
and Dachau*

JAMES BACHNER

McFarland & Company, Inc., Publishers
Jefferson, North Carolina, and London

LIBRARY OF CONGRESS CATALOGUING-IN-PUBLICATION DATA

Bachner, James, 1922–
    My darkest years : memoirs of a survivor of
Auschwitz, Warsaw and Dachau / James Bachner.
        p.   cm.
    Includes index.

    ISBN-13: 978-0-7864-2962-2
    (softcover : 50# alkaline paper) ∞

    1. Bachner, James, 1922–   2. Jews — Germany — Berlin —
Biography.   3. Jewish children in the Holocaust — Germany —
Berlin — Biography.   4. Holocaust, Jewish (1939–1945) — Personal
narratives.   5. Berlin (Germany) — Biography.   I. Title.
    DS134.42.B33A3   2007
    940.53'18092 — dc22   2007010954
[B]

British Library cataloguing data are available

Cover photograph ©2006 Flat Earth Photos

Manufactured in the United States of America

McFarland & Company, Inc., Publishers
  Box 611, Jefferson, North Carolina 28640
    www.mcfarlandpub.com

Table of Contents

I dedicate this book of memories to Marilyn,
my wonderful wife and life's companion.

*Her love and inspiration gave me the courage
to put the story of my darkest years on paper.
Lovingly, she spent countless hours
correcting my mistakes, again and again,
until we completed this seemingly endless task.*

Preface

The idea of writing my life story began like a tap on the windowpane. After fifty-five years, the idea became a pounding on my door that had to be answered. The time had finally come for me to share my experiences with my family and many friends.

I am not trying to analyze or find the reasons for the Holocaust. Historians are far better qualified to bring us answers to the countless questions the Holocaust has raised.

This is my story. It begins in the early 1920s in Berlin when Nazism first raised its ugly head. It tells of my happy childhood filled with love and comfort and the changes brought about under Nazi restrictions. It recalls my being a refugee in Poland and my confinement in concentration camps where cruelty, torture, and death were my daily companions. Those were the most awful years of my life, but miraculously I survived them.

I needed years to complete this project as it opened wounds that I thought had healed long ago. I would like to thank my wife Marilyn, for her love and understanding which brought me happiness and sunshine, and removed some of the shadows of my nightmares.

With love and admiration I give honor to the memory of my beloved mother, and members of our family and friends who perished during the Holocaust.

I further dedicate these pages to our son Evan and his lovely wife Lisa, who has been like a daughter to us, our son Robert and his wife Connie, our grandsons Joshua and Stephen, and our granddaughters Allison, Emily and Jessica.

Preface

I hope that my experiences will strengthen the resolve of future generations to practice and promote tolerance and understanding toward all people. We must do all we can to prevent another Holocaust from ever happening again.

Introduction

At the end of World War I, in 1918, Germany experienced an enormous political upheaval. The Kaiser and his dreams of conquest were in ruin. To save his life, the Kaiser fled to neutral Holland. He left behind a country politically divided, economically devastated, and burdened by demands for reparations from the Allied victors. The after-effects of this war, and the resulting inflation, eroded monetary values to the point where trillion mark banknotes were almost worthless. An item purchased on one day could not be had for the same sum of money on the following day. Jobs were very hard to find and the morale of the German people was very low. The newly formed Weimar republic, named after the city in Germany where the meeting to establish it was held, had to deal with the formidable task of bringing prosperity and normalcy to a war-ravaged country. A number of political parties, ranging from the extreme right to the far left, fought for power and acceptance. One election followed another but none produced a clear majority for any party. Coalitions were organized, and there were many such coalitions, but in spite of all good intentions, they fell apart as rapidly as they were formed.

Among the disillusioned and unemployed was a house painter and former army sergeant named Adolf Hitler. He surrounded himself with people who, like himself, were unhappy and in search of someone to blame. Hitler developed a style of public speaking which mesmerized audiences. His ideas attracted many followers including former jail inmates and others of questionable repute. They found courage in each other and organized themselves into a political party known as the Nationale Sozialistische

Introduction

Deutsche Arbeiter Partei (National Socialists German Workers Party), Nazi, for short. "Die Juden sind unser Unglück" (Jews are our misfortune) was Hitler's theme. "Hate and punish the Jews," he proclaimed. "They are behind the international conspiracy to destroy Germany. Jewish financiers control the International Press, the Communists, the United States of America, England, and France!" He repeated these rantings over and over again, and his message was readily accepted by the poor and unemployed masses. Forgotten were the ruinous policies of the Kaiser which led to World War I, the real reasons behind Germany's difficulties. Blaming Jews for all the problems in the world was nothing new in Europe. Throughout history Jews have been falsely accused, segregated, tortured and killed. Hitler used his own distortions to feed the flames of anti–Semitism which prevailed in Europe. With daily attacks against Jews and political opponents, the Nazis made front page news on a regular basis.

Fewer than 550,000 Jews lived in the midst of 63,000,000 Germans at that time. Even though there was a *Numerous Clausus* (quota system) in place at German universities, many German Jews attained prominence in business, education, the arts, medicine, and other sciences. Their achievements and contributions to the culture of Germany far outweighed their numbers.

Nazis — *SA* men in brown and SS men, the elite troupe, in black uniforms — congregated in *Bierhalls* (bars) and created constant disturbances on peaceful neighborhood streets. Their uniforms were highly visible and forbidding. Always in groups, they stood with collection boxes in their hands calling for donations to build, "die Einbahn Strasse nach Jerusalem" (the one-way street to Jerusalem). Forcefully they pressured passers-by to donate money; not placing a coin in their collection box was a sure way to start a fight.

In earlier national elections, Nazis were never more than just a small minority and no one ever believed that they would become a major factor in German politics. But continuing poverty and the inability of the parties to find a positive solution created a perfect opportunity for the Nazis to succeed. Their propaganda filled with lies and deceptions took hold. Their smear campaigns, as ridiculous as they were, were repeated again and again to the point where people began to believe them. Hitler's party grew in size and strength and in time attracted major industrialists who recognized the potential for their own benefit. If Hitler could resurrect Germany's military power, they would be able to restart their dormant steel and war machinery plants. These industrialists pressured the aging president, General Paul von Hindenburg, to appoint Hitler as the new *Reichskanzler* and form a new German government.

The date was January 30, 1933, a date never to be forgotten. The Jewish community, like the majority of Germans, was shocked by this development. Still, people familiar with politics counseled not to worry. They said like all other governments before the Nazi regime, they too would fail to get the country back on its feet. They estimated that the Nazi government would last a few days, maybe a few weeks at most ... it lasted twelve years.

1
Childhood

On the dresser in my room stood two photographs of similar size, each framed beautifully in fruitwood. One of them showed my parents holding me, their firstborn, with smiles and sparkle in their eyes, a scene of perfect happiness. The other photo was my baby picture, resting on my stomach, on top of a bear rug, my head raised high and my face beaming with joy. And why not? I was blessed with loving parents and a wonderful family. I have many fond memories of my early years. Unfortunately, those pictures and many other mementos of happy days were destroyed and are gone forever. Although I can't share them with anyone now, in my mind they live on and on.

I was born in Berlin in 1922 during the unsettled times after the end of World War I. My father was a manufacturer of men's clothing and our family lived a very comfortable lifestyle. Our eight-room apartment was huge and occupied the entire third floor of 30 Kaiser Wilhelm Strasse, a street which extended into the famous Boulevard unter den Linden. High ceilings, large windows, and a spacious corridor connected all the rooms. It was so huge that on bad weather days my friends and I would use our corridor to play ball. Of course we had to move some furniture and protect the mirrors before we played. The real problem was keeping our volume down so the adults would not be disturbed by whatever sounds could penetrate our heavy doors.

From our balcony we had a beautiful view of the Rathaus Tower, the famous Berlin City Hall. Looking to our left we saw the Bülow Platz, an area of great significance in the life of Berlin in the 1920s and 1930s.

It was here that many political parties assembled for marches either to celebrate or protest. Brass bands and singing masses marched past our windows on their way to the Lustgarten. There, on one side of the park, loomed the Alte Museum with its many steps leading to the building, providing a perfect backdrop for political rallies. Speakers used the top of the stairs to address thousands of marchers who had gathered in front of them.

Facing the museum was the Kaiser's Palace with a balcony used by the Kaiser to greet the people gathered below in the park. Incidentally, this balcony has a special place in the history of our family before I was born. After World War I, during the time of extreme instability, this platform was used by newly elected governments to address the masses. Politicians made promises that could not be kept and the ruling party of the day was quickly voted out of office. Papa, a member of the Social Democratic Party, accepted an appointment as police commissioner of Berlin during one of those very short-lived administrations. He, too, used the kaiser's balcony to speak to the assembled Berliners. During the upheaval and takeover by a new party, Papa nearly lost his life. I vividly remember my mother telling me every detail of this dreadful episode when I was old enough to understand a little bit about politics.

One day, not yet of school age, I stood in our pantry with Mutti, as I affectionately called my mother. I asked her why our pantry was so different than those I had seen in the homes of relatives and friends. Our pantry was wallpapered with bank notes. Real money, in denominations of one hundred thousand marks and some with even more zeros after the first number. Innocently, I asked Mutti, "Why don't you keep the money in the bank?" She explained to me that those banknotes were worthless leftovers from an inflation that was out of control. Continuing to explain the meaning of inflation to me, she pointed to her piano standing in our living room. "You see," she said, "Papa was negotiating the purchase of an apartment house with the money he had saved. Day by day the purchasing power of our money decreased, and by the time negotiations were completed, the only thing his money could buy was this piano. Now that the banknotes you saw in the pantry were without value, we decided to put them to some use and decorate the walls with them."

Opposite: **My parents' wedding picture. Berlin, September 1920.**

My Darkest Years

My father was always impeccably groomed, a respected businessman, and well versed in politics. My beautiful mother was loving and caring and enjoyed having an open house for friends and family. Although I was the oldest, I was not the first born. My parents explained to me that there was a little girl ahead of me who unfortunately was stillborn. I can't help wondering what life would have been like with an older sister around. I think I would have loved it. In retrospect, I know that she was certainly spared a lot of pain and hardship.

Dr. Sadger was the dear friend of the family who delivered me into this world. A little more than three years later, he again assisted my mother in giving birth to my brother. Fred arrived on Yom Kippur eve, just as everyone was getting ready to go to synagogue for Kol Nidre services. I was so little, yet I still remember the excitement in our apartment. I could hardly wait to see my new brother, but I was made to wait for what seemed an eternity before I could see both Mutti and baby Fred. I recall being told that the delay was caused by the stork who had been waiting outside the window until someone had noticed him. It was only then that he could come inside and make his delivery. It's remarkable how things have changed. I wouldn't dare tell such fairy tales to my own grandchildren.

Our lives revolved around our family and friends who lived in our neighborhood. Opa and Oma, my grandparents, had an apartment only a short bus ride away, but many times when Opa came to take me to his home, we walked the entire distance. He thought it was much quicker to walk than wait for a bus. Quite often I slept at their home over the weekend and on Friday evenings we would go to his synagogue, sometimes on Saturday mornings, too. I had finished nursery school at the age of five and had just started Hebrew lessons. Opa was so pleased when I began to recognize the Hebrew letters and took special delight in pointing to each word in the prayer book so I could follow the cantor's chanting. I can still picture his smiling face when he used his grandfatherly bragging rights to show me off to his friends.

When I stayed with Oma and Opa, Gretchen, our maid, took care of my little brother so my parents were free to visit and enjoy an evening with their friends. They loved the theater, opera, and other cultural activities. Berlin was a center of culture in Europe and in fierce competition with Paris for the number one spot. There was always so much to see and do. While broad masses had a difficult time making ends meet, the more fortunate people filled the cabarets to the last seat for entertainment. It was the time when Lehar's operettas took Berlin by storm. Tenor Richard Tauber and soprano Fritzi Massary were the darlings of Berlin's society. The many cabarets presented humor and satire that was unique, mirroring Germany's society and its problems. Though I was much too young to attend any of these places, I was old enough to be told that there was a lot of truth behind the clever jokes of the comics.

Our Sabbath meal was always something very special either at home or in my grandparents' apartment. I still can picture the warmth and comfort of sitting together around the table and eating the delicious food that was served. Invariably, even if well stuffed, I was told not to waste any food because so many poor children in the world had nothing to eat. After our meal, Opa would take me into the living room to rest and talk. I loved to hear Opa's experiences during World War I. He was a sergeant in the Austrian army and was captured by the Russians during combat. He told me of the hardships he had endured when imprisoned in Siberia and how bitterly cold it had been. The conditions for work and sleep were unbearable and many people actually froze to death. For me, the most exciting part of his story was when he told me how he had managed to hide in a railroad car and escape from Siberia. When he came to farmhouses, he pretended to be deaf and dumb because he didn't know the Russian language, and speaking German would have been disastrous in enemy territory. He walked from one isolated farm to another, worked for a few days at a time, and eventually made his way back to Berlin. It was a huge journey which took him more than a year. Oma completed the tale by describing the surprise the family had one day when the door bell rang and Opa stood in front of them. The shock was incredible, as Opa had been listed as missing in action and presumed dead.

My father's business was located fairly close to our apartment and he routinely came home for our main meal of the day. The telephone had just become popular and our home was one of the first to have this new marvel. Every day Gretchen let me climb onto a chair to reach the phone and help me call Papa. She needed to know when Papa would be home so she could be ready to serve our meal. I simply lifted the receiver and had the immediate attention of the operator at the exchange. Giving her the five-digit number was enough to get Papa on the line. The operator even recognized my voice after a while and always had a nice word for me.

My Darkest Years

I recall many other things that were so different from the way we live today. Evenings, at dusk, a man would come down the street carrying a long pole. He stopped at every lantern on his way and turned on the gaslight. In the morning, I would see him again as he turned the lights off. Our apartment also had gaslight fixtures when I was young, but converted to electricity as soon as it was available. It is truly amazing how much progress was made in the twentieth century. I especially remember the wonderful times my family enjoyed together in Berlin. Sundays we would start the day with a late breakfast in the dining room, a little formal perhaps, but fun nonetheless. Then, providing the weather was pleasant, Papa would call for a *Droschke* (taxied horse and buggy) to take us for a ride in the park. We would drive down Unter den Linden, through the Brandenburg Gate and into the Tiergarten (a huge park in the heart of the city), and along the way we would greet friends who traveled leisurely on a similar route. After spending time in the park with our relatives or friends, we would end our day with a snack at the Konditorei Dobrin. My favorite treat was *Apfelkuchen mit Schlagsahne* (apple cake with whipped cream).

Many times the tranquil streets were disturbed by groups of congregating Communists or Nazis. They roamed about shouting their slogans, soliciting donations, or vying for votes for the next election. Wherever they met, they were immediately embroiled in a commotion. Other than anti–Semitic slogans shouted by the Nazis, there was little difference between Communists and Nazis although they represented the extreme opposites of the political scene. Many onlookers were sympathetic and offered encouragement to one group or the other. Some simply commented that those hoodlums should be in prison. Anyway, it was always wise for us to get out of their way when we saw them gathering.

I was six years old, in 1928, when my parents enrolled me in the elementary school operated by the Jewish community of Berlin. My first day in class was very special for me and I felt so grown up. I thought class was fun, but what I really looked forward to was the treat that awaited me after school. The moment I walked through the gate I spotted Mutti, and like all the other mothers she carried a *Zuckertüte* (a cone-shaped colorful container, much like the horn of plenty, filled with lots of candies and toys). It was customary that after the first day of classes, parents brought their children goodies to show that education had its sweet rewards.

1— *Childhood*

Once I had conquered my ABC's, my parents started me reading the daily newspaper delivered to our home. Most of what I read was beyond my comprehension, but it was good exercise anyway. As I got older, in the evenings, Papa would explain some of the things I had read about. He knew a lot about politics, and spoke to me about the various parties and their programs to revitalize Germany.

One by one, my classmates joined the Jewish sports club Maccabi, and so did I. Soccer and track and field competitions were my favorites. My father, no athlete himself because of physical problems, encouraged me to participate in these activities. I enjoyed the time I spent in the gym or at the sports field, but my parents never failed to caution me not to neglect my schoolwork if I wanted to be accepted into a school of higher learning. Universities enforced a quota system and only a small number of bright Jewish students were allowed to attend classes. Being accepted to a good school was what they both wanted for me, and at the end of my four years in elementary school, they had me apply to the nine-year program at the gymnasium (a German secondary school) in our neighborhood. I was proud as could be when my letter of acceptance finally arrived. My parents and grandparents were thrilled as well. If I would have asked them for the moon, they would have tried to get it for me. However, I had only one simple request; I wanted the official school cap showing the colors of my gymnasium. Not wasting any time, Mutti went with me that same afternoon to buy my cap. After that day, I never left the house without wearing it. It was only a cap, but it created a bond among the students and was a sign of being accepted. There were a few Jewish and Catholic students in my class, but the majority were Protestant. Regardless of our religious background, we still shared a common pride and became good friends. We would study, play soccer, and laugh at our jokes and pranks together.

Among my parents' friends there was constant talk about the political uncertainty and lack of direction in Germany. There were no less than twenty-seven active political parties, I was told, all of them were fighting with each other. They each claimed to have the formula for bringing back prosperity to Germany. From 1919 to 1933, a period of fourteen years, countless governments tried to restore stability to the country and failed. The aging President Hindenburg had grown weary of this situation and on January 30, 1933, he appointed Hitler to be the new *Reichskanzler*.

Everyone was taken by surprise, especially since the Nazi party had never received a majority of votes. People commented that whatever numbers the Nazis lacked in votes, they made up for with street fights and demonstrations. After the initial shock faded, people reasoned that Hitler's government would quickly fail, too. This time they were wrong. The ink on the newspaper headlines had hardly dried when changes in our lives could already be seen and felt.

I was halfway into my second year at the gymnasium when Hitler became Germany's *Reichskanzler.* The friendly atmosphere in our classes changed overnight as one by one my classmates joined the Hitler Youth organization. Following their Nazi indoctrination, they made it very unpleasant for Jewish boys to be with them. It was painful to be shunned by former friends, but my fellow Jewish students and I knew the importance of our education and tried to make the best of a bad situation. Our teacher, Dr. Blaese, started wearing his Nazi party emblem openly in his lapel, but his attitude toward all the boys did not change. He was one of the few who made no distinction between Jewish students and all others.

Soon after Hitler came to power, a countrywide boycott against Jewish businesses was organized. In full Nazi regalia, SA men (short for *Sturm Abteilung, assault unit*) posted themselves in front of targeted stores and prevented anyone from entering. They would shove and beat those who tried to defy them. The smallest neighborhood shops suffered as much as the giant department stores of Herman Tietz and Wertheimer. All the stores were badly defiled with Nazi slogans painted across the store windows. Slogans like "Kauft nicht bei Juden" (Don't buy from Jews) and "Wer beim Juden kauft ist ein Verräter" (Whoever buys from Jews is a traitor) appeared often. Pictures of these actions appeared in the foreign press but had little effect. The German press was totally under Nazi control and all news items reflected only Nazi policy. The one place to get objective opinions was in international newspapers available for patrons in coffeehouses. Papa's favorite place was the famous Kaffee Kranzler, where he would meet his friends and talk. They read and discussed the items of interest as they appeared to the people living in other countries. This of course was on days when the Nazis failed to confiscate the papers. The international press reported the shocking boycott in great detail and condemned the Nazi action. For a while, this seemed to slow Nazi activities and we resumed a somewhat normal life. Still, even walking down the street stirred some fear in all of us. The Jewish people had simply become fair game for harassment and threats wherever we went. We were made to feel like thieves, just because we were Jewish. It felt strange walking along the street and hoping that no one would recognize us. Germany always had some anti–Semitism, as did other European countries, but this was different and alarming.

The bloody pogroms of Czarist Russia and Poland were things of the past, or so we believed. This was the twentieth century in Germany. Germans were a cultured people who had always held intelligence and civility in high regard. At first, name-calling and fighting were seen as election propaganda, but when many Germans started accepting Nazi lies and supporting Hitler, it became serious. Nazi slogans like "Juden Raus" (Jews get out) or "Wir bauen die Einbahnstrasse nach Jerusalem" (We are building the one-way street to Jerusalem) and similar expressions were everywhere. As far back as I can remember, there was always some political discussion in our home, but with Hitler's rise to power, politics became the most important topic of conversation. Our family and friends carefully scrutinized Hitler's programs and discussed how they would affect us. If the people of the world had actually read Hitler's *Mein Kampf,* they certainly would have understood the Nazi agenda. Everyone believed that the Western powers would exercise their strength and put a halt to Hitler's schemes. After all, it wasn't just the Jewish issue that was of concern, it was the entire treaty of Versailles which Hitler repudiated.

Starting with their first day in office, the Nazis were well organized. Swiftly, they eliminated the opposition and arrested their leaders, placing them in hastily built concentration camps. Sachsenhausen, near Berlin, and Dachau, near Munich, were among the first camps in operation. From the beginning, there were rumors that inmates in these camps were tortured and later they were proven to be true. Some of Papa's friends knew of families who received urns containing the ashes of their loved ones. Notes usually accompanied the urns with an explanation that the individual had suffered a heart attack, died, and was cremated. No one thought it possible that so many healthy, able-bodied men could die so suddenly and of the same cause. There was no recourse and nothing the families could do. Adding insult to injury, a charge was levied on the family for the cremation. Before long, the existence of such camps was known to all and served to intimidate the public into submission.

One day, on my way home from school for lunch, I turned the corner into our street and saw it crowded with uniformed SA men. Occasionally, I had witnessed the vandalism they were capable of, but in the company of my parents I felt safe. Now I was alone and very frightened. I saw them painting Stars of David on Seidman's leather goods store while others were yelling, "Juden raus," or "Kauft nicht bei Juden" (Jews get out, — don't buy from Jews). Two of the brown-shirted thugs were beating a man in front of the store who had chosen to ignore these hoodlums and tried to enter. Policemen were nearby, but our guardians of the law deliberately looked the other way. Some passers-by even offered encouragement to the SA men while others rushed past the ugly scene, shaking their heads in silent disapproval. What a relief it was for me when I finally reached the safety of my home.

In the spring of 1933 our class went on our annual outing, and some of the boys wore the Hitler Jugend (Hitler youth) uniform and brought with them a Nazi flag. We, the Jewish students, were very uncomfortable and commented about our feelings to Dr. Blaese. "Don't worry," he said, "the party will soon change their attitude toward Jews and you will be treated no different from the rest of us." It was customary to take a class picture on these trips, but now the Nazi flag was center stage and all the students were told to encircle the flag. My parents were very disturbed when they saw the photo of me standing together with happy Hitler Youth in uniform.

My friendship with Hans-Heinz, one of my closer friends in class had cooled. We lived across the street from each other and often did our homework together. Once I asked him why he had changed so toward me, and he answered that his parents preferred that we didn't see each other anymore. "Why?" I asked. "You are Jewish," he replied, "and Jews and Gypsies are all cheats." I told him that he was being fooled by Nazi propaganda but he maintained that he couldn't be around Jews and that was final. I was hurt, but I had to accept the situation. All my Jewish classmates had similar experiences and we consoled each other with comments heard at home. "The Nazis can't last much longer."

As I was coming home from gymnasium one day, I spotted some uniformed SA men standing in our lobby. They looked at me but let me pass without incident. Impatiently, I waited for the elevator to take me to the third floor. When I entered our apartment I saw Mutti with fear written on her face. I knew that something was dreadfully wrong. Mutti told me that Gretchen had answered the doorbell a half hour earlier and three SA men had pushed her out of the way. They came in looking for Papa but somehow Gretchen was able to make them leave when they saw that Papa was not home. It was obvious that those SA men I had seen must have decided to wait for Papa in the lobby of our building. Mutti was frightened and called Papa at the office. He told her not to worry because he could get help from Mrs. Metner, one of his trusted employees. She was outraged at the vandalism occurring in the streets of Berlin and found it hard to believe that Germans, a sophisticated and cultured people, could behave like that. She got in touch with her husband, a party member, and persuaded him to bring some friends in full uniform to escort Papa home. Eventually, Papa and his escorts arrived and were followed closely by the waiting SA men. It turned out that one of them had worked for Papa, had been fired for incompetence, and now came seeking revenge. Harsh words were spoken at first, but soon things quieted down. With handshakes and clinking of glasses filled with schnapps, a bad situation was averted. Still, life as we had known it — our freedom, happiness, and comfort — were suddenly gone.

This episode left us all unnerved, yet we could do nothing to prevent these things from happening again. No longer did we have the police to protect us as they had orders to ignore complaints made against any Nazi. Almost overnight it seemed that the Nazis had gained control over our lives. It took Papa time to recover from the shock and he stayed home for days while his experienced employees ran the business. Though I was still a youngster, that scene had a marked effect on me, too. It was thoroughly discussed by family and friends and everyone agreed that it was best for all of us to keep a low profile and limit our outside activities.

Economic conditions were so bad that the Nazis were able to capitalize on this difficult situation. To obtain a better job or a higher rank within the party, some people thought nothing of denouncing a neighbor, friend, or relative. There were brothers who denounced brothers. Even children were known to have denounced their parents for personal gain. The fear of being arrested and imprisoned in concentration camps was reason enough for many Germans to fall in line with Nazi policies. More and more stores, restaurants, movie houses, and other places of entertainment started displaying signs at their entrance doors that read, "Juden und

Hunden ist der Zutritt nicht gestattet" (Off limits to Jews and dogs). Other signs used different words but the message was the same. Some Germans did feel embarrassed when they had to exclude their Jewish friends or business associates from their lives and would apologize to them in private and explain the need to cooperate with the regime for their own protection. "Please bear with us," they said. "Just be patient and understand that Hitler and his policies won't last much longer." Papa, Mutti, Fred and I dressed and looked like everyone around us. We spoke like real Berliners, which we were, and blended easily into our surroundings. Occasionally we even dared to take chances and travel out of our neighborhood for a movie or to a coffeehouse. Even though we believed that no one would recognize us as being Jewish, we were never at ease. Our lifestyle had changed drastically in such a short time. No more Sunday morning rides through the Tiergarten or public outings. Everything we did was geared to a low profile and keeping out of sight.

Papa's cousin Herman Wellner, his wife Mali, and their two daughters, Edith and Ilse, lived down the street from us. Our families were close friends and the girls were close in age to Fred and me. Uncle Herman and Aunt Mali, as I respectfully called them, had a very successful fur manufacturing business which required much traveling, buying raw pelts and selling their products. During one of these trips in 1934, the girls, Edith and Ilse, went with them to enjoy a short vacation in Switzerland. Routinely, Uncle called his office, and was told by his manager that a Nazi official had come to announce that a *Treuhänder* (trustee) would soon be in control of the business. Not wasting any time, Uncle Herman made immediate preparations to relocate the entire business to Amsterdam. Aunt Mali went back into Germany, and over a holiday weekend, she was able to load the factory, literally everything they owned, into railroad cars and ship it all to Amsterdam. What a surprise for the Treuhänder when he came to claim his business. This bold action made the headlines. The Wellners were wanted by the Gestapo and anyone able to provide information about them was to be rewarded. It wasn't an easy task for Aunt and Uncle to restart their business in Holland. They had little knowledge of the language and customs, but with the help of the wonderful Dutch people they became successful again.

As the Nazis became more and more confident in their positions, they issued all kinds of restrictions. One of them concerned Jewish immigrants from Eastern Europe who settled in Germany before, during, or after World War I. They were stripped of their German citizenship and became stateless, exposed to the mercy of German authorities. Exceptions were made for naturalized German Jews who fought and were decorated during World War I. My father and mother were among those who lost their citizenship because they were born in a territory that had become Poland after World War I. This was a very frightening development. Individuals with foreign citizenship, even Polish passport holders, had some sense of security as they believed their consulate would help them in case of harassment and arrest. Any kind of protection was better than none, and so my father applied for and obtained Polish citizenship for our family.

Other proclamations removed Jews from civil service jobs. Professors at universities could no longer teach. Artists, even the most famous ones, were banned from the German stage. Painters could no longer exhibit. Judges were removed from the bench, and on and on. Edict after edict, all were designed to make Germany *Judenrein* (free of Jews). The most spectacular action, which attracted international attention, was the burning of books written by Jews or others who opposed Nazism. Pictures published in the press showed smiling SA men throwing books by the carload into the fire.

In 1935, the city of Nuremberg was chosen as the place for the largest gathering of Nazis, the *Reichsparteitag*. Thousands upon thousands of goose-stepping marchers in full Nazi uniform were surrounded by a sea of flags and standards. Those banners and swastikas provided an impressive background for Hitler to proclaim an additional list of edicts. They became known as the Nuremberg Laws, and affected the activities and rights of all Jewish people throughout Germany. We were no longer permitted to mix with Germans in a movie house, theater, concert hall, or other public place. Also, we now were not permitted to employ females under the age of forty-five in our homes. This restriction was hard on my mother, as our maid Gretchen was considered part of our family. With tears in all our eyes, Gretchen had to leave our home.

My mother's brother, Uncle Alfred, had settled in Amsterdam at the end of World War I. He was very concerned about the conditions in Germany and insisted that my grandparents leave Berlin and move to Amsterdam to be near him. It was relatively easy for him to obtain the required papers and he was sure that they would be comfortable in their new home.

When Oma and Opa left Berlin, my family became very depressed. Gone were our lovely visits with each other and sharing joys that only a close family can understand. Our relationship was reduced to letter writing, an occasional phone call, and a visit in the summer or on holidays. Our feelings for one another other would never change, but there is a difference when one is just a few streets away, or separated by hundreds of miles and strict borders.

Aunt Mia, Mutti's younger sister, remained in Berlin. She was an independent young lady with a fine job at the Dresdner Bank, and head over heels in love with her best girlfriend's cousin, Robert. Originally a race car driver for Mercedes Benz, Robert now had a car dealership in the city. Unfortunately he was not Jewish and our family was very upset to see Mia marrying outside our faith. Undeterred by the new laws which prohibited a German to wed a Jew, they did get married. Aunt Mia dyed her hair blond to look even more German, quit her job at the bank, and together they rented an apartment near my uncle's business where no one knew them or had any idea of her Jewish background. Uncle Bobby was a perfect

Left to right: Uncle Bobby, me, Mutti, and Fred. Berlin, 1934.

Aunt Mia and Uncle Bobby's favorite car. Berlin, 1929.

gentleman who always had a smile on his face. When he saw me or my brother Fred, he generously pushed a banknote into our hands and said, "Here is some extra spending money." Many weekends Aunt and Uncle came to take Mutti, Fred and me and drive us to their weekend home at Motzen-See. We just loved it. Regrettably, Papa couldn't accept his non–Jewish brother-in-law and never joined us on these outings.

2

Life as a Teenager

Shortly after I entered my third year at the gymnasium, I was summoned to the principal's office. There, without comment or explanation, Prof. Dr. Dyckhoff handed me a note addressed to my parents which advised them that I would have to leave school because available records showed that my father was not a soldier during World War I. For similar reasons, other Jewish students were also ordered to leave school. This action was really no surprise to us since rumors had been around for some time that Jewish pupils would soon be expelled from schools. Still, I was hurt and upset when it actually happened. Fortunately, the leaders of our Jewish community anticipated this order and were ready to increase class size in Jewish schools. Classrooms designed to accommodate thirty-five pupils now had more than fifty students in attendance. Our classroom was extremely crowded, but we were grateful for the opportunity to continue our education. Ironically, the finest educators, professors, and instructors, forced to leave their jobs at universities, were now teaching our classes.

Purification of the German "Aryan" race was one of the Nazi propaganda tools. It served to promote the idea of the German super race, one superior to all other ethnic groups. The Aryan stereotype became the basis for Hitler's policies and the excuse to eliminate feeble-minded and sick people. Race became so important that many Germans were forced to search their own ancestry for proof of racial purity. A single grandparent of Jewish background made anyone subject to the same restrictions imposed on all Jewish people.

Posters visible throughout the country depicted tall, strong, blond, blue-eyed Germans. Every time I saw such a poster, I wondered why neither Hitler nor many of his advisers resembled the image of such a pure Aryan. I couldn't help but think of how many Germans actually knew the meaning of *Aryan.* I checked the *World Book Encyclopedia* and here is their explanation:

> ***ARYAN:*** *Aryan is the language spoken by a people who are supposed to have lived long ago on the Iranian Plateau of southern Asia. All Europeans speak the Aryan tongue except the Turks, Magyars, Basques, Finns, Laps, Estonians and small groups in Russia. The term Aryan can be used only to describe a language. Other words meaning the same thing are Indo-European and Indo-German. There is no such thing as an Aryan race. If there ever were a distinct people, their characteristics have been thoroughly mixed with those of other peoples.*

How could the educated, cultured German population have been so gullible to accept such Nazi propaganda?

My father's business began to decline and he had to reduce the number of people he employed. He was not happy about it, but reasoned that a lower volume of business would delay the takeover by a German trustee. He was still convinced that Hitler and his Nazis would soon disappear and thought it best to be patient and wait a bit longer. Tightening the belt a little would be far easier than uprooting our family and moving to another country. Like so many of his friends, Papa shared the belief that, in time, change would eventually come from within the party, and it almost did. Ernst Rhöm, one of Hitler's earliest followers and chief of the SA, became disenchanted with some of Hitler's actions. He gathered a number of like-minded men and planned to assassinate the *führer,* Hitler's title. Unfortunately, someone squealed and Hitler ordered his loyal elite SS guards to arrest Rhöm and his associates. There was no trial and those arrested were executed without delay.

This incident happened on a Sunday morning in 1934 and I remember it well. I was on my way to the sports complex in Grunewald. Even before I could take a step out of our building, a policeman yelled from across the street that I must get back into the house and stay there. I was startled and ran back to our apartment. Hiding behind window drapes, my family watched the activities on the street below. Policemen and Hitler's SS guards roamed the streets ready to shoot anyone who acted suspiciously. We had no way of knowing what was happening until late in the day when we heard the special newscast announcing the failed insurrection. A few tense days followed, but the entire episode was soon forgotten. Still, hope for a successful insurrection remained alive among our friends and family.

Hardly a week went by without a letter from Oma and Opa asking us to come and spend our summer vacation in Holland. They were anxious to see their Berliner grandchildren. At first reluctant, Mutti finally convinced Papa to let Fred and me go to Amsterdam that summer. We were excited at the prospect of seeing our grandparents, having a vacation at the seashore, and getting to see Holland, a place we had heard so much about. Also, there was the added excitement of an eight-hour train ride and crossing the border into another country, all by ourselves. To make such a trip without our parents required individual passports and visas for us. Our newly acquired Polish citizenship caused endless paperwork for my parents, but finally the day came when we boarded the morning train to Amsterdam.

Mutti spoke to the conductor, gave him a few marks, and asked him to keep an eye on us. I was all of twelve years old and Fred was barely nine. He was a friendly man and came to our compartment frequently to make sure that we were all right. The train ride was thrilling as we watched the beautiful landscape from our compartment window. At the border, the customs officer who checked our car was very thorough and examined everyone carefully. When he came to us, we told him that we were on our way to visit our grandparents and that brought a little smile to his face. He didn't suspect that we were Jewish. Why would he? We looked, spoke, dressed, and had names like any other German youngsters. When he questioned whether we had money or other valuables, I showed him the one hundred mark note that Papa had given me for the two of us. He seemed amused and wasn't interested in looking at our luggage. Other passengers did not fare as well. Their luggage was searched thoroughly, making a mess of all their possessions. The customs officers were primarily looking for gold and other valuables which were not permitted to be taken out of the country. Once the train was cleared, we continued across the border where local Dutch passengers came aboard. Among them was Uncle Alfred who had come to meet and escort us to Amsterdam. Our ride to Amsterdam seemed to take no time at all because we had so much to tell and he was anxious to hear it all. At the Amsterdam railroad station, we were greeted by Oma and Opa, Aunt Yetta, and our little cousin Mary, whom we had never met before.

Our grandparents lived in the heart of the city, a short taxi ride from the station. Their apartment was on the second floor of a four-story building and I remember being intrigued by the narrow and steep staircase. Their home was so different from the spacious apartment they had left in Berlin. At first we had difficulty getting our suitcases up the stairs, but Opa showed us how to step sideways, and once we got the idea it was easy. He explained that space was at a premium in Amsterdam, and so everything had to be rather small in size. The apartment was comfortable, but a long way from the luxury they enjoyed in Berlin. Oma's hospitality had not changed and her table brimmed with all kinds of goodies for us. It wasn't very long before family and friends arrived to welcome the grandchildren they had heard so much about.

I gave the hundred marks to Opa, the maximum the two of us were permitted to take out of Germany. Fifty marks per person was really next to nothing and could hardly purchase a thing. The Nazis had limited the amount of money one could take out of the country because Germany only had a small amount of gold in their treasury and German currency was completely worthless in international trade. To add some value to their currency, the Nazis had ordered that all gold bars and gold coins in private possession had to be exchanged for paper money. People not complying with this directive would be severely punished. The mere mention of a concentration camp put fear into everyone and made all Germans follow the new orders.

To have some income, Opa had started a delivery route for bread, rolls, and other baked goods. He had to get up before dawn, go to the bakery, and load his big tricycle with morning orders. Riding his heavy load up and down the narrow streets and over steep bridges was really hard work and not befitting an elderly man. So, after delivering his first load, he would come home to get a little rest. Sitting with a cup of coffee at the table, he would tell Oma the latest news that he had heard in the street. Soon he was gone again to complete his rounds for the day. Oma had worked as a dressmaker in her youth, and with this talent she was able to supplement their income doing alterations for her neighbors.

To make our summer vacation memorable, Oma and Opa rented an apartment in Zandvoort, a seashore resort not far from Amsterdam. On weekends, Opa joined us for fun at the beach and took us into the frigid waters of the North Sea. Holding us, one on his right and the other on his left, we would jump in unison over huge oncoming waves. He held us with all his strength because he feared that the strong undercurrent would pull us out to sea. Fred and I had never been to the seashore before and we couldn't get enough of the water and sand. Our cousins, the Wellners, came to spend a few weeks in Zandvoort, too. They stayed at a hotel on the boardwalk and we saw each other often, just as in the days when we all lived in Berlin. It was the most wonderful time we could imagine. There were no restrictions on Jews living in Holland and we were allowed to go anyplace we chose. Language, however, presented a little problem for us. Remembering German actions during World War I, the Dutch people were not fond of hearing anyone speak that language. Therefore, we tried to avoid speaking German in public. What a strange situation I thought. In Berlin, I was discriminated against for being Jewish and not German. In Holland, I got dirty looks because, in their eyes, I was a German. Oma and Opa had learned a few words of Dutch, and with added words of Yiddish, they got along surprisingly well.

The weeks went by and before we knew it Fred and I had to return home. It was the year before my bar mitzvah and Opa and Oma were distraught that because of conditions in Germany they could not attend their first grandson's bar mitzvah. Although my big day was still months away, I was able to chant some of my Torah reading for them, and just as Mutti thought, they beamed with pride at their grandson's accomplishment. With smiles on their faces, they showed me the gold wristwatch they had bought for me but would keep until my bar mitzvah day. This I thought was sort of a bribe and incentive for me to do well.

Their friends and neighbors came to say goodbye and made us promise to come again soon. It was Uncle Alfred who took us to the train, where he again asked the conductor to keep an eye on us. The trip to Amsterdam was fun and exciting, and traveling home was more of the same. As the train pulled into the station in Berlin, we looked out the window and saw Mutti and Papa waiting on the platform. We waved to each other, and with luggage intact, we made our way home.

The Nazis kept their promise to create employment and provide food for every German table. The infrastructure, roads, and factories were being rebuilt, but the people couldn't enjoy the things they worked for. Many products made in Germany had to be shipped abroad to pay for the most essential imports. Seeing so many of their products disappear, the German people became disenchanted. They wanted more than just bread on their table. It was then that Herman Göring, Hitler's friend and appointed *Reichsmarshall,* made his famous speech saying, "Let's have cannons instead of butter." Those remarks confirmed to the world that Germany was indeed building factories for the production of military equipment. The huge amount of such equipment exceeded the limitations imposed by the Treaty of Versailles, but the Western countries were sound asleep or didn't care.

In contrast to the limited prosperity enjoyed by Aryans, our people were continually losing their jobs and sources of income. But in spite of all the difficulties, most of us somehow managed to maintain a reasonable lifestyle. German theater, opera, concerts and other cultural events were off-limits, so activities of the Jüdische Kulturbund (the Jewish culture society) were expanded to fill the void and provide us with pleasant things to do. Since many of the finest internationally known artists were Jewish, there was first-rate entertainment available to us at the Kulturbund.

Money to pay for activities in our Jewish community came from the religious tax. A percentage of the income tax collected by the government was forwarded to the institution of the taxpayer's affiliation. Unfortunately, this system proved troublesome to the Jewish people since everyone had to reveal their religious affiliation on their tax returns. Now, the Nazi government had a complete dossier on the entire Jewish population. As the income of Jews declined, so did the revenue forwarded to the Jewish community. At the same time, the need to expand schools, hospitals, and care for the aged became overwhelming. Equally important was helping those who had documents to leave Germany, but there was not enough money to help pay for their ship passage. Additional money now had to be raised by means of personal appeals.

Though our schools were maintained and operated by our community, they, like all other schools in the city, were supervised by the regional superintendent. On one of his visits, he observed that we had a much more extended curriculum than other schools in his jurisdiction. At first we were angry at our teachers because we had more than the usual amount of homework. It left little time to prepare for bar mitzvah, to practice our musical instruments, and so on. It was only many years later that I understood why the great push was necessary. Our teachers, realizing that drastic change could come at any time, tried to push as much knowledge into our heads as we could absorb. I, for one, am grateful to my teachers for the efforts they made on my behalf. With all my studies, I still managed to spend some time in the gym, play soccer and compete in 1,500-meter races.

Barred from membership in German athletic clubs, Jewish athletes needed to join Jewish clubs; Bar-Kochba and Hakoach were the largest among them. With so many added members, the need for a larger sport facility was very evident, and the sports field in Grunewald was just perfect for such an expansion. A group of *Chalutzim* (Zionist pioneers), learning to work the land in preparation for moving to a *kibbutz* (Zionist cooperative in Palestine), built a beautiful new sports complex for us in a relatively short time; three soccer fields, lockerrooms with showers, and a snack shop were ready to be used. The center stadium was the main attraction for our soccer games or track and field events. It became a very busy place as schools and clubs competed regularly. Since we were not permitted to compete against German athletes, we challenged Jewish sport clubs from other cities. Their athletes and friends were hosted in our homes and, in turn, we enjoyed their hospitality when we visited them. Our stadium turned into a wonderful place for families and friends to spend a few pleasant hours and forget our troubled lives.

Criminal actions against Jews were no secret to the outside world, but no country was willing to defend or protect us. Gradually a few of Papa's friends who had been terrorized started to look for ways to leave Germany. They paid no attention to the discouraging letters coming from friends who had migrated to the States or other places. Many immigrants complained of difficulties in their new society and were sorry they had left home. "Stay in Germany and wait until political changes make life pleasant again," they counseled. Obviously, they were not aware of the many new hardships we had to face daily since they had left Berlin.

June 1, 1935, was the date set for my bar mitzvah. Festivities after services were to take place in our home, and for days on end, my aunts were busy helping my mother in the kitchen. They prepared food for kiddush (a ceremonial blessing) at the temple and the festive meal to be served at our home. Having such a large party was quite an undertaking; even the bathtub was off-limits to us for days because of fish swimming in the tub. Every bit of our furniture had to be moved to make room for those invited. I had often heard that nothing ever works exactly as planned, and my bar mitzvah was no exception. I was supposed to read my Torah portion at the Alte Synagogue in the Heidereuter Gasse, the synagogue where we had our seats. Unfortunately, the Jüdische Kultusgemeinde, who oversaw the conservative synagogues in Berlin, assigned Rabbi Dr. Singermann, my teacher and friend of the family, to officiate at another synagogue. I was disappointed because I wanted to be in my synagogue where I sang in the Temple choir and had so many friends. But it would have been very awkward not having Dr. Singermann next to me on this occasion, so changes had to be made. Much to my regret, we had our *Simcha* at the Golnow Strasse Synagogue. Incidentally, our choir at the Alte Synagogue was recognized as one of the finest in Berlin, and being a member of the choir was not just prestigious, but also a paying job. It was the first money I had ever earned.

The gathering of so many people in our home after services needed to be registered with the local police. So, not to draw unwanted attention from our neighbors, my parents thought it wise for only two or three guests to arrive at a time. The plan worked well, and no one was accosted in the street. We celebrated the afternoon with singing and eating a most delicious meal. Even the weather was perfect. The customary gifts to a bar-mitzvah boy at that time were books, fountain pens, tie clips and the like; I received my share of them. Aunt Mia and Uncle Bobby gave me the gold watch they had taken along from my grandparents on their last visit to Amsterdam, and they presented me with a beautiful gold ring with engraved initials. I treasured these two pieces of jewelry, not just because they were beautiful, but because they were from my very special relatives. Soon after everyone had left, I called my grandparents to thank them and tell them all about my special day. Mutti took the receiver from me and told Opa that I read the Torah beautifully and that they had good reason to be proud.

The anticipated Olympic games of 1936 in Berlin were nearly a year away, but the newspapers were already filled with reports about the preparations for this event. Competitions, tryouts, and names of athletes from all over the world selected to compete in Berlin were constantly in the news.

The Nazis were determined to make the Olympic games in Berlin a showcase for the New Germany, and the best sporting event ever seen.

At the same time, hidden behind Olympic headlines but getting stronger all the time, there were stories of demonstrations in the Saarland. This territory, taken from Germany at the end of World War I, was placed under French rule. Under the Treaty of Versailles, there was to be a vote on whether the people would like to continue under French rule or be part of Germany again. Hitler, who was very anxious to get the coal and iron mined in this region, got ready to test his strength against the Western nations. Not willing to wait for voting day because the outcome could be embarrassing, the Nazis smuggled loyal party members into this demilitarized area and staged pro–German demonstrations. Hitler accused the French government of discriminating against the German people and surprised everyone when he ordered the German army to occupy this territory on March 7, 1936. Staged pictures, issued by the German press, showed local girls carrying bouquets of flowers and embracing their German liberators. The Western world was stunned by such brazen action but did nothing more than file a protest with the League of Nations. There were talks of a more vigorous protest, even boycotting the Olympic games in Berlin, but nothing ever materialized. This inability of the Western world to restrain Hitler's activities was a serious matter and a great reason for concern.

3

Restrictions

When Papa was only three years old, he lost his father in a terrible accident at the family store in Spytkowice. My grandparents, the only Jews in the village, had a good relationship with their Polish neighbors and operated the local general store. Milk, clothing, kerosene, even harvesting equipment were all sold there. The store was open all day during the week but closed on Saturday when the family observed Shabbat, and Sunday, when all their neighbors attended church. One Saturday, a neighbor ran out of kerosene for the lamps in his house, but waited until after sundown before going to my grandparents for help. My grandpa went to his store, which was across the street from their home, but while pumping the highly flammable liquid from a barrel, his kerosene lamp fell to the ground. It ignited everything instantly, and by the time the volunteer fire brigade arrived there was nothing left to be saved. Grandpa suffered severe burns all over his body and died a short time later. My grandmother was devastated. She was left a young widow with three babies. My father was three, his brother Israel, two, and sister Klara was not even a year old. The business was in ashes and there was a farm that needed constant attention. Grandpa's brother Samuel and wife Marie assisted Grandma during this tragic time, and to make it easier for her they took my father to live with them in nearby Chrzanow. His cousins, who were of similar age, were like brothers and sisters to him.

Soon after Papa's bar mitzvah, Uncle Isaac, grandfather's other brother, and Aunt Rosa asked Papa to come and live in Berlin with them and their children, Robert, Regina and Klara. Papa loved the idea of moving to the big city where he would have more opportunities to make something of himself. Many times he told me of his life in Berlin as a young man. He spoke of his schooling and the wonderful things he was able to enjoy. He was good friends with his cousins and Aunt Rosa's younger brother Edward, too. They were constant companions until Edward was drafted into the army. He was a lieutenant when discharged from the Austrian army after World War I, but didn't relish living in Berlin any longer. He kept on looking for a new challenge in his life, and much to the chagrin of his sister, found it in Buenos Aires, Argentina. There he became a successful businessman, and as conditions for Jews in Germany became intolerable after 1934, he asked the family, including us, to move to Buenos Aires. It wasn't difficult getting a visa to Argentina at that time if it involved a first-line relationship such as parents and child, sister and brother, or husband and wife. But, since there was no blood relationship between my father and Edward, getting visas for us involved a waiting period. We had to hope that when our Uncle Isaac became a permanent resident in Argentina our waiting period would be cut short.

Restrictions imposed on us made our lives in Berlin very unpleasant and Uncle Isaac and Aunt Rosa followed her brother's urging and moved to Buenos Aires at the end of 1936. As soon as they were settled, the necessary documents were prepared for their children and grandchildren to join them there immediately. He also filed the required documents for us but, as expected, we were put on a waiting list for entry permits. The first to receive their documents was Regina and her family. They liquidated their home and were devastated when their valuable furnishings were now almost worthless. The market was so overloaded with furniture and household items of other Jewish families trying to dispose of their belongings that their finest possessions were purchased by Germans for a mere pittance.

The new German laws didn't differentiate between those who left the country for only a short time or those who left Germany permanently. No one was permitted to cross the border with more than fifty reichsmark. Since this was a meaningless sum of money, trying to retain some real assets required great ingenuity. It was an extremely dangerous undertaking, but they had no other choice. Willy Seiden, Regina's husband, bought diamonds and gold on the black market. Cleverly he had his gold cast into buttons, colored them to match their garments, and sewed them in place of regular buttons. Diamonds without settings were hidden in their coat seams, knowing that these valuables could be converted into cash any place in the world. Unfortunately, someone denounced Willy and he was summoned to appear at the feared gestapo (abbreviation for **GE**heime **STA**ats **PO**lizei, the German secret state police) headquarters at Prinz Albrecht Strasse 8. Since few people ever returned from such an interview, the family packed whatever they could take along and fled to Poland that very same day.

In the family hometown of Chrzanow, Uncle Samuel and Aunt Marie opened their home to them. Regina, Willy, and their children expected to be there for only a short time, but the bureaucratic nightmare kept them in Poland for many months. They had booked passage on a ship leaving Hamburg for Buenos Aires, but now they didn't dare go back to Germany to board the ship. All their documents had to be transferred to Poland and new ship passage had to be booked. After six months and many trips to the Argentinean consulate in Warsaw, the end was in sight. They left aboard a Polish freighter from the port of Gdansk on the long journey to Buenos Aires.

In Berlin, the Olympic games were about to begin and the city put on its most festive look. Unter den Linden, the grand Boulevard leading to the Brandenburg Gate, and all other major thoroughfares were decorated with Nazi flags and banners. It was an impressive sight. On the day prior to opening ceremonies, I passed the large radio store on Alexander Platz and saw a huge crowd gathered in front of the window. Curiosity made me stop, too, and what I saw was fantastic. In the center of the window was a small TV screen transmitting pictures from the Olympic stadium showing workmen preparing for the opening ceremonies. Everyone was awed and marveled at the achievements of modern technology. It was the first TV broadcast ever seen publicly in Berlin.

The games went off just the way the Nazis had planned and the mood in the streets was jubilant. People from all over the world came to visit our city and watch the games. Nobody seemed to notice or care that the decorations were all swastikas and Nazi flags. On opening day, my friends and I ventured out to see the activities on Unter den Linden. We came to this main thoroughfare in the city just as Hitler and his entourage drove down the street. The crowds lining both sides of the road went nearly mad as they waved little Nazi flags and shouted excitedly, "Heil! Heil!" again and again. It was truly amazing to see so many people nearly hypnotized by Hitler's presence. It was the first and only time I had actually seen Hitler in person. Cautiously at first, but with more confidence as the games progressed, my friends and I went to places normally off limits to us. With so many foreigners around, we reasoned that nobody would pay attention to us in the crowds. Incidentally, most of the signs reading "Juden und Hunde nicht erwünscht" (Jews and dogs not welcome) had been moved to less conspicuous places. The Nazis succeeded in putting their best foot forward and foreign visitors were impressed by the cleanliness and order that they saw. Stores were stacked with merchandise and Germany indeed looked prosperous.

My friends and I had purchased tickets for the track and field competitions, and as luck would have it, it was the day when Jesse Owens was to receive his award for his record-breaking 100-meter dash. Hitler, who usually attended such award presentations, abruptly left the stadium when Jesse Owens, an African American, was called to receive his gold medal. Hitler could not accept that other races or nations, not only his Aryan race, had good athletes, too. Hitler's action, an insult to athletes from nations around the world, was not appreciated. There was even talk that some countries might withdraw their athletes from further competitions in response. As a young athlete myself, I was in awe of Jesse Owens and his achievements. Little did I know then that I would meet Jesse some forty years later when he was public relations director for a client of mine in Chicago.

The successful completion of the Olympic games was still on everybody's mind when Italy's fascist dictator Mussolini came to visit Hitler in Berchtesgarden and received a royal welcome. On October 25, 1936, they signed a friendship pact which became known as the Berlin–Rome Axis. It was also the time when the much touted League of Nations, established after World War I to prevent all future wars, watched helplessly while modern fascist Italy overpowered the underdeveloped country of Abyssinia in Africa.

My friends and I became involved in Zionism, and together we joined the Zionist scouts club Maccabi-Hatzair, an affiliate of the Maccabi sports club. Our group met on Saturday afternoons in the clubhouse, actually just an apartment in the center of the city. The meetings were learning sessions as we became familiar with the geography, history, social and economic conditions of Palestine, our Jewish homeland and Theodor Herzl's dream. The land of milk and honey had been turned into a desert under Turkish rule and it was up to us, the new generation of *Chalutzim* (pioneers) to make our land bloom again. It was a wonderful group of boys and girls and I enjoyed being with them immensely. Our meetings, trips, and all our activities had to be registered with the gestapo. Names, date, place, and time as well as the topic we planned to discuss had to be submitted. Scouting or the need to rebuild the barren land of Palestine were topics acceptable to the authorities and often a Gestapo officer would come into our room, sit down, listen to us for a while, then leave us alone. Of course he didn't know that we had a lookout outside who alerted us to his coming. By the time he had walked up the stairs, we were in the midst of discussing the registered topic.

This clubhouse became a very important place, not only for us, but for out-of-town comrades who needed temporary shelter. Many of them had run away from home because they were afraid of being arrested on some trumped-up charges. The apartment also served as an overnight stop for comrades on their way to work on farms in preparation for work on a kibbutz (cooperative farm) in Palestine. We knew that the apartment was under surveillance by the gestapo yet we managed to camouflage sheltering our friends for a long time. It was inevitable though that we would get caught someday, and we did. The gestapo came one afternoon and surprised two members who were "wanted for questioning" in their hometown. They were arrested and we never heard from them again. The gestapo closed our clubhouse after this incident, but we continued to meet privately in our homes. As any gathering of more than five people had to be registered with the gestapo, we met in small groups of three or four. Our parents were uneasy about our activities but realized how important they were for the Jewish cause.

One afternoon I nearly got myself into big trouble. Eight of us had met in my home and somehow weren't as careful as necessary. A neighbor must have seen my friends arriving and informed the gestapo. A few days had passed when I received a summons to appear at gestapo headquarters. This was serious business and the possible consequences were well known to us. My parents were beside themselves and so was I. Anticipating problems such as this, we had to be prepared with reasonable excuses. My explanation was a simple one and well rehearsed with my friends. I told them that I wasn't feeling well at school on Friday, and one by one, my friends came to visit me; the timing of their visit was sheer coincidence. I arrived at the gestapo building and was ushered into a room as I fought my fears. Soon after all formalities like name, address, and age were completed, two men, in rapid succession, fired questions at me. Before I could finish my answer to one question, the next one came at me. They were trying to confuse me, hoping for a slip of the tongue. They knew that all of us who had gathered in our apartment were members of the same Zionist organization and wanted to know what we were talking about. Schoolwork, sports, and other safe topics was what I told them. After what seemed an eternity, I was released and warned not to have so many people in my home again.

Since Gretchen was no longer with us, our huge apartment became too much for Mutti to take care of. Also, Papa's business was hurting and we needed to lower our expenses. We moved into a smaller apartment in a building with two units on a floor. Our neighbors and their children greeted us at first with smiles and a friendly "Guten Tag" (Good day) but soon the friendly smiles were replaced with a slight raise of the right arm, and in time, became the Hitler salute.

Like most other youngsters, our new young neighbors joined the Hitler Youth and our elevator and staircase were always filled with their visiting friends. Seeing uniformed boys and girls going up or down constantly was unnerving, so we tried to stay out of their way. Before leaving our apartment, we would look through the peephole in our door to be sure that we would be alone on the floor.

Our entertainment was curtailed even more when our Kulturbund (culture society) performers accepted contracts for concert, opera, and theater stages all over the world. We were happy for them, but it left us with a void when we needed more amusement desperately to lift our morale. Even our sport activities in Grunewald were in danger because Hitler Youth groups opened a camp nearby and we were constantly being harassed. Frequently, the gestapo would just close the access road to our facilities, and we never knew about it until we arrived.

During our spring vacation we planned a bicycle trip to visit Maccabi friends in Magdeburg. Our teams had visited each other many times, but on this trip we planned to camp out and sleep in tents. Like all our other activities, this, too, had to be registered with the gestapo. Sigi Brenner, our leader, applied, never thinking that our request would be approved.

Much to our amazement, we got permission and were even allowed to wear our blue and white scout uniforms. On our second day out it rained so heavily that pitching our tents would have been almost impossible. We finally found a youth hostel in the area to spend the night, but as luck would have it, the place was crowded with Hitler Youth groups. The owner expressed his regrets that his place was filled to capacity. We were disappointed but would have been uncomfortable sharing quarters with Hitler Youth anyway. Our uniforms were of a different color and they surely would have asked us questions and recognized that we were Jewish. Just as we were mounting our bikes, the owner called us back. He didn't have the heart to send us out into the pouring rain again and offered us his barn to bed down on the straw which was stored there. This suited us just fine. In the morning we watched the Hitler Youth groups have their roll call and march away. As soon as the last troop left, Sigi went to pay the bill and we prepared to leave, too. The hostel keeper said to Sigi, "I am very impressed with the behavior of your group. You are so much more orderly and quiet than most others who come here. Your uniforms are a different color than the other troops. Tell me, which organization do you belong to?" This was the question we had tried to avoid. Sigi told the man that we were a Jewish scout group and the hostel keeper exploded with laughter. "That's the funniest thing I've heard," he blurted out. He went into his office and told us to wait. He returned with a copy of the newspaper the *Stürmer* in his hand. "This is what Jews look like," he said. "Jews have big noses, wear beards, side curls, and hats. They are dirty, smelly and don't look anyone in the eye." As we left, he called after us, "Have a good day and beware of Jews." (*The Stürmer* was a weekly Nazi publication to excite the German public and promote hatred toward Jews. The paper was filled with despicable caricatures and wild stories that only a sick mind could invent.)

There was no use telling him that he was a victim of Nazi propaganda, and regrettably he was one of many duped the same way. Every German was exposed to this tabloid filled with trash. Bulletin boards displayed the pages of the *Stürmer* throughout the country and people stood in front of this garbage and gobbled up every word. One time, I stood among them to see their reactions to what they read. Some shook their heads in disbelief while others said that they knew of similar stories and that they were true. Some just stopped, looked for a moment, and quietly walked away.

They were obviously embarrassed and afraid to voice their opinion. After our experience with the hostel keeper, I often wondered how many Germans had actually ever known a Jewish person.

As the months passed, we prepared ourselves for a move to Buenos Aires. We began to learn Spanish and gather information about the country which would become our new home. Unfortunately, our plans and preparations were useless. While our papers were in transit, the government of Argentina closed the border to all except first-line relatives. Our family tried to console us, writing that they hoped this new ordinance would change, but when? We were so sure of moving to Buenos Aires that we hadn't even thought of looking elsewhere. Sometimes things don't go as they are planned, but in 1936, "sometimes" seemed to turn into all the time.

Mutti began searching for Opa's older brother who had moved to New York many years before. The family had lost contact because staying in touch meant writing letters that took weeks in transit across the ocean. The time between letters steadily increased, and eventually they stopped completely. Finding Opa's brother in New York was no easy task, but Mutti was persistent and eventually successful. With his address in hand, she wrote him immediately. At the same time, Mutti spent many hours visiting the offices of HIAS and JOINT, pleading for assistance. These Jewish relief organizations, headquartered in the United States, had offices in countries where help was needed. They did their best to help us leave Germany, but without countries willing to provide visas, there wasn't much they could do. Still, like so many others, she waited endlessly in reception rooms to speak to a representative. Most of the time, she went there to follow up on rumors that a few entry visas to some country had become available. This was often true, but those visas were to third-world countries looking for special craftsmen able to help their lagging economy. They were not desirable places but, for a few people imprisoned in concentration camps, it was a way to obtain freedom. If the family could secure such a visa and pay a handsome ransom, there were instances when a prisoner was released. The family then had to get him out of Germany within a twelve-hour period and he was sworn to silence about the things he saw in the concentration camp. Warned that his family would suffer great consequences if he would speak, he kept quiet.

There were also underdeveloped countries who offered some visas to capitalists. Any individual who came to them with a first-class ship passage and in possession of at least $5,000 cash was welcome. There weren't many who could muster such a sum in foreign currency, and only those who had wealthy relatives outside of Germany had a chance to actually leave. This, too, didn't last very long as political pressures made these countries also close their borders.

Our parents traveled to Amsterdam quite often. Essentially they went to visit Oma and Opa, but they made sure to visit all the Jewish organizations in Amsterdam as well. They thought that being outside of Germany and pleading with these people in person would help us find a place to relocate. Each time they returned home more and more frustrated as all their efforts were fruitless.

Finding a country in which to settle was really only the first step. It was also important that we think of ways to earn a living once we got there. I had shown artistic talents at school and my teacher suggested that I develop these talents. Hearing this, my parents wanted me to study commercial art and enrolled me for afternoon classes in art school. I learned a lot in class, but with art classes, regular and Hebrew schoolwork, violin lessons and sport activities, my days and evenings were filled to capacity. Mutti was eager to learn a craft so that she too could help rebuild our home, wherever it might be. During a conversation with our downstairs neighbor, Mr. Goldberg, he mentioned that a Treuhänder had taken his business from him, and he planned to start a small workshop with his wife and daughter producing neckties. Mutti asked if he could use her help and he replied that it would be his pleasure to teach her to make ties. Whenever she had time, Mutti went to his shop and learned as much as she could. Wherever we went, Papa, Fred and I wore the prettiest ties, all made by my mother.

We hadn't heard from Opa's brother in New York since he replied to Mutti's original letter, and we had given up hope of hearing from him again. What a surprise it was when one day we received another letter. Excitedly, Mutti opened it, but she couldn't read it since it was written in Yiddish. We had to wait for Papa to come home and read the letter to us. The first few sentences were an apology for the long-delayed reply. He and his family were not financially secure, and to make an affidavit for us to come to the States, the government required his guarantee that we would not become a burden to the country. To satisfy this demand took him a long time, but with the help of his children he got the required documents.

He said that they were in transit and should arrive at our home shortly. After all the disappointments we had gone through, we really needed this bit of good news. We were so touched that even in his financial situation he did his best to get us this affidavit. "Honestly," Mutti said, "I never gave up hope. The shirt is closer to the skin than the vest, and here is proof once again that family ties are something special."

There is no way to describe the joy in our home when the envelope with those precious documents arrived. We could hardly wait to bring these papers to the American consulate the next day. Approaching the building, we saw a long line of people waiting their turn to enter the consulate. Some people were in line like us to register, and others came to see how much longer they'd have to wait before their quota number would be called. Our excitement soured quickly when we heard how long some had been waiting for their registration number to be called. The clerk who registered us didn't give us much hope either. He gave us our number and told us that the Polish quota was filled for the next five or six years. We would have to wait at least that long. Fred and I were born in Germany which had a larger and less used quota, but the clerk insisted that we were minors and must be registered under the Polish quota. We came to the American consulate with great joy in our hearts, but walked away in utter despair.

In 1937, less than half the total of our former Jewish community was still in Germany. Roughly three-hundred thousand people like us could not find refuge in any country in the world. Adding to the worsening situation, Great Britain issued a White Paper, further reducing the number of visas for Jewish people wishing to settle in Palestine. England had a mandate over Palestine from the League of Nations after World War I, but as Arab concern grew about the Jewish influx into Palestine, they threatened to cut the flow of their oil to Great Britain. Forgotten was Lord Balfour's declaration, approved by the government, promising a national homeland in Palestine for the Jewish people. Dr. Chaim Weitzman received that promise in recognition of the special gunpowder he developed for use in World War I. It was his accomplishment which led to a speedy conclusion of that war.

The Jewish Agency (Jewish government in exile) received a limited number of visas and issued them primarily to the Youth Aliyah movement. Jossy, Max, Sigi Brenner, and all my close friends applied for these visas and left for Palestine early in 1938. I was the only one in our group left behind because Papa was adamant that our family must stay together. I pleaded with my parents to let me join my friends, but after many long and tearful "discussions," my parents still didn't want to hear of it. They were too protective and didn't think that a pioneer life was in my best interest. They hoped that some countries might still open their borders to us and let us stay at least until our U.S. quota number would be called.

I was very lonely and sad — my closest friends were gone, and my cousins and some schoolmates had left Berlin, too. Adding to my loneliness were the restrictions imposed by the Nazis at our sports facility in Grunewald. It was closed more often than open. My parents were also unhappy when more and more of their friends who were registered under the German quota left Berlin for places overseas. For some amusement, my family went to movie houses in other neighborhoods where we were less likely to be recognized. Still, I wasn't comfortable doing what was against the law. We always had to consider the consequences of someone recognizing and denouncing us. People were so eager to improve their standing in the Nazi party that they denounced others indiscriminately.

Radio and newspapers reported world news, but only those stories approved by Nazi censors glorifying the Reich. To understand what was really happening, one had to read between the lines. The lead stories began to mention demonstrations in the streets of Austrian cities. There was little doubt that these demonstrations were organized by German Nazis. They asserted that Austrians shared a common language with their German neighbors and wanted to be part of *das dritte Reich* (the third Reich). Austrian Chancellor Kurt von Schuschnigg, a nationalist and strongman himself, had seized power from the socialists after the assassination of Chancellor Dollfuss. He was not about to relinquish his power to a union with Hitler. However, the Nazis exerted such pressure that Herr Schuschnigg had to visit Hitler at the Eagle's Nest (Hitler's retreat in Berchtesgarden). Rumors surfaced that the chancellor had been kept there for a few days against his will, but then was permitted to return to Vienna. Shortly thereafter he was made to resign when the German army marched into Austria. News reports and pictures were reminiscent of the German reception after they "liberated" the Saargebiet in the Rheinland earlier. No sooner had the German army crossed the border into Austria when anti–Semitic demonstrations and violent acts against Jewish people made front-page news. Boycotts and restrictions were much the same as those suffered by the Jewish communities in Germany. True, there was anti–Semitism in Austria long before the *Anschluss* (joining), but the nationalist government had kept anti–Jewish activities somewhat under control. Now, all violence against Jews was acceptable. To stifle any opposition at all, Chancellor Schuschnigg was arrested and imprisoned by the Germans.

Henrietta Szold, a prominent American Zionist, president of the Women's Zionist organization Hadassah and director of the Jewish Agency's Youth Aliyah program, was a name well known to us. So was her very close associate Recha Freier, our rabbi's wife, who headed the Youth Aliyah program in Germany. These two women, especially Henrietta Szold, used their influence in having the British government permit ten-thousand Jewish children to come study in England. The Jewish community in England agreed that they would provide shelter and food for all these children. What a magnificent and unbelievable development. In Berlin, registration for this program started even before it became official. Lotte, Mutti's cousin had lost her husband David to diabetes earlier that year, and because of their existing hardship, her children Julius, Jack, and Heinz were among the first to be accepted for this program. There were lots of tears as Lotte and the three boys said goodbye to each other. She hoped that their separation would only be a short one and prayed that there would be a way for her and her six-year-old daughter Ruth to join her sons.

Encouraged by the success in Austria and lack of serious opposition, Hitler next set his sights on Czechoslovakia. The Skoda plants in that country produced cars, trucks, tanks, and other heavy equipment which the Nazis wanted and needed to augment the German arsenal. As they had done so successfully in the Rheinland and again in Austria, the Nazi party organized ethnic Germans in the Sudetenland (Bohemia) to stage protests. He claimed that the ethnic Germans were being discriminated against because of their background and insisted that it be stopped. If it was not, the German army would enter Czechoslovakia and liberate his German people. Czechoslovakia was a strong democracy, well armed, and had no intention of submitting to Nazi demands. They asked for and received promises of support from England and France, which at long last recognized the danger Nazi Germany presented. Instead of organizing a strong, united European front to force Hitler to abandon his reckless policies, they sent their prime ministers, Neville Chamberlain and Pierre Daladier, to meet and negotiate with Hitler in Munich. This meeting turned out to be a fiasco. Instead of staying their position, they accepted Hitler's empty commitment that freeing Sudetendeutsche from Czechoslovakian intolerance was his only goal. No sooner were the prime ministers out of Munich than Hitler ordered his troops to march into the Sudetenland. As in previous conquests, staged pictures showed German soldiers being greeted with flowers and parades, while the Jewish community then suffered the same violence that befell the German and Austrian Jewish communities before them.

In Germany, Jews were ordered to appear at their local police station to have a red letter "J" stamped on the front page of their passports. This was just another act to humiliate Jews because an earlier edict already required males to add Israel as a middle name, and Sara to females, on all documents and signatures. Stores still operated by Jews were ordered to prominently display the full name of the owner on the store window to alert Germans not to patronize the establishment. Neither one of these laws affected my family because the Nazis had no jurisdiction over foreign passports. Just the same, the scene was reminiscent of the Middle Ages when Jews had to wear yellow hats or other types of identification.

Reacting to domestic pressure, a few world leaders began to look at the Jewish problem a little more seriously. In 1938, a small number of governments attended a conference in Evian, at the beautiful Lake Genève, in France. The purpose of this meeting was to find ways to absorb Jewish immigrants from Germany into their economy. The delegates met, talked for days, and couldn't even agree on a future meeting date, let alone find a solution to the problem before them. Hitler flaunted the results of this conference with newspaper headlines claiming, "Nobody wants the Jews! Why should Germany be saddled with them!"

The German people were euphoric; one success after another. Hitler had restored Germany's strength and everything was pointing upward. Newspapers were filled with pictures of smiling German families on vacation as part of the "Kraft durch Freude" (strength through pleasure) program. This program was a showcase featuring deserving workers and party members, implying that life under the Nazis was wonderful. Everyone was employed. Everyone enjoyed life. Marching bands played while Nazi flags

Our last formal family picture, on the occasion of Fred's bar mitzvah, October 9, 1938. Aunt Mia and Uncle Bobby saved this and the other family pictures shown on previous pages while hiding in Amsterdam during the Holocaust.

decorated the streets. Almost every German was proud of what had been accomplished. Germany was on its way to conquer Europe!

Encouraged by virtually no opposition, Hitler looked for additional conquests. The Polish corridor and the German city of Danzig were territories taken from Germany at the end of World War I and given to Poland. This time the people weren't Saarländers or Sudetendeutsche, they were Volksdeutsche, people of German ancestry who lived in that territory. Using Volksdeutsche as their weapons, the Nazis began protests against the Poles, and the Western world finally reacted. England and France signed friendship pacts with Poland agreeing to cooperate and assist each other in case of German aggression. Hitler took notice of this agreement, but did not change his plans.

During the year 1938, everything seemed to go from bad to worse. The only bright spot was planning Fred's bar mitzvah in September. Just as my parents had made a beautiful celebration for me, they wanted to do the same for Fred, and they did. Since so many of our friends and relatives had left Germany, there was only a small group of people left to share our Simcha. But, as before, kiddush was served at the Temple and an elaborate meal enjoyed at our home. Fred did a wonderful job reading his Torah portion and we were all so very proud of him. His presents were similar to mine and we all shared a beautiful day of pleasure and good wishes for the future.

4

Arrest and Escape

Friday, October 28, 1938, seven o'clock in the morning — a moment in my life I will never forget. I had started the day a little earlier than usual. There was an orchestra rehearsal scheduled and I needed to practice a difficult passage on my violin before school. Time and again my fingers moved over the strings of my instrument. Then I heard the sound of the doorbell. This was pretty routine for a Friday morning and my mother quickly answered the door. However, instead of the girl's voice delivering our daily milk and rolls, I heard a masculine voice in the foyer. This was strange, I thought, as I opened my door into the hallway. There was a policeman speaking to Mutti, and her face had turned ashen white. For years we had lived in fear of such a moment, but when it actually happened my heart felt as if it were jumping out of my chest. Turning to me he said, "Sorry to disturb you so early, but the lieutenant would like to ask you and your father some routine questions and asked me to bring you to the station." Mutti had recovered from the initial shock and asked the policeman to be seated while Papa, who was still asleep, could get dressed.

When I first heard the policeman speak, I thought he had asked for Abraham and Johannes Bachner. To mispronounce my name was not unusual because the German pronunciation for James sounds much like Johannes. My curiosity made me ask him to show me the warrant which he still had in his hand. There was no mistake, the warrant read Johannes. I went for my passport and showed him that he was looking for the wrong person. Obviously, this was a mistake, he acknowledged, and he would have to come back with the corrected warrant. He smiled understandingly when I told him not to bother because I wouldn't wait for him. In my room I took a suitcase and quickly began throwing some of my things into it. When Mutti came in to help me, she whispered, "Close the case and hurry to Uncle Robert's home. Papa left already via our service entrance to the apartment and was on his way to Robert, too." Actually, Uncle Robert was my father's cousin who had not yet left for Argentina to join the rest of his family. I closed my case and said loudly so the officer could hear, "I'll say goodbye to Papa in the bathroom," hoping that this would give Papa a few extra minutes to get away. Moments later, I grabbed my things, kissed Mutti goodbye, and ran down the stairs. I had done nothing to break the law, yet I felt like a criminal as I ran from the police, away from the home which I would never see again.

At the corner of the street I got into a taxi, and since traffic was light in the early morning, I arrived at Uncle Robert's home about ten minutes later. Mutti had called him by then and he was expecting us. Someone, he told me, had mentioned to him last night that the police had orders to arrest Polish citizens in the morning. Since it could have been just another rumor, he didn't pay attention to this one. Anyway, he was still a German citizen and this news did not affect him. Waiting for Papa, Mutti, and Fred to arrive, we had telephone calls from Aunt Hella's relatives and friends, all of them bringing more bad news. Aunt Hella's two brothers had been arrested and other reports told of people who were taken off streetcars, buses, and taxis simply because they looked Jewish. I was so scared as I waited for my family to arrive. It seemed an eternity had passed before Mutti and Fred finally entered the apartment. Mutti told us about the frightening moments after the policeman realized that Papa had escaped. Essentially, he told Mutti that he did not expect such treachery from her and left with the threatening words, "We'll get them soon, anyway!"

With every passing minute we became more and more concerned about Papa. He should have been at Uncle's home even before I got there. When he finally walked in, he told us that he had stopped at Rabbi Dr. Singermann's home. There he learned that the action was a response to a Polish deadline of October 28. This date was set by the Polish government to strip Polish citizens of their citizenship if they lived outside of Poland for more than six months at a time. This affected nearly all the Jewish people living in Germany who carried a Polish passport. We were pawns in the dispute between Poland and Germany over the corridor to East Prussia, and the Nazis seized this opportunity to rid itself of thousands of Jews.

It was barely eight o'clock in the morning on that fateful day, and we all sat around the table in Uncle Robert's dining room. Inconceivable but true — with a ring of our doorbell we had lost our home and future. Papa and I were fugitives and afraid of getting caught by the police and taken to a concentration camp. Going back to our home wasn't even an option, and hiding in Berlin was out of the question, too. Our passports were invalid and we didn't even have a chance to obtain a visitor's visa to escape to Amsterdam. Smuggling ourselves across any border was also hopeless as they were all tightly guarded. The one and only option we had was to try to get into Poland. We had to hope that a reasonable excuse for missing the deadline by just a few hours would be acceptable.

Leaving Berlin without being arrested was the first problem for Papa and me. The railroad station wouldn't be safe, so Mutti quickly arranged for Aunt Mia to drive us to Frankfurt/Oder, some eighty kilometers from Berlin. There we could catch the next train to Poland. Only two trains daily traveled from Berlin to Krakow via Frankfurt/Oder, and since time was of the essence we wanted to catch the mid-morning train. This would get us to the border only a few hours past the deadline. We got to the station just in time to see the train pull in. Running all the way, we got to the platform just as the station master was giving the signal for the train to move. With no time to purchase tickets, we had to pay a penalty and buy them from the conductor.

Luckily, we found a compartment all to ourselves. Papa could no longer contain himself and started crying like a child. We hugged each other lovingly and eventually he regained his composure. Everything that he had worked for all those years was gone. All his plans for our future had evaporated into thin air. Our family was torn apart and the immediate future depended upon finding refuge in Poland so that Mutti and Fred could join us. Occasionally we opened the door of our compartment and stood in the aisle, staring at the German landscape as we sped along. At one point Papa gave me a nudge with his arm and motioned that I take a look at a man coming down the aisle. He wore a brown shoe on one foot, a black one on the other, and carried a small overnight case in his hand. He, too, must have left his home in a hurry and was in a situation similar to ours. Papa and I spoke little to each other, but our emotions were evident as a million thoughts raced through our heads. We had nothing to eat all day and decided to make our way to the dining car. Walking past other compartments, we saw many people who looked as forlorn as we did. Everybody seemed to be avoiding eye contact and no one was anxious to be drawn into conversation. One never knew whom you could trust. At the stop in Breslau, a man came into our compartment making us feel even more uneasy. Luckily, he began to read his newspaper and left us at the next station in Oppeln. We were alone again — alone with our heavy hearts.

Finally the train slowed down as we approached the German-Polish border town of Beuthen, O/S (Oberschlesien). As we had passed this crossing many times before, we knew that it was never a simple task. The German passport control officer boarded the train, inspected the passports, and rubber-stamped a page documenting that we were leaving Germany on that day. He was followed by the inspector who checked for valuables and cash. I had completely forgotten about the money Mutti had given me as I packed my suitcase. Papa had also taken some money along in his wallet, but took a chance when he answered that we had nothing to declare. The German control was surprisingly fast and then the Polish inspectors entered the train. As always, they were the most unpleasant ruffians. It may have been because we didn't speak their language, but every time we crossed the border, they made us open our suitcases and rummage through everything with a vengeance. They never believed our word, and were always hoping to find something that we were smuggling into Poland without paying duty. It was no different this time. The last to enter our compartment was the Polish passport control officer. From shouts and commotion we heard in other compartments, we knew that passport after passport was being rejected. Nearly everybody was refused entry into Poland and we fared no better. We refused to get off the train as instructed by the Polish guards, and they had strict orders not to let any of us enter their country. This was a stalemate if ever there was one. The train sat in the station for a long time and eventually German border police came back on board. They spoke to us in an almost friendly fashion and tried to make us believe that they were trying to help us! "We know you want to go to your homeland and we will help you. Please, don't be afraid and trust us," they said. Now we had no choice in the matter. The Germans helped us get off the train and led us to the waiting room at the station. There, we met many others who like us had been removed from an earlier train. In that room, under German police control, we were indeed prisoners.

We could walk freely on the platform of the station, but we were not permitted to go anywhere else. Late in the evening, a senior police officer called us together and explained his plan to us. Three police trucks, waiting for us outside the station, would take us to a nearby border crossing. German guards would open the gate and we were to quietly walk across the no-man's land into Poland. All we could do now was to take our suitcases and find a place on the truck. A short ride brought us to the border outside the Polish community of Chorzow. The commanding police officer then remarked, "See, we kept our word." He pointed to the Polish guardhouse and said, "Move quietly, don't disturb them!" The Polish guards watched the activities on the German side and when they saw us moving in their direction, they stormed out of their guardhouse, pointed guns at us, and ordered us to go back at once. When we started returning to the trucks, we had another surprise in store for us. The German policemen were now reinforced with vicious shepherd dogs and with guns pointing at us yelled, "Don't you dare cross back into German territory." Emphasizing their orders, they fired shots into the air — we were in no-man's land and helpless!

At the end of October, the weather in that part of Europe was cold and damp. The night of Friday, October 28, Sabbath eve, was no exception. We huddled on the side of the road seeking protection from the wind blowing across the open fields. Like all the others, I was tired but could not sleep. A few people in our group spoke Polish, and one by one they approached the guardhouse. The guards refused to get into conversation with anyone except to say that nothing would be done until the morning. Then, and only then, would they be able to communicate with their superiors. There were women and children among us, and as the hours passed the need for comfort stations became desperate. A request to give us access to the sanitary facilities inside the guardhouse fell on deaf ears. Spotlights from both sides were trained on us, and we were in full view of the guards on either side. The Germans warned us not to stray into the fields to relieve ourselves or the dogs would come after us. Occasionally, a truck would travel the road, crossing the border, but they were warned not to stop. However, at about midnight, one of these drivers had the courage to stop his car as he crossed into Poland. He spoke briefly to one man and promised to tell the local Jewish community about our situation in no-man's land.

Sitting at the roadside, waiting for the first light of a new day, my thoughts wandered to the sermon Rabbi Dr. Freier delivered only a few weeks earlier during Yom Kippur services. It was a story taken from our midrash (a compilation of stories with special meaning). The story told of a poor man who lived with his family in a little village. His wife became ill, and by the time he had come home from work with his horse and wagon, her condition had gotten worse. Her pains were unbearable. Tired and exhausted, he still decided to take her to the doctor in the city nearby. It was already evening by the time he hitched his tired horse to the cart again. For his wife's comfort, he placed a bale of hay in the cart on which she could rest. The road into the city crossed a river where a ferry took people, carts, and horses from one side to the other. No matter what he did, the tired horse just couldn't go any faster, and by the time he came to the river, it had turned dark. The ferry was closed for the night. The poor man and his wife were desperate. He saw the watchman guarding the ferry on the far side of the river and he called across to him, "Please help me." The man on the other side yelled back, saying that he couldn't navigate the river at night. He watched his wife's condition get worse and called to the man on the ferry once more. "How soon before the ferry moves again?" The guard responded, "You must be patient and wait until the morning!" Desperate, the man called across again. "How much longer do we have to wait before the new day dawns?" From the other side came the answer, "The new day can't come until we have total darkness, and midnight is yet to come." Dr. Freier used this story to tell us that as bad as things seemed to be, it could get even worse before conditions improved. How befitting our current situation in no-man's land.

At the first sign of approaching daylight, we heard people on the Polish side arguing with guards. Eventually the arguing stopped and we could see a horse-drawn cart followed by a few bearded men and guards coming toward us. The cart brought us blankets, hot coffee, bread, and news that things would get straightened out very soon. This was just wishful thinking, but just hearing those words made us all feel better. The rabbi of the community, so we were told, was informed about our predicament, and during the night he went from door to door gathering people, blankets, and food. Even though it was Shabbat, he said that it was a greater mitzvah (observance of the commandments) to help us, rather than spending the day in prayers. The Hasidic rabbi set the example by riding in the first cart to bring us help. They said there was little else they could do for us now, since all government offices were closed for the weekend. Papa asked one of the helpers to contact Dr. Ignatz Schwartzbart, one of Papa's childhood friends, and a member of the *Sejm* (Polish parliament). He was one of an extremely small number of Jews ever to be elected to the Polish government. Luckily it didn't rain that morning, but still we were all chilled to the bone from the dew and cold night we had endured. As the day wore on the community brought us more supplies, but Papa's request for help from Dr. Schwartzbart was unsuccessful because he was out of the country.

In the afternoon our situation took a turn for the better when an influential man in the community used his position to get us off the road and into the gym of the public school. The local police accepted responsibility that no one would escape. Once inside the building we were able to thaw out and the warm food given us revived our spirits. Soon we were asked to get in line for registration, but Papa had some other thoughts. He told me to take my suitcase and ask the guard for permission to use the toilet and change out of my damp clothes. Living at the border, the policeman spoke German and allowed me to do as I had asked. Papa watched me leave the gym and he, too, approached the officer for permission to use the restroom. I turned and saw the policeman walking back toward the registration desk. Papa and I made a fast turn to the right, and were soon outside the entrance door. Luckily, no one in the gym knew our name, and we were not listed on any official papers. We knew we would not be missed.

By now it was evening, and with only a few street lights illuminating the neighborhood, it was easy for us to disappear into the darkness. After walking a few short blocks, we found the railroad station and, like thieves hiding in the dark, we waited for the train, any train, to arrive. It felt like an eternity, but eventually one did come and we managed to lose ourselves among the people getting off and on. We didn't care where the train would take us, we just had to get away from this border town. We had no tickets and no Polish zlotys to buy them, but good fortune was with us as the train was crowded and the conductor hadn't gotten to us before we arrived in Katowice, the first stop on the main line after crossing the border from Germany. We were free and out of immediate danger.

The first thing we had to do was get in touch with Mutti. She hadn't heard from us for thirty-eight hours and must have been frantic. Unfortunately, there was no way for us to make a call. We couldn't even contact someone to make a call for us. None of our relatives in Chrzanow had a telephone, nor the need for one. Telephone service, except for business, was limited and, at best, cumbersome. One had to go to the post office for someone to contact the other party and set a time for all to be at their respective post offices. To complete such arrangements took hours, but that was the only way a call could be completed.

Two orthodox Jews were also waiting, as we were, for the train to Krakow via Chrzanow, some forty kilometers away. Papa spoke to them in Yiddish and they were happy to help us by exchanging some German marks for zlotys. We had no time to purchase tickets, but with Polish currency in our pockets Papa knew he could deal with the conductor for our fare. Now I was about to have quite an interesting lesson. P.K.P. are the initials decorating every railroad car, station, locomotive, curtain, and all that was connected with the Polish railroad. These initials stood for Polskie Koleje Panstwowe (Polish State Railroad), but people who used the railroad attached a different meaning to these initials. To them, P.K.P. meant "plac konductorowy polowe" (pay half a fare to the conductor). The train wasn't very crowded and the conductor approached us soon after we boarded. Not saying another word but Chrzanow, Papa handed him a five-zloty note and pointed to me and himself. The conductor just nodded his head and we were on our way. Forty hours had passed since we had left our home and, physically and emotionally exhausted, we fell asleep in our seats. The conductor's voice announcing Chrzanow, and the jolt of the train stopping, brought us back to reality. It was after 10 o'clock in the evening and we were the only passengers to get off the train.

When we had visited our family in Chrzanow before, we had always arrived during daylight hours and a host of *fiakers* (horses and buggies) would be waiting there for customers. I remember the excitement when nearly all the drivers would rush toward us. Each would grab at least one of our suitcases and stow it away in his cab, hoping that Papa would select his buggy. All drivers wanted Papa to choose their cab because they knew they would be rewarded generously. Since Papa knew most of them and their families, it was always a difficult choice for Papa to make.

This late at night, there was only one buggy waiting for a possible late-comer. No sooner did we come through the gate when the driver recognized us and started shouting the blessing in Hebrew and Yiddish "Borooch Habah, Geloibt zu Gott as ihr sayjnt doo!" (Blessings to the one who came, praise to God that you are here). It was a greeting that surely came from his heart. He took our suitcase, made us sit down, covered us with a heavy blanket to protect us from the cold air, and repeated over and over again, "Geloibt zu Gott!" As soon as he got to his seat, he started telling us that everyone in town knew about the raids in Germany and that we were the first ones to arrive in town.

It was only a short ride to Uncle's home and soon we were making our way to his apartment. The sound of a *fiaker* at that time of night brought all his neighbors to their windows, and some came rushing through their doors to greet us. They were genuinely happy to see us safe. Aunt and Uncle couldn't wait to get us inside where we were hugged and kissed and asked a million questions. After catching our breath, we told them all that had happened to us during the past forty plus hours. But still we had not contacted Mutti, and at this late hour there was no hope of doing so.

Mutti had managed to call Uncle Samuel on Friday to tell him that we were on our way to Chrzanow, but when she hadn't heard from us by Saturday, she called the owner of the local hotel. He was a good friend of the family, and knowing the situation, he offered to relay her message even though it was Shabbat. In a community like Chrzanow, news traveled unbelievably fast, and though the hour was late, news of our arrival spread like wildfire. Many townspeople who had relatives in Germany were concerned about their safety and came to question us. We told them what we knew, but really we couldn't ease their anxiety.

I woke up late the next morning and heard Papa in conversation with Aunt and Uncle. Uncle had finished his morning prayers, but when he saw me he offered me his teffillin (phylactics) so that I could pray, too. Aunt looked at my reaction and Papa gave me a wink that made words superfluous. "Of course, what a great idea!" I responded. Ever since the day of my bar mitzvah, Papa made me use my teffillin on Sunday for my morning prayers. I wasn't particularly happy to do this but realized this was an issue I couldn't win. He made it clear that he wanted me to know and understand our Jewish heritage, customs, and tradition. It was a case of "do as I tell you," rather than "do as I do." On that morning however, in Uncle's home, I was happy to show them that Papa had taught me well. I knew, too, that the kind of meals I would be eating would be different from those we had at home, because Uncle's home observed kashruth. The rules of keeping kosher were familiar to me, but restrictions imposed on us by the Nazis had forced Mutti to discontinue our kosher kitchen years before.

Soon after breakfast we made our way to the hotel to thank Mr. Bochenek for his help with messages. He then graciously offered us the use of his phone to call Mutti. The long-distance operator made the connection, but no one was home. Now it was our turn to be concerned. Next we called Aunt Mia and she was delirious to hear from us. I had to speak to her with great caution because I knew that calls from outside Germany were most likely monitored by the Gestapo. Casually I mentioned that I was visiting Uncle and that Abe (Papa) was here with me, too. I tried to contact Erna (Mutti), I said, but there was no answer. She replied that Erna and Fred were visiting cousin Rosa because she was so lonely with her son away on business. We now knew that Mutti was afraid of staying at home because of possible danger to herself and Fred and that Rosa's son Isi had been arrested.

The marketplace in Chrzanow was the same as other marketplaces in small towns all over Poland. People would gather near Mr. Bochenek's hotel at any time of day to hear news, exchange ideas, or simply gossip. But now, as we left the hotel, we were surrounded by people anxious to get first-hand information about the fate of their relatives. There were no Yiddish newspapers on Shabbat and the Polish papers had only sketchy reports about the raids against Polish Jews in Germany. On Sunday however, the Yiddish papers reported all the available details about the arrests. All we could do was tell the townspeople of our experiences, which confirmed what they had read in the papers.

We were not alone in our difficult days. Many other families had also lost their home and worldly possessions at a moment's notice. In Berlin, they arrested only men, but in other cities they took women, too. With only a suitcase or two packed with what they could gather, they were put on trains, headed for the Polish border. Hearing these stories, we realized that as bad as it was for us, others fared far worse. We heard about trains arriving at the Polish border town of Poznan and forced to stay there when the government refused them entry. Many days later, the Polish government let them off the trains and interned thousands at a camp in nearby Zbaszyn.

Getting Mutti and Fred out of Berlin was now our greatest problem. They had no valid passports, and neither did we. To begin with, we had to legitimize our being in Poland. Wasting no time in obeying the law, Uncle took us to register at the police department on Monday morning. The clerk took our passports, looked at them, and the first question out of his mouth was, "When did you get here and how? There is no stamp in your passports to show you entered Poland legitimately." Uncle, a member of the Jewish community council, knew this clerk, but there was no way he could convince him to apply his stamp to our registration and make us legal residents. Having authority over a rubber stamp turned a government clerk into a powerful person. This clerk wanted his pound of flesh, and after days of endless discussions, Uncle Samuel gave him the bribe he demanded and the official stamp was placed in our records. This was the first step in an endless chain of papers and documents we needed in order to get Mutti and Fred to join us.

In Berlin, Mutti and Fred had returned to our apartment and packed a few cartons of clothing for Papa and me. Sending them to us, however, was not so simple. As per Nazi government restrictions, cartons had to be a certain size, and one person could send only one package a month to any specific address. To get around these restrictions, Mutti went to various post offices and mailed packages, intended for us, to a number of our relatives. As a result, we had packages all over the city which we had to collect.

Chrzanow was as good a place as any to live under the circumstances. This provincial city hosted the county government, and according to 1938 statistics, more than thirty-five thousand people, almost half of them Jewish, lived there. Compared with other towns in Poland, it had a strong Western European influence. Some streets were tree-lined and all of them had sidewalks. There were some very old one-level structures, but there was also a very modern section with three- and four-storied buildings. In the center of town there was a marketplace where peasants came to sell their produce. Krakowska Street was the main thoroughfare from east to west and formed one side of the marketplace quadrangle. The prettiest and most prestigious street was Aleja Henryka. It was a wide street with trees, government buildings, and beautiful residences where people took leisurely walks on pleasant afternoons. Especially on Shabbat, everyone went there to see and be seen by friends as they strolled along, smiling, and exchanging pleasantries. The town had a cosmopolitan flair, a remnant of its Austro-Hungarian past. Many residents had relatives who lived in Berlin, Paris, Vienna, and other major European cities and they came to Chrzanow frequently. It wasn't the place I had envisioned spending the rest of my days, but for now we found refuge there until things could get sorted out. The people were all friendly and very sympathetic.

Aunt Marie and her daughters, Sala and Sarah, had a store on Krakowska Street which sold Polish and Yiddish newspapers, cigarettes, tobacco, and candies. It was a busy little place since the bus linking Katowice, some forty kilometers to the west, and Krakow, a similar distance to the east, stopped directly in front of their store. It was a convenient place for people to wait for the bus, and for want of anything else to do, Papa and I spent many hours there. Well-meaning friends and neighbors offered names of people and places they thought could help us cut through bureaucracy and speed up the paperwork for Mutti and Fred to join us. We left no suggestion untried; we traveled to Krakow, Katowice and other places too, and received lots of sympathy and promises, but unfortunately nothing else.

Uncle Samuel and Aunt Marie always thought of Papa as another son and insisted that we stay in their house as long as necessary. Grandma too wanted us to stay with her at the farm, but while we enjoyed vacationing there in the summer, the winter season was something different. We did go to see her, and though it was only thirty kilometers away, it was a three-hour ride because of switching trains in Oswiecim (renamed Auschwitz by Germany) and the long wait between trains. We spent the day with Grandma and visited four of Papa's brothers who had settled in Zator, a small town about ten kilometers from Grandma's farm. They also insisted that we move in with them and make it our temporary home. Papa was very touched by their warmth and sincerity, but eventually they agreed that it was easier for us to be in a larger city like Krakow or Chrzanow. There we could be near government offices and had a better chance of accomplishing things. Their counsel and help was heartwarming and I was very proud to be part of such a loving family. Every time I got to see one of my uncles or aunts, they put money in my pocket, just for candy, a movie or ice cream, they would say. I knew their gifts came to me from the bottom of their hearts, and since our resources were extremely limited, they were greatly appreciated.

On November 7, 1938, we were at cousin Clara's home when Trudi, their maid, came out of the kitchen to tell us that a special news bulletin would be broadcast shortly. We turned our attention to the radio, but the announcement was in Polish, which neither Papa nor I understood. It was so frustrating. Papa had spent the first thirteen years of his life in what was now Poland, but at that time Chrzanow was part of the Austro-Hungarian empire and people spoke German and, of course, Yiddish, too. Everyone motioned that something very special had occurred and they would tell us the details when the news was completed. Watching their faces, I wasn't sure whether their reactions were happy or fearful ones. At the end of the broadcast they told us that the third secretary of the German embassy in Paris, Herr von Rath, had been shot. Herschel Grynszpan, a Jew from Berlin, had been caught and arrested. Herschel Grynszpan was one of the students at the Jewish community school, Grosse Hamburger Strasse, which I had attended. He was a year ahead of me and I had seen him occasionally. After graduation, without being able to find work in Berlin, he went to Paris on a visitor's visa. Like so many others, his visa had expired and he became an illegal refugee. Depressed about his misfortune — no home or job, and hearing that his father had been arrested and deported to Poland, he looked for a place to vent his anger. He somehow got a handgun, went to the German Embassy, and shot Herr von Rath.

Nazi reaction to this assassination was swift. Pretending to the world that this was the people's reaction, Hitler ordered his SS and SA men to seek revenge. On November 9, 1938, a date never to be forgotten, his henchmen broke into Jewish stores, apartments, businesses, and synagogues all over Germany. Everything that wasn't nailed down found its way out the window and into the street. According to available records, twenty-six thousand Jewish men were arrested and sent to concentration camps, and ninety-one people were killed. Seventy-five hundred shops and businesses were destroyed and one thousand synagogues were set on fire. In addition, the Jewish community had to pay one billion mark as payment for removing the debris and cleaning the streets after this "reaction of the German people to the assassination." The night of November

9, 1938, became known as "Kristall nacht" (crystal night), the night of broken glass. It was the beginning of the Holocaust.

In France, Grynszpan was arrested, tried, and sentenced by the courts. In Germany, there was no punishment for the hoodlums. I'm sure that every German knew what had happened that night and even if they didn't participate they certainly had heard about the destruction and saw the many pictures in all their papers. What had happened to morality and law? Isn't the one who watches a criminal act without doing anything about it just as guilty as the perpetrator?

Needing to know if Mutti and Fred were safe, I spent hours trying to contact Aunt Mia to get some news about them. It was easier for me to speak with Aunt because Papa still had a strained relationship with her for marrying outside of our faith. Eventually, when I got connected, she told me that Mutti and Fred were unharmed, but there was nothing left of our apartment. Our home and business had been destroyed. We were able to arrange for Mutti to call us the next day and what a joy it was for us to hear her voice again. She tried to sound optimistic, but we weren't even sure if we would ever be together again; certainly not in the foreseeable future. It was an emotional conversation and it took Papa a long time to recover from this trauma.

5

Caring Relatives

My life, formerly so busy and exciting, was now boring and unproductive. The only bright spot was the arrival of Sigi Singer, a former classmate of mine. Like me, he too was welcomed by relatives with open arms, but as they were busy with their own lives, we were soon left to our own resources. We didn't speak or read Polish and couldn't even pass the time studying or reading books from the library. We were just hanging around, waiting and waiting. All we could do was play chess in the afternoons, but our minds were not on that, either.

At cousin Clara's home I met their neighbor's son Szlamek, who was about my age. He invited Sigi and me to join him on a Saturday afternoon to attend a meeting of the local Zionist Youth Group. We were delighted and looked forward to meeting youngsters our own age. There were about seventy-five boys and girls in attendance and we were warmly welcomed. We conversed with nearly all of them in Yiddish, as this was the language used in their homes. Familiar Hebrew songs started the afternoon program and made us feel right at home. However, soon their discussions began in Polish, and we were at a loss. Not being able to participate, we felt out of place and excused ourselves from the meeting room.

As I had been instructed by Aunt Mia, I waited a week before calling my grandparents in Amsterdam and was surprised when Aunt Mia answered the phone. She told me about all the difficulties Mutti and Fred had suffered since Kristallnacht. Our apartment and Papa's business were in ruins. Mutti and Fred had moved in with cousin Rosa, who was also alone after her son Isi was interned in the Polish camp in Zbaszyn. More bad news involved Oma, who had suffered a mild stroke. Not wanting to add to Mutti's problems, they kept Oma's condition a secret until Oma recovered enough to tell Mutti herself what had happened to her. Aunt Mia then told me how she and Uncle Bobby fled Berlin the day after Kristallnacht and how they intended to remain in Amsterdam legally, if possible, or illegally, if they must. Uncle had been concerned for a long time that someone would find out that Aunt was Jewish, so he had made preparations for them to leave Berlin in a hurry, if necessary. Working after hours in his shop, when he was alone, he built hiding places into one of his cars. The day after that awful night of November 9, they took all they could stow into the altered car, left their home and business, and drove to Amsterdam. Uncle was so ashamed of being German that he vowed never to step foot into Germany again. Mutti came to say goodbye to them and brought with her the only piece of crystal and a silver tray that were not destroyed on that fateful night. Miraculously, these two valuable mementos survived the war and are now treasured possessions in my home.

As a German business couple, Aunt and Uncle had crossed the German–Dutch border many times before. It was never really simple, but this trip was really a most complicated one. Their car was fully loaded and a suspicious border guard might take a closer look at them. To reduce the risk, they stopped in Emmerich, a German town near the Dutch border, where they rented a hotel room and unloaded many of their belongings. The car was now only half full as they continued across the border to Amsterdam, just an hour and a half away. Uncle unloaded his car, and a few days later went back to Emmerich and brought the rest of their possessions to Amsterdam. This was a very dangerous and courageous move on his part. There weren't many Germans who were willing to give up a successful business and trade it for the life of a refugee.

A letter arrived from Mutti telling us of her frustration because she couldn't visit her mother in Amsterdam. Her passport was invalid and the request for a visitor's visa on an emergency basis had been rejected, too. It was heartbreaking, separated from each other, living in different countries, and then not being able to visit a sick mother.

Papa telephoned Mutti to commiserate and to offer hope. He told her that we were on our way to Krakow to meet someone who was well connected and possibly able to get her and Fred out of Berlin quickly. This news was good for her to hear. She then suggested that we visit Aunt Paula, Oma's twin sister, while in Krakow. Sadly, the meeting with our contact, Mr. Zonenszein, was full of promises, but as usual, led nowhere.

We visited Aunt Paula and had dinner with her, her son Alek, and his charming wife Sidonia. Since we had seen Alek last, he had been made vice-president of a major chemical and coal mining company. He was also a member of the Jewish Community Council in Krakow, and well informed about the current situation in Germany and Poland. He volunteered to help us in any way he could, and suggested that I might join the Kinder Transport to London. He said that he could arrange it easily and quickly. Papa didn't like this idea when we were in Berlin and still hadn't changed his mind. "Our family must stay together," he said. Next, Alek suggested a move to Shanghai, a journey he could possibly arrange for us. Such a trip involved a dangerous land route via Russia and would be a long and arduous undertaking. More than that, the differences in culture and language, Papa commented, would make it most difficult for us to adjust. Anyway, we really couldn't plan anything until Mutti and Fred were out of Germany.

When Alek heard that I was interested in advertising art, he called the studio that did work for his company and arranged for me to meet the art director. I had no work permit and couldn't get one, but this might be an opportunity for me to gain some valuable experience. I'd be doing something constructive with my time while waiting and hoping for something good to happen. If everything worked out, Alek and Sidonia would let me use a room in their apartment and Aunt Paula added that I could have my meals with her. The following day I met the art director who, unfortunately, didn't speak German. Still, I understood that he wanted to please Alek and asked to see samples of my work the next time I would be in Krakow. This was the first positive thing that had happened to me since I left Berlin. As soon as we were back in Chrzanow, I wrote Mutti about our visit to Aunt Paula and how well we were treated. I asked her to send some of my art samples, provided any of my work had survived Kristallnacht, so I could go back to Krakow and visit the studio once again. I had no materials or even a place to produce any samples in Chrzanow, so my hopes depended on Mutti finding a few pieces of my work, and luckily she did.

On the twenty-eighth of November, one day prior to Poland's Independence Day celebration, Papa and I went to Krakow again. I showed

A visit from Aunt Paula, Oma's twin sister from Krakow. Seated from left to right: Opa, Aunt Paula, Oma. Standing in back: me, Mutti, and Fred. Berlin, 1928.

the samples of my work to the director and received many compliments. He invited me to come the following Monday and work as an apprentice, of course without pay. Nevertheless, I was very happy with this latest development. We visited Aunt Paula, thanked Alek profusely for the opportunity, and made arrangements for me to stay in Krakow. As we left Aunt's building, we saw a crowd gathering to watch a parade of soldiers coming down the street. Papa and I were early for our bus, so we watched the parade, and what we saw was nearly unbelievable. Papa turned to me and said, "Oh my God, is this the Polish army that is going to fight the Germans?" There was a unit of mounted cavalry ahead of six World War I vintage tanks rattling along the street. They looked and sounded like equipment found in a junkyard. Behind the tanks was a marching band followed by a battery of cannons. Each cannon was pulled by eight horses, and at the rear a detachment of infantry soldiers shuffled along. After having seen German parades, this one was indeed a pitiful sight. German tanks didn't rattle along the streets; they were well maintained. Their cannons were mounted on fast-moving vehicles and German soldiers marched with discipline. Heaven forbid, we thought; if ever there was a war, the Polish military was certainly no match for the Germans. Back in Chrzanow, Papa commented about what we had seen, but no one was happy about Papa's "unpatriotic" remarks. They suggested that we didn't see the real thing, but we were not convinced. Reading the news and listening to all the saber-rattling, we were very uncomfortable with the European situation. Since war might break out soon, we were afraid of getting caught in the middle of it all. What a terrible time for us — Mutti and Fred in Berlin, and us on the other side of the frontier.

I started my job in Krakow and moved into Alek's apartment. The view from it was absolutely spectacular. Located on the top floor of the newest and tallest residential building, I looked across the Vistula, Poland's largest river, flowing directly below me. On the opposite bank I could see the Wavel, the old castle and fortress protecting ancient Krakow. What a magnificent panorama of this important Polish city. I had been in Krakow a number of times visiting relatives, but I never saw the real city. There were modern sections with the latest plumbing, central heating, electricity, and conveniences, in sharp contrast to the areas dating back to the days of King Kazimierz and the Middle Ages. The numerous marketplaces and cobblestone streets with open sewers were still there — along with open wells in the courtyards for residents to fetch their water.

I was nervous yet anxious to start my new job. The art studio was in the heart of the business section and not far from Alek's apartment. It could easily be reached by trolley, but to save money, I decided to walk. Not used to such cold weather, my ears, fingers, and toes were frozen by the time I reached the studio. I was embarrassed that on my first day at work I was more concerned about warming my limbs than trying to make a good impression. To make matters worse, there was no one who spoke German when I arrived, and no one seemed to know anything about my working there. While thawing out and waiting in the reception room, I saw samples of the work for such well-known companies as Omega, the Swiss watch company, and Suchard, the Swiss chocolatier. I was impressed. The owner finally arrived a little later and greeted me with a friendly, "Dzien dobre" (Good day or Hello). He motioned for me to be patient as he made arrangements to place another desk in the room. Then he seemed to be explaining my presence to his employees, and a few smiles came my way, making me feel a little better. There I was, only seventeen years old, surrounded by people who did not understand me and that I could not understand, either. Not able to exchange a thought or two made me very uncomfortable, but I was determined to learn and gain experience. I was not willing to pass up this rare opportunity.

On one of my walks to and from work I noticed the clubhouse of the Maccabi Sports Club and decided to go in and look around. As soon as I came through the door, someone greeted me and, recognizing that I didn't speak Polish, spoke to me in Yiddish. As a member of their sister club, Maccabi in Berlin, I was welcomed by all. On my second visit to the club I met a girl that looked so very familiar to me. Her name was Esther Widmann, exactly the same as my mother's maiden name. What a coincidence! She turned out to be the daughter of my grandfather's younger brother. I knew Opa had a brother in Krakow but I had never met him.

Coming to Aunt Paula for dinner one evening, I saw that she had been crying and was terribly upset. She finally told me that Sidonia, Alek's wife, had been arrested. This was not the first time, but because of the current political situation, this was serious. Sidonia was an active member of the Communist party and very outspoken in her opinions. Just as the Polish regime was opposed to Germany and Nazism, they were also opposed to Russia and Communism. To prevent demonstrations in the country, they arrested all known activists and Sidonia was one of them. Her arrest would have been the end of my staying in Krakow if not for my grandfather's brother. As soon as he heard about Sidonia's arrest, he asked me to come and stay with his family and I readily agreed.

The city was preparing itself for the Chanukah and Christmas season and vendors in the marketplace had begun selling Christmas trees and toys and gifts for the holidays. It was the season for joy and excitement, but I was lonely without my family and friends. On the day before Christmas, when everyone was gearing up for the holiday, the owner of the studio called me into his office. There, his wife, who spoke some German, explained to me that economic conditions were so bad that they had to lay off some of their artists. They were concerned and afraid of having trouble if I were to return for the new year. I was disappointed and saddened as I packed my belongings and said goodbye to my wonderful relatives who were so helpful to me. I thanked them again for all they had done and took the next bus back to Chrzanow.

Newspapers and radio broadcasts were full of Hitler's demands directed toward General Smygly Rydz, the Polish prime minister, and at the same time the Germans were renewing their provocations against Czechoslovakia. As many of us expected, Hitler reneged on promises he had made to the English and French foreign secretaries in Munich, and used the sixth anniversary of his appointment as Reichskanzler to threaten the world. We heard his tirades as we sat around the table and listened to the radio at Clara's home. One of his threats was directed at us, the Jewish people of Europe. We heard him say that if ever a war were to erupt, it would mean the end of all Jews. We pooh-poohed his statement, still convinced that when the first shots were fired, the Western world would make a quick end to Hitler and his Nazis.

The first detainees from the camp in Zbaszyn had been released, and among them were two people from Chrzanow. They confirmed the stories we had heard about terrible living conditions in the camp. They spoke of inmates who had no relatives in Poland to contact for assistance. Even for people with close family ties, it was complicated to get through Polish bureaucracy and their inbred anti–Semitism to get someone released. We were told of demoralizing experiences when men, women, and children had to live together without privacy under the constant surveillance of Polish guards who detested their Jewish prisoners.

Cousin Isi was among those who were released, due in part to the help of his mother's sister Hella. It still took more than five months, all through that terrible winter, for him to be freed. When it was arranged for him to stay in Krakow with his aunt, we told him about the Kinder Transport to London and that he must make sure he got in touch with Alek, Aunt Paula's son. A few weeks later, Isi was on his way to England.

There were many people who made their way to Chrzanow from camp Zbaszyn, and among them were Isi Rosenzweig and Salo Feiler. Sigi and I knew them from Berlin, but in Chrzanow we really became close and spent our days together. The others we had met through the Zionist organization had little time for us as they were either in school or at work. We, on the other hand, had nothing but time. All we could do was take long walks, discuss politics, science, and other subjects we had studied in class and, if the weather was inclement, we would play chess or cards in our families' homes. Often we compared our lonely days with conditions of our friends whom we had heard from by mail. They all complained about their difficulties in foreign countries as refugees and it seemed that we were the luckier ones with relatives who had made a place for us in their homes.

Even though expected, it still shocked us greatly when Hitler's army marched into Czechoslovakia and occupied the country on March 15, 1938. Again, Hitler got away with his aggression. Hitler badly wanted the industrial plants of Czechoslovakia to supplement German production of tanks, planes, and other war materials. The signal for things to come was loud and clear and our worries about Mutti and Fred's safety became unbearable.

The weather had turned mild, and on one beautiful Shabbat afternoon walk, my three friends and I were involved in a heated debate and didn't realize how far we had wandered. As we walked down the country road, past the local railroad station, we never noticed the group of Polish youngsters at the edge of the forest on the far side of the road. We only became aware of them when they began throwing stones at us. They yelled and threatened us, but not understanding Polish, we didn't know what they were yelling about. However, the word *zyd* (Jew), shouted over and over again, was easily understood by us. As we were dressed for Shabbat, we were not eager to get involved in a fight, and more than that, we couldn't afford to ruin our best clothes. We remained passive for quite a while, but there came a point when enough was enough. We were not weaklings, good athletes in fact, and very capable of giving a good account of ourselves. Removing our jackets and ties, we gave them what they asked for. This was the first time that we had ever dared to defend ourselves against the Polish youngsters in town. It was a wonderful feeling as we bloodied their noses and landed many good punches.

Someone in the community must have witnessed the fight, because when we returned to the city, everyone on the street greeted us with a smile. We were told that a few girls had been attacked in that same area before and it was good that we got back at these hoodlums. We were treated as if we were the returning heroes! Being seventeen or eighteen, we enjoyed a flirting smile from a pretty girl, but soon the shy smiles became a bit bolder. It wasn't easy to resist their charm, intelligence, and beauty, but in a small town where everyone knew everyone, it took a lot of discipline on our part to keep our distance, yet remain friendly. Starting a friendship that didn't develop into a permanent relationship would be embarrassing to the girl and blemish her reputation. Neither my friends nor I had any intentions

67

of tying ourselves down, so we kept very much to ourselves. We could understand why the local girls had their interest in us, why not? Big city boys were enticing, and if things ever returned to normal, they might be able to leave the small town and come along with us to our original home cities. There were times when matchmakers approached us individually with offers of substantial parental assistance for a good liaison. We had our laughs as we compared notes, but I can't say we weren't flattered. It was a nice lift to our egos, but "no thank you" was our answer. I was raised in a different environment and tying myself down at such an early age and under these circumstances didn't make much sense to me.

Joel, a nephew of Uncle's neighbor, and our cousin Sala, were in love and planned to get married as soon as Joel was discharged from the army. As the possibility for war became ever more real, they advanced the date of their wedding. The family believed that, as in World War I, married men would not be the first ones to be called into service. Now, with Joel's discharge only weeks away, the family was busy making wedding plans. Joel was stationed in the army barracks at nearby Oswiecim (Auschwitz) and came to visit Sala whenever he was off duty. It was a happy time for all the family. Papa tried to use the family wedding invitation to expedite Mutti and Fred's joining us, but once again the authorities denied our request. What was the Polish government gaining by keeping families apart? What purpose did it serve? Why couldn't a wife and minor child join her husband in a country in which they were all citizens?

Aunt Marie and Joel's aunt were busy cooking and baking. Using their adjoining apartments, they rearranged furniture to make room for all the people they had to invite. Not only family, friends, and neighbors were to share the festivities but, as was customary, homeless strangers in town were asked to join us for the special meal, too. It was the first time I was to attend a wedding, a modern orthodox one at that, and I was looking forward to the experience. The wedding was planned for a Tuesday because, describing the days of creation in our Torah, it says, "God looked upon his work for that day (Tuesday) and described the creation as 'good, good.'" It is the only place in the scriptures where the word *good* appears twice, indicating that this day was very special and a lucky beginning. The weather cooperated and it was a most beautiful afternoon for the ceremony, which was held in the courtyard of their building. Sala was in her room, off-limits to everyone except the women who were busy preparing the bride. Joel was at Clara's home, surrounded by all the men in the family. A *Battkhen* (Yiddish rhyme maker) and *Klesmers* (musicians) entertained us in the apartment and then accompanied the entourage as they danced down the streets leading Joel to the *chuppah* (wedding canopy). Once Joel was in place, the women in the family led Sara seven times around him before the rabbi pronounced the blessings. The customary glass, a reminder of the destruction of our holy temple in Jerusalem, was broken and the good wishes of "mazal tov" completed the ceremony. Everyone then went upstairs to the apartments and enjoyed their festive and delicious meal.

Holding the corner of a handkerchief to avoid bodily contact, men danced in one room and women in another. This was something I had not seen before, but truthfully I had more fun when I joined the younger group in another room where they danced to records of ballroom music. One of Joel's cousins insisted on dancing with me and wouldn't accept my excuse that I had never danced before. She was persistent and taught me my first waltz and tango steps. Once I knew what to do, I did enjoy myself. Some elders showed great concern about modern dancing and came into our room now and then, just to check that we didn't get too close to each other. We didn't care — we laughed and continued having fun. The wedding was a highlight not just for the family, but for the community as well. We talked about it for days after.

Not long after the wedding, the front door of Uncle's apartment opened and there stood Aunt Marie's youngest brother, waiting for his sister's welcoming hug. Instead of greeting him, Aunt Marie, not hiding her anger and disappointment said, "Now you're coming? ... The wedding was last week!" Stunned, he looked at her and answered, "What wedding?" He then sat down and began to tell his tale of woes.

He was an international dealer of diamonds with offices in Vienna and Prague. Soon after Hitler's army marched into Vienna, they confiscated his business and expelled him from his suite in a residential hotel. He escaped to Prague and continued business from there until the Nazis occupied Czechoslovakia. Again, he was pushed out of his business and home and never received the invitation to Sala's wedding. It took him a long time to get to the Polish border and along the way he was robbed, leaving him with only his attaché case and enough money to pay someone to escort him across the Polish border at night.

The telephone call we had been so anxiously awaiting finally came at the end of May. At long last Mutti received a note from the Polish consulate in Berlin that the new passport for her and Fred was ready to be picked up. Our joy and happiness were indescribable. She needed two days, so she said, to complete some minor details, pack whatever was left into cartons, and send most of them through the mail. That, she said, would be much easier than carrying a lot of luggage with her. We now had two days to set up a place for the four of us to live. Anticipating this day, Mr. Weinberg, a friend and a regular at the evening gin games at Clara's home, told Papa not to worry about an apartment. As soon as Mutti and Fred arrived, he'd gladly rent us the small apartment his daughter had vacated. It was a modern two-family house and the rent he asked from us was minimal since he knew of our circumstances. The family was so happy to hear our good news, and it seemed that everyone had a chair or piece of furniture they just didn't need anymore. By the time Mutti and Fred were due to arrive, we had managed to have a small home prepared to welcome them.

The hours moved especially slow on the day we made our way to the station in a *fiaker*. We got there early so we could see the train arrive. Mutti and Fred stood at the door and we eagerly ran to help them with their luggage. We looked at each other in disbelief as we hugged and kissed again, again, and again. It was a most joyful reunion.

On the way to our apartment, Mutti began telling us the gruesome details of their life in Berlin after we had left. Choking with emotion, she described the infamous *Kristallnacht* to us. Seeing the vandalism raging in the street, Mutti decided to hide what she could between the dirty laundry, and as the hoodlums entered, she and Fred fled the apartment via the service entrance. Being afraid that someone would recognize them, they rode the streetcars for hours. The mezuzah on our front door was a sure giveaway, but our neighbors knew that we were Jewish anyway. Could they have prevented this destruction? Maybe, but they were afraid of getting into trouble themselves. Returning home late that evening, Mutti and Fred found the front door had been forced open. When she entered the apartment, she couldn't believe what she saw. The glass cabinet filled with our precious crystal was turned over and everything in it was smashed to pieces. Porcelain figures were broken, leather furniture was ripped, and most of the fine china dishes were gone, too. It was a disaster. Papa and I had known about the destruction from Mutti's letter, but hearing about it from Mutti's mouth made it so much more painful. Papa quoted Aunt Marie who had said to him earlier, "Geld verloren — nichts verloren, Hoffnung verloren — alles verloren," (Losing money is like losing nothing at all, but losing hope is like losing everything). It was more important that all of us were healthy and together again. We would face the future as a family and give each other the courage to get through these awful times. We had a comfortable home before, and we were sure we could create one again. In time, it would all work out — so we hoped.

With hardly any time to regain our composure, we were whisked off to Aunt Marie's home for dinner. The entire family had gathered to give Mutti and Fred a loving welcome. Uncle and Aunt had a very special affection for Mutti and were hugging and kissing her endlessly. In conversation, Mutti told us how some desperate people found ways to get out of Germany. Wives accepted positions as maids or governesses, while their husbands took positions as butlers or gardeners in English townhouses. These few positions had become available through the Jewish emigration services. Others gave serious thought to traveling to China, and some people actually made that difficult trek. She also heard of people with relatives in the States who paid American citizens to visit Germany, marry their relative, then get divorced once they were in the United States. It may not have been an ethical arrangement, but it worked well for some.

One of the Jewish relief organizations, Mutti was told, had made arrangements to bring a ship filled with refugees to Cuba. Only first-class passengers could apply and they had to show sufficient capital outside of Germany to be accepted. With help from relatives in Holland, Mutti thought that we, too, could possibly get passage. However, when she finally got an appointment to speak to someone at the agency, every cabin on the ship was already booked. Not long after Mutti came to join us in Chrzanow, that ship, the S.S. *St. Louis*, owned by the German-American line, set sail for Cuba. This journey became a bitter chapter in Holocaust history. By the time the *St. Louis* reached the harbor in Havana, heavy pressure on the Cuban government forced them to rescind landing privileges to all on board. Throughout the Americas, Jewish organizations tried everything in their power to have the ship land at any place on the American continent. Regrettably, all the doors remained locked. Even the great humanitarian President Roosevelt turned a deaf ear to their plight. After weeks of trying to have the refugees disembark, the ship and all its passengers were forced to return to Germany, the place they so desperately wanted to leave. Hitler gloated and boasted to the world that nobody wanted the Jews; why should Germany be the one stuck with them? Some of those aboard the ship couldn't bear the thought of going back to Germany and committed suicide. It was destiny, I suppose, that my family was not among those aboard the doomed *St. Louis*.

My grandma insisted that we come and spend time with her on the farm. The weather was beautiful and Mutti could certainly use a vacation and some pampering. It would be nice to relax and enjoy life for a change,

Summer 1934: Vacationing on Grandma's farm in Spytkowice. Standing from left to right: Papa, me; Papa's siblings *Pincus, Herman and Regina; Grandma's second husband, Eli Herszteil. Seated from left to right: *Uncle Samuel, *Aunt Marie, *Grandma. Seated on the ground from left to right: *Cousin Dollek Fischler, my brother Fred, Cousin Lusia Fischler. Resting on the ground: *Cousin Henry. *Killed in Auschwitz.*

if only for a short time. We spent our days lounging in the garden, wandering in the fields, or even fishing in the brook near the back of the house. We were oblivious to world affairs because we had no radio and the Polish newspapers we had were outdated. It was a time to calm our nerves, relax, and get back to being ourselves again. I would lounge under a tree and watch the cows and goats grazing ever so peacefully. At other times I would read one of the books Mutti had brought with her, all the while enjoying the smell of freshly cut hay. The only sounds heard were the occasional moos of the cows, or the sound of the village church bells as they chimed every fifteen minutes. On rare occasions, I would hear the engines of a plane flying overhead. To break the monotony, we would take the horse and buggy and drive the few kilometers to nearby Zator and visit Papa's brothers. They had radios and current newspapers that brought us up-to-date, but none of what we heard was good.

One morning, Oma asked me to take the bicycle and visit Uncle Moniek. He had his law office in Zator and she asked me to pick up a package from him. Riding through town, I stopped to say a brief hello to other relatives before I returned to the farm. I was almost outside of town when a policeman came chasing after me. He yelled for me to stop and had his gun drawn, ready to fire. At first I thought he was chasing someone else, but when I stopped he put handcuffs on me. Even though I didn't speak Polish, I understood enough to recognize that I was accused of being a German spy. A Polish peasant, so it seemed, had overheard me speaking German to my relatives and accused me of being a spy. Encouraged by newspaper articles, radios, and local priests, Polish people were told to watch out for spies and report anything to the police that was suspicious. This peasant did what he was told to do and no one can fault him, but I still believe that this was more a case of anti–Semitism than catching a spy.

Zator was a small town where everyone knew our family. Certainly the people had seen me in town before and knew I was there to visit relatives. News traveled fast in Zator and my Uncle Bernhard heard about my predicament and raced to the police station to help me. I had barely passed through the door of the station house when he came in, too. The policeman's attitude changed quickly when, with the customary handshake, Uncle slipped him some money. The officer suddenly remembered that he had seen me before in Uncle Bernhard's store and apologized for this "misunderstanding." My handcuffs were swiftly removed and I was free to leave. I was really lucky that Uncle was at home and could come to my rescue. Otherwise, I could have been in big trouble. Back on the farm, I told my parents what had happened, and after much discussion they thought it would be much safer for us to be in the larger city of Chrzanow, where the Krakauer, Laufer, and Meltzer families had been reunited during our absence. They were part of my parents' circle of friends in Berlin, and now they would have each other to share their thoughts and frustrations.

As in the Saarland, and again in the Sudetenland, Nazi infiltrators crossed into the Polish Corridor, which included the city of Gdansk, (Danzig) territory lost to Poland after World War I. The Nazis encouraged Volksdeutsche (people who identified as German) to claim discrimination against them by the Polish government. These people became ever more aggressive and charges and threats between Germany and Poland were daily occurrences. The radio was full of this news and, at the top of every hour, all activity in town or at home came to a virtual halt so people could hear the latest developments.

Soon, draft orders for the military reserves were issued without regard to status. It made no difference if one was single, married, with or without children. Cousin Sala's husband Joel was also called back into service and garrisoned in Oswiecim again. One time, cousin Sala asked me to take a package to him and I was glad to oblige as I wanted to learn what I could about the Polish army's readiness for war. Individually, the soldiers were high-spirited and full of confidence. However, when I saw soldiers using their own bicycles or primitive horse-drawn wagons for transportation, it was very disappointing. Remembering my experience in Krakow when I watched the big military parade, I couldn't imagine how Poland would be much of a challenge for the disciplined and mechanized German army. It came to me suddenly that if war were to break out, I too would find myself in this place as a Polish soldier. How ironic it was that some years later, I would be in those very same barracks when it became the nucleus of the infamous death camp, Auschwitz-Birkenau.

At home that evening, I told my parents what I had seen. Again we tried to reassure ourselves that the combined strength of the French, English, and Polish armies would surely succeed. We placed our hopes in the newly signed treaty that England and France would declare war on Germany and come to Poland's defense if it was needed.

On the twenty-third of August, a news bulletin interrupted the regular program and took the world by surprise. The announcement stated that Herr von Ribbentrop, the German foreign minister, and his Russian counterpart, Litvinov, completed a nonaggression pact. This was unbelievable, yet seemed to be true. How could two such sworn enemies, extreme opposites on the political spectrum, agree to live in peace with each other? What was behind these maneuvers? Did this development suggest that Hitler may have changed his policies toward Jews as well? There must be more to this. We were anxious to hear more details, but we had to wait for the evening when our shortwave radio could receive the BBC news broadcast from London. What we heard that evening was all bad. Earlier, unsuccessful negotiations prevented Russia from joining the Allied camp, so once again Hitler had outmaneuvered the Allies.

One week later, Friday morning, September 1, 1939, as I was on my way to the store, I heard the unusual sound of many airplanes flying overhead. Looking up, I saw a squadron of German Stuka bombers flying east, and only minutes later I heard the sound of explosions ripping through the air. Huge clouds of smoke filled the sky as the German bombers crossed into Poland and attacked many strategic places. The oil refinery in Trzebinia, just six kilometers from Chrzanow, was one of their targets.

6

Blitzkrieg

Smoke could be seen for miles and everyone in the street ran home to listen to the radio. So did I, but not speaking Polish well I was unable to understand the details of the broadcast. The confusing news coming over the airwaves included code words and numbers obviously meant for the Polish army. How primitive I thought, as I recalled a newspaper article I had read about Italy's campaign in Abyssinia a few years earlier. The story told about how Italy had deciphered the radio code by which the Abyssinian army received orders, and Mussolini's son-in-law, who directed the campaign, had his enemy's plans for the day presented to him at breakfast. What we did hear on the radio confirmed that Germany's newest airplanes, the *Stukas*, had dropped bombs at several locations throughout Poland causing severe damage. Outraged, Prime Minister Smygly-Ridz went on the air and declared that Poland would respond in kind to this attack. "Nie damy guzika" (We won't give as much as a button) were the words he used. Those words were repeated sarcastically for years to come — the prime minister didn't give a button, but gave all of Poland instead. In response to this attack, England and France demanded that Hitler cease hostilities at once, and when their demands were ignored, they honored their commitment and declared war on Germany.

There was a total lack of official information during the first few days of fighting. Rumors made the rounds with everyone adding their own personal version of what they had heard. One of the tales was a report about a Polish cavalry unit repelling an incursion by German tanks. This unlikely story was heard again and again and must have been just wishful thinking or the miracle of miracles. I, for one, didn't believe in miracles, but easily accepted the wishful thinking explanation. More and more people gathered in the marketplace hoping to hear some factual news in this serious matter. We were only fifty kilometers (thirty-five miles) from the German border and advances or retreats would definitely have a powerful impact on the people in Chrzanow.

On Saturday, the second day of fighting, people, and I among them, stood in the marketplace exchanging rumors and gossip. Polish soldiers were seen traveling through the city on bicycles and nobody paid much attention at first. We assumed that they were reservists on their way to join their unit. But then, we thought it strange that they were all heading eastward, while the German border was to the west of us. Late that afternoon, the number of soldiers we saw increased remarkably. Not only did we see bicyclists, but soldiers traveling in horse-drawn wagons away from the front lines. All of them looked exhausted and seemed to be traveling without a commanding officer. They were in a hurry and stopped only briefly for water offered to them by the local citizenry. When questioned, they replied that they had orders to regroup in a small town halfway between Chrzanow and Krakow. This information was not encouraging; in fact, it was most disappointing. Was the Polish army so weak that they couldn't hold back the Germans for even a few days? Our situation was worsening by the minute.

Joel, Sala's husband, arrived the following morning in uniform, with rifle and sidearm, but no ammunition. He never got to use his gun because, like most others, he never got any bullets. It was an act of sabotage executed by Volksdeutsche in the area, so he thought. Neither his, nor any other fighting units ever received live ammunition. There were no real plans for fighting the Germans, and like many others, he too decided to walk to the east. Exhausted and anxious to get out of uniform, he was afraid of being captured as a Jewish soldier. To the best of his knowledge, the German army had broken through the Polish lines and the Polish army was not capable of defending our area. He estimated that they would close in on Chrzanow within a day. There was confusion all around us, but we still hoped that by regrouping near Krakow, the army would be able to take a stand. Why Krakow and not at the border was the big question, but not ours to explain. We began putting our most essential belongings into packages that we could carry, but had no idea where we should go.

We couldn't even be sure that any of us would ever return to Chrzanow again.

Earlier that day I had passed the railroad overpass near our street and saw one train after the other facing toward the interior of the country. None of them were moving, but all were filled to capacity with people who had fled from border towns. It was useless for us to even consider getting on a train. Locomotives were under steam but there were no engineers to operate them. Many of the engineers were Volksdeutsche, and their desertion had brought the entire railroad system to a complete standstill. With no instructions from anyone and no government official to tell us what to do, we had no answers to our questions. Do we evacuate or not? If we left our homes, where were we to go? How would all these people on the road get their next meal or find some rest? Afraid of falling into German hands, people just ran and left everything behind. When one family moved out, all others followed blindly. Lacking knowledge of roads that would lead us to safety, our family joined neighbors and friends walking east, further inland. Roads were overcrowded with people pushing or pulling anything that had wheels. It was slow going because small children and the sick and elderly all needed support from able-bodied members of their family. These people were holding back others who might have been able to walk faster.

There was only one paved road leading to Krakow, so to speed up our travel my family headed across the fields and country roads. They were dusty, but we did move along at a better pace. An abandoned farmhouse and a barn filled with freshly cut hay served as shelter for the night, and as we were completely exhausted, we fell asleep almost at once. In fact, we slept so soundly that none of us heard anything taking place around us. Soon after dawn we continued our flight, but didn't get very far because German paratroopers had landed all around us during the night and blocked the roads. A German officer, speaking Polish like a native, instructed all civilians to squat on both sides of the road and wait for further orders. Four days after the war had started, we were crouching in the ditches of a road, watching the German army roll into the heart of Poland without a challenge from our Polish defenders. After the last tank had rolled by, one of the officers addressed us. In a friendly manner, he told us not to worry and turn around and go back home. As the main road was used by the German army, he instructed us to use side roads only. German efficiency was astounding. They had detailed road maps of the area to guide them, while Polish soldiers coming through Chrzanow needed to ask us for directions. Like others in our group, dejectedly we turned around and walked back home. Although we were away for only one day, we were now greeted by posters pasted on every street corner telling citizens of restrictions imposed by the occupying Germans. No one was permitted to be on the street after six o'clock in the evening, nor before seven o'clock in the morning. All stores had to be opened. Weapons and radios were to be surrendered immediately. Anyone found in possession of such contraband would be executed on the spot. No religious services or any kind of assembly was permitted. On and on went the many lists of restrictions to make our lives more difficult.

New proclamations were added nearly every day, and many of them were specifically directed to the Jewish citizens. One such restriction ordered all Jews to wear a white armband, ten centimeters wide, with a blue Star of David across the full width. We were now clearly recognized as Jews, even at a distance, and the Nazi occupation forces could easily terrorize us at will. At random, they came into a street, closed off the block, and forced Jewish people onto their trucks. Sick or not, old or young, they took us to work wherever they needed us to do manual labor. Sometimes it was only for a few minutes, but more often it took hours and sometimes even days to complete our tasks. Unless someone had witnessed the round up and was able to inform the family, no one would ever know what had happened to a loved one. To end this terror, members of our Jewish Community Council approached the military commander. The best they could do was to accept an arrangement whereby one hundred men would have to report to the Community Council every morning and be available for any German units in need of physical labor. Rather than take us off the street, their trucks would come for us at the home of the Council. This arrangement eliminated raids in the street, but we still never knew if or when we would ever get back home. Our Council had a list of all the people in town and they promised us that the work details would be shared equally by all. It wasn't long however before we realized that some of us were called to serve in this labor pool more frequently than others. Our suspicion of foul play grew stronger every day, and my friends and I began to voice our objections to such unfair treatment. Our objections had no effect whatsoever and we became a thorn in their side and placed on the Council's black list.

Life had settled into a strange but calm routine as stores were ordered to reopen their doors and continue doing business as before. Polish newspapers, fully censored by German authorities, were being published again and told of an agreement between Germany and Russia, unthinkable only a short time ago, allowing Russia to occupy the eastern half of Poland. To some families, this presented an opportunity to leave the Nazi occupied city and join their relatives in the area now under Russian rule. In their eyes it was the lesser of two evils.

Even though there were travel restrictions in place, confusion near the newly established German/Russian divide created an opportunity for some people to travel east and then come back to Chrzanow if they wished. From them we heard about German soldiers terrorizing Jewish people in many of the small towns. According to the stories told, in some Jewish communities the entire population was taken into the forests and killed in most barbaric ways. It could not be confirmed, but if this was true, Kristallnacht faded in comparison.

Not long after we heard these reports, we had a demonstration of Nazi-German bestiality. I was in my cousin's store when we heard shouting and painful cries coming from the corner of the marketplace. I went to the door and saw a few motorbikes with sidecars, typical Waffen SS transportation, parked in the street. The soldiers had gotten hold of a few Hasidic Jews and lined them up against the wall and cut off their *tsit-tzees* (fringes worn on undergarments). Not satisfied having these pious men so shamefully humiliated, they pulled their beards and side locks until hair and skin were in the attackers' hands. These poor people were bleeding and crying out in pain as Hitler's stormtroopers laughed, cajoled, and amused themselves. Polish peasants stood nearby and watched this spectacle with delight, while some others shook their heads and observed this brutality from a safe vantage point. As quickly as they came into town, the SS mounted their motorcycles and disappeared. It was only a short visit by the Waffen SS, but it had a long-lasting effect on all of us.

Outraged by this incident, our Council president, Mr. Zucker, contacted the German authorities. Earlier, he had been told by the military commander that he would ensure the life and safety of all residents and that rowdy or obnoxious behavior by German military personnel would not be tolerated and should be brought to his attention. But when he was told of this shocking attack, he simply shrugged his shoulders and said that he had no authority over the Waffen SS. On the day following this action, a new ordinance was posted all over town demanding that Jews be clean-shaven at all times.

The Jewish Community Council in prewar Poland played a very important part in every city. It was the local organization that assisted those in need, educated children, and helped the sick. It was supported by members of the community and by funds received from overseas. Unfortunately, under German occupation, the role of this Council changed dramatically, including its name. The Nazis named it Judenrat, and it became the executor of German orders. Most of the original members elected to this position of honor were uncomfortable with their new role and, rather than be handmaidens to the Nazis, many, including Aunt Marie's brother, Samuel Kluger, resigned. Others, who were trying to ingratiate themselves with Police Lieutenant Schindler, were swiftly appointed to the council to replace those who had left.

Police Lieutenant Schindler was a very clever businessman. Using his position in the military government, he found reasons for ordering the closing of a few selected Jewish-owned stores. In desperation, these merchants approached two of the characters who had been appointed by the lieutenant to fill the vacancies at the Judenrat. A payoff was arranged and the stores then reopened. Soon other stores had to close and, after payment to the lieutenant, they too were permitted to reopen. Schindler and his friends now had a very lucrative business. Mr. Weber and Mr. Wachsberg, the two henchmen, had no misgivings and declared that they were actually performing a service to the community. What a farce! Incidentally, neither of these two men survived the Holocaust.

Flour and other supplies to keep Leo Fischler's bakery operating started to run low and he needed to reorder the most essential supplies. He received his allotment of flour from the military command, but also got news that a German treuhänder (trustee) would soon be appointed to take charge of his bakery. To forestall this takeover, Leo hoped that Trudy, their maid of many years, could be of assistance. She was honest, trustworthy, and treated as part of the family. She was of German background (Volksdeutsche) and capable of handling the business. Rather than a strange trustee, Leo made Trudi a partner. As the new owner, she was obliging and helpful at first, but changed her attitude very quickly and began acting as if she had never even known the Fischlers.

The German government annexed the city of Gdansk (Danzig) and the province of Upper Silesia into the German Reich. All communities in those territories were renamed and Chrzanow now became known as Krenau. In line with this annexation, all businesses were ordered to change the signs above their storefronts into German. A sizable application fee was to accompany the architect's drawing and the lettering for such signs had to be in German Gothic.

Before the war, the city had one sign painter, but he had left Krenau for eastern Poland. Suddenly I had an opportunity to earn some desperately needed money. While still in Berlin, Papa's cousin, Sigi Wellner, had me come to his sign shop to get some experience doing lettering and learning his trade. Commercial art was fine, he had said, but hands-on experience making signs would increase my chances of supporting myself some day, wherever that might be. I was glad that I had listened to him; the things I had learned in his shop were about to pay off. With the need to change the signs, and no sign painter in town to do the work, I became involved in a bustling business. I connected with a tinsmith who had the necessary permits, and as soon as I had the signs painted, he took care of the installation. Our small apartment, with absolutely no room to spare, now became a sign shop. Spread across chairs, on top of beds or tables, signs were all over the place. The smell of paint constantly permeated the air. At night, the signs dried under our beds, on top of our closets, and in every other place we could think of. We were very uncomfortable, but under the circumstances, earning money was paramount. We simply had to accept the hardship to make ends meet.

The deadline set for changing signs was approaching rapidly, but many people still were without the required permits. Mr. Printz, the only remaining architect in town, was overwhelmed by the amount of work he had to do. Making drawings was simple enough, but the legwork involved in getting approvals kept him away from his desk most of the day. To ease his problems, I suggested that I could make the drawings and then he could spend his time obtaining the permits. It made sense to him and added nicely to my income. I did his work in the office during the day, and painted the signs I had on order in the evening and late into the night. I knew this was only a temporary situation, so I tried to make every moment count.

One of the new ordinances published replaced the white armband with a yellow Star of David attached to the left side of our outer garment. It felt like living in the Middle Ages when Jews lived in ghettos and wore yellow stars and yellow hats. There were other ordinances to harass and humiliate us as well. Jews had to step off the sidewalk and walk in the gutter whenever we passed German soldiers in the street. Furthermore, to show respect, we had to greet them by tipping our hats. Some Germans objected to being greeted by a Jewish person and beat us for doing so. Then again, if we didn't tip our hat, some soldiers started screaming and beating us for not following orders, not showing proper respect. We were damned if we did and damned if we didn't. So, prior to turning a corner, we had to make sure that no soldier was in the street and hoped that none would come along.

To avoid problems, our family always made sure to be home at least one hour before curfew. But one evening, the curfew hour was long past and Mutti and Papa had not returned home. My brother and I became more and more concerned with every passing minute because this was so unlike my parents. We could only hope they had stayed over at one of our relatives after spending the early evening with them. Many hours into the curfew, our doorbell rang and there stood Aunt Pearl. Totally out of breath, she came to tell us that our parents were in her home. Papa and Mutti had been attacked and beaten by drunken soldiers soon after they had left her. Bloodied and in pain, they managed to get back to Aunt's apartment where she tried to help them. She believed Papa had a broken shoulder and should see the doctor in the morning. Mutti was also beaten badly, but she thought her bruises were just superficial ones. They were resting at her home and she had come to tell us what had happened. As a midwife, Aunt Pearl had permission to be in the street during curfew hours, but when challenged she had to prove her reasons for being out so late. Coming to us was not that kind of emergency and she had taken a great risk in coming to our apartment. Aunt remained with us overnight, but as soon as the curfew was ended we hurried to help our parents. Papa was in great pain, but Mutti, who had a swollen face and bad bruises, was able to tell us about their horrible experience. They had left Uncle's apartment early enough to get home before the curfew started, but when they turned the street corner they saw a few drunken soldiers coming toward them. It was too late to turn back, so in compliance with the latest ordinance, they stepped off the sidewalk but were attacked anyway. The soldiers cursed and kicked the "dirty Jew," each one trying to prove that he was the tougher Nazi. Mutti pleaded with them to let Papa go, but they were too drunk to hear anything and kicked and beat her, too. When the goons finally had enough, they left my parents on the ground, crying and bleeding.

The medication Aunt Pearl had given Papa hardly helped him and he was in agony. That morning, we went to the one and only physician who remained in town and were lucky that he could X-ray Papa's shoulder at the hospital. The film showed a broken collarbone and fractured rotator cuff. They set his shoulder and immobilized his arm, but he was still in great pain for a long time. After many sessions of physical therapy, he regained some motion but was never able to lift his arm above his head again.

The following day, I accompanied my battered mother to the military commander of the city to file a complaint. This was the same officer who had proclaimed that law and order would be observed in his city, and Mutti reminded him of his promise. All he could tell us in reply was that these soldiers were not under his command. They were just traveling through the city and he had no jurisdiction over them. He warned us not to make such frivolous accusations again.

Without a letup, German soldiers conducted searches in our homes, day or night. Coming out of nowhere, vehicles suddenly blocked the street and soldiers scattered into the buildings. Seeing them with their sidearms mounted was scary, but listening to the sound of their jackboots reverberating through the hallways was chilling. Again and again they came searching for hidden weapons, radios, or transmitters which could send information to the outside world. Unfortunately, on one such raid, they uncovered a radio in a neighbor's home. This brave man had been listening to BBC broadcasts at night and keeping the community informed of happenings around the world. The poor soul was dragged from his home, accused of being a spy, and without further inquiries shot in front of his family and neighbors.

Chrzanow, now Krenau, continued to be the seat of the county government and German administrators and their families moved into our city. To house them, our Judenrat was ordered to requisition a number of homes and apartments in all the better neighborhoods. The homes had to be left the way they were except for personal items such as clothing. At a moment's notice, people had to leave and move in with relatives, or be assigned to families living in predominately Jewish neighborhoods. We were told that such requisitions would continue and the Judenrat would be faced with many tough decisions. Not only did they have to select the families who were to give up their apartments, but also, they had to find others willing to share their homes. The anger and friction in our community was indescribable. "Why us? Why were we selected and not the other family?" Those were the questions heard over and over again. It was sad to see families leaving their beautiful surroundings, taking only a few suitcases of clothing and personal items with them. I sympathized with those people and could understand their tears and anguish as they lost their home and privacy. My friends and I volunteered to help those who had to resettle and shared their painful experience.

German administrators tried to calm the community by telling us that this was only a temporary situation and all homes would be returned as soon as the war was won. We had different opinions about our situation. We believed that these moves were the first step in establishing a ghetto, as had been done in other cities. When questioned, Police Lieutenant Schindler denied such intentions and said that Chrzanow had been incorporated into Germany. "You know," he said, " there are no ghettos in Germany."

The community had barely recovered from the first resettling when once again the Jews in Krenau were made to share living space with other families. This time it involved Jewish people who were forced from their homes in Katowitz and smaller communities near the former German border. We knew that our Judenrat could not prevent the influx of these refugees, but the way they handled the problem was now in question. Accusations of bribery and preferential treatment were rampant. Still, the need to house and help people was more important than protesting the activities of our leaders. We couldn't accomplish anything with our protests and it could only serve to aggravate a bad situation. "There, but for the grace of God go I," was the attitude of most people in Krenau. When our leaders called for volunteers to assist the unfortunate ones, I was among the many who offered their services.

Using pushcarts and wheelbarrows, we walked the distance to the railroad station and helped people carry their meager belongings. With only the few suitcases and cartons they had, they came with us to our Jewish Children's Home. Our calming words of compassion seemed to be appreciated as our Judenrat arranged for refreshments and handed them assignments to their new residence. Day after day people arrived in this resettling program and eventually all of them had a roof over their heads. The social part of this relocation now became the next big problem. Apartments, small to begin with, had to house at least twice as many people as they were originally designed for, and strangers were forced to share kitchen and sanitary facilities. It was no surprise that people found it difficult to accept and live with each other under such conditions. Serious arguments arose daily in most apartments. As the need for German living space increased, space for our Jewish people decreased even more. The modern and elegant heart of Krenau was made *Judenrein* (without Jews) and the old part of the city became the only neighborhood relegated to the Jews. No matter what the Nazis called it, it was definitely a ghetto.

Among the newcomers to Krenau were several boys and girls who were my age. Since they grew up in a city that was more German than Polish, we had much in common. It was now early spring and pleasant weather encouraged us to enjoy the outdoors. Whenever we were not on work detail we spent our time with each other, walking and talking and playing ball in the meadow. But most of all, we constantly complained about the unfair treatment we were receiving from our Judenrat. We were summoned to the daily work detail much more often than others, and our anger at them was fierce. We complained about their injustice and bribery loud and clear, but nothing ever changed. It just raised us to the very top of the Council's blacklist.

Food grown locally and always in abundance became scarce as the produce was taken from the farmers and shipped to Germany. To no one's surprise, black-market activities began to flourish in spite of German proclamations warning us against it. As it was impossible to exist on the food rations we received, we were forced to buy what we could on the black market. We knew that punishment would be severe if we were caught, but hunger was a strong incentive for us to take that risk.

Once, during a raid at Mr. Rath's home, German soldiers found a bag of sugar in the pantry. Mr. Rath owned and operated the other bakery in town, and like our cousin Fischler, he too lost his business to a trustee. His son, a teenager, was home alone during the raid. When the soldiers found the sugar, a leftover from his bakery, the boy was immediately arrested and ordered to be hung in public. The entire Jewish community was made to appear in the square and witness the heart-wrenching execution. To make sure that no one would miss their display of brutality, soldiers went from door to door chasing everyone into the marketplace.

The Polish daily newspaper, now published by the military government, reappeared on the streets. It was censored, yet we always looked for clues to see if England and France were ready to fight Hitler. Every day our hopes sank one notch lower. Hitler's army invaded Denmark and Norway and conquered them within days. The bad news continued when the Nazis overran Holland and Belgium, too. In no time at all, German soldiers were in back of France's impenetrable Maginot Line and the French guns and armaments, set in concrete pointing east toward Germany, were useless when the Nazis came through Belgium. They conquered the Maginot Line without much resistance.

French and English forces were in disarray, while the German army advanced faster than the Allied forces could retreat. By the time the English and French got to the coast at Dunkirk, the Germans were right on their heels. Every available vessel, be it powerboat, sailboat, rowboat, in fact anything that could float, was used to move as many soldiers as possible across the English Channel. It was a disaster that ended with France surrendering to Hitler. These developments destroyed any hope we had that this war would be over soon.

Not long after the French surrender, we saw German troops and equipment heading east. That was strange, we thought, because these troops traveled at night, and no soldiers headed west. If there was no action in the east and troops were being exchanged for those who had occupied Poland earlier, why wouldn't we see military transports traveling west in their battle against England. Could it be that the friendship pact between Germany and Russia wasn't as solid as we were led to believe? Would there be another battle on the Eastern front ?

In October 1940, our Judenrat received orders to gather eight hundred young and strong men to work at a project in Germany. They said we would be well fed and well housed for the duration of the job, said to take a few months to complete. We were told that after the work was done, all the men would return home. Thinking about the rumors we had heard where transports were taken from Jewish communities and the people never seen again, we were very suspicious of the German plans for us. To calm our fears, members of the Judenrat, with assurances from the

Germans, told us that we would even be able to write and receive mail. We could only hope that such promises were sincere.

Gathering such a great number of people meant that most of the Jewish households in our city had to part with at least one family member. The offices of the Judenrat were filled with people trying to have their family members excluded from this selection. Some had good reasons for being excused, while others were able to pay their way out of the selection. Aunt Marie's brother, who had resigned from the Council before it became the Judenrat, tried to use his influence on my behalf, but whatever influence our family had at one time had disappeared. There was nothing he could do for me, especially since I was one of those who criticized the Council's shenanigans. In fact, my friends and I were the first on their list. It was an easy way for them to get rid of us.

As expected, the summons was delivered to me personally and ordered me to appear at the local high school that same afternoon, November 1, 1940. Along with this summons came the threat that noncompliance would result in severe punishment for my entire family. Even so, my friends and I, like most people throughout the city, agreed that we would ignore the summons. Consequently, only a handful of men appeared at the schoolhouse that afternoon. As soon as the authorities realized that we were not complying, they conducted raids to fill the quota. Army trucks suddenly appeared in the streets and soldiers with mounted sidearms worked us over with rifle butts as we were herded onto their trucks. Young and old, healthy and sick, strong and weak were all hauled to the school building where we were supposed to have come voluntarily. A soldier took my name and address and sent me into a classroom to join others who had been picked up earlier.

Our families received instructions to bring us work clothes for the winter months and the most essential personal items. There wasn't a home in the city that wasn't affected by this action and everyone had his own tragic story to relate. Young fathers were worried about their small children and the hardships their wives would have to endure. Others had sick parents and wives at home who depended on their personal attention and support. We were prisoners, and for now there was no one to help us. Late in the afternoon, relatives came to the building delivering hastily packed suitcases which they deposited at the front door of the school. From my classroom window I saw Mutti trying to find me, and when she finally spotted me she waved. As windows and doors were shut tight, we communicated with sign language until the guards chased her away. As the afternoon turned into early evening, members of the Judenrat brought us food along with our suitcases. Again and again they tried to reassure us that we would be fine and return home as soon as we completed our assignment. It was in our interest, they said, to complete the project as quickly as we could.

We spent the night in the classroom, but none of us could sleep. The following morning, officials from the Judenrat brought us food again and took with them a few elderly and sick people from our midst. None of us objected to that as there were more than the required eight hundred men in the building. However, when others who obviously had paid a bribe to the Judenrat were dismissed, we were outraged. All we could do was verbalize our displeasure and yell at the members of the Judenrat with us in the building. They just turned a deaf ear to our complaints. I can only imagine how my parents must have felt when they found out about the Judenrat's sneaky dealings. Though we were told that our work would only last a few months, deep in our hearts we knew that this parting would separate us from our families for a long, long time. We received our food rations, but no one had the desire or appetite to eat. All through the day, I watched as people were taken out of the classrooms and others were taking their place. I knew that I definitely would not be one of those rescued. My parents did not have the money required to pay a bribe, and since I was on their blacklist there was no chance that they would release me. The following morning, the third of November, we were taken outside and onto waiting trucks. Guarded by German army personnel and local militia, we were driven to the railroad station and ordered to board the passenger train waiting for us. Once we were on board, the doors were all locked from the outside and, although we could move around freely within the car, we were indeed prisoners. The train stopped in Katowitz where a little jolt made us realize that other cars were being hooked on. When we then continued traveling west into Germany, I couldn't help but look at the landscape I had seen so many times before. Two years earlier, with Papa at my side as we were fleeing Nazi Germany, it had never even entered my mind that I would be coming back as a prisoner.

7

Slave Labor

Being locked into a railroad car and hauled back into Germany was a very emotional experience for me. Now I was on my own and had no one to confide in or ask for advice. I felt like a criminal captured on foreign soil who was on his way back to the scene of his crime. But I was not a criminal; quite the contrary, I was a law-abiding person. What had gone wrong in this world of ours? What was the crime that I was accused of? Just having been born to loving and respected parents of Jewish background — was that a crime?

Lost in my thoughts, I wasn't aware that our train had stopped at a station named Gogolin O/S, a place I had never noticed when traveling through this area before. The locked doors were suddenly opened and we were ordered to leave the train. Waiting for us on the platform were SA men in their brown uniforms, a frightening sight, just as I remembered them from my days in Berlin. At that time they didn't carry weapons, but now, with rifles slung over their shoulders, they looked even more threatening. Surprisingly, there was no shouting or shoving as we were ordered to get into formation, standing five abreast. Once it was determined that we were all present, we were divided into three groups and made to board army trucks which took my group to nearby Ottmuth O/S. We huddled close together, and tried to protect ourselves from the wind of a chilly November afternoon. The air had an obnoxiously sweet smell which we later learned was the by-product of a paper manufacturing plant in town. As we approached the camp that was to be our home, we saw barbed wire fences and armed SA guards opening the gates for us. It was clear now that the stories we were told at home were all lies. We were definitely not just workers.

Counted once again, in groups of twenty, we were assigned to our quarters. Every room had free standing double tiered bunk beds with headboards lined up against two facing walls. Tables stood in the center of the room and two chairs were placed at the foot of every bunk bed. The wall facing the door had two windows, and in between them was an iron stove. We selected our bunks and received instructions to fill a bag, the size of a small mattress, with straw for our use. Fresh army bed linen and a blanket completed my bunk; my small private space in this cold barren room.

I had barely finished putting my bunk in order when we heard a shrill whistle. We had no clue as to what the whistle meant or what we were supposed to do. Suddenly, all hell broke loose. SA men appeared in our barracks, kicked and yelled for us to hurry and report to the Appell Platz (roll-call square) on the double! We were all confused but learned rapidly what this was about when we had our first contact with the *Lager Kommandant* (camp commander). He stood there like a statue with legs spread wide and firmly anchored. With clenched fists resting on his hips, he was visibly furious. He waited for the right moment, and then came the explosion. "I'll teach you discipline," he shouted. "Liegestütz" (push-up position) was his command. My Polish- and Yiddish-speaking comrades didn't understand the order and looked for clues as to what to do. The explanation came quickly when the guards, who stood on the sidelines, were suddenly in our midst. Using their jackboots and rifle butts, they made us understand the meaning of this command. Everyone was shocked; we were supposed to be workers and not soldiers in an army training camp. Some middle-aged men found it difficult to perform this exercise but finally we all completed the ten push-ups and were then ordered to return to our barracks.

No sooner did we get inside than the whistle sounded again, signaling another exit. Our response obviously wasn't fast enough to please our commander, so he repeated the push-ups a few more times and seemed to be greatly enjoying the power he had over us. When he eventually tired of his game, he assigned us permanent roll-call positions based on our room location. Barracks number one was to stand facing the roll-call square, and barracks number two would then face number one. With the blowing of his whistle, and chased by our guards, we scrambled into our assigned places. As I looked straight ahead, I thought I was hallucinating when I saw my Uncles Moniek and Herman, Papa's younger brothers facing me. I was absolutely stunned to see them, but had no way to catch their eye. I could hardly wait until we were dismissed after receiving our long list of rules. Essentially, they were the strict rules observed by the German army. The wake-up whistle would give us thirty minutes to get ready and the *Stubenälteste* (room orderly), appointed by the commander, had to select two people to get coffee from the kitchen for everyone in the room. Our quarters had to be swept and dust free at all times. The next whistle meant that we had to take position for roll call. At night, all our clothes had to be neatly folded to form a cube and placed on the chair in front of our bunk. We were warned that if, on inspection, the officer found any traces of dirt on his white glove, the entire room would be turned upside down and we would miss our meal.

At the end of his tirade he introduced Mr. Winskovitz, the *Judenälteste* for our camp, appointed by the Judenrat in Sosnowitz. This arrangement was set up by the German authorities, and made the Judenrat agents for Jewish affairs in the annexed areas of Upper Silesia. We listened as Mr. Winskovitz continued with additional information. He told us that a number of girls from our hometowns would be working in the kitchen and camp office and housed in a separate barrack, off-limits to us. Mr. Tischauer, a pharmacist and medic during World War I, would be in charge of the emergency room. To avoid problems for those who couldn't understand German, he translated a few German commands into Polish. He told us that the word *Achtung* (attention) precedes every command, and that "Achtung — Mützen ab!" meant to remove our caps and "Mützen auf!" meant to replace them.

The *Lagerführer* (camp director) was next in line to address us. He wore civilian clothes but boldly displayed his party membership pin on the lapel of his jacket. He explained that our assigned task was to build a section of the *Reichsautobahn* (turnpike). He was in charge of the camp, and would see to it that we were housed and well fed. He thought it important to stress that the entire German nation was working hard to support the soldiers defending Germany against the aggressors. He ended by warning us not to do anything foolish like trying to escape. Controls throughout Germany were extremely tight, he said, and we would not get very far. When we were caught, we would be executed on the spot and our families sent to Auschwitz. This was the first time I had heard such a threat, but we were all aware that Auschwitz (formerly Oswiecim), housed the newest concentration camp. He ended his remarks with "Achtung — Abtreten!" (Dismissed!).

At last I could make contact with my uncles. They had recognized me during the Lagerführer's address but we could only nod as a greeting to each other. They were as surprised to find me in this place as I was to see them. They told me that they had been forcibly moved from their home in Zator to the larger Jewish community in Wadowice, and that Uncle Moniek was extremely nervous about leaving Aunt Mania and two babies all alone in strange surroundings. With our spirits low, we walked together to the mess hall for our meal. The chef placed a ladle of food in each bowl and added a small piece of bread. The food was edible, but we were much too tense to eat. Instead, we spoke of our experiences and how we had become part of this transport. As far as they knew, their other brothers and sisters were still in Wadowice. While still in the mess hall, Mr. Winskowitz announced that he had postcards for sale and urged us to write home immediately so our families could be at ease. A short message, he suggested, would be best, because our guards, who would censor the cards, could read them quickly. There were no restrictions as to the number of cards we could send or receive, and we were also permitted to receive a package from home every week.

After mealtime, Moniek and Herman went to their room and I made use of the community washroom. The water from the few available faucets was icy cold on that frosty November night; the boiler room and showers were not yet operative. In fact, we waited several weeks before we could take a real shower. The toilet was a culture shock, too; I never imagined that such primitive facilities still existed. Two elevated boards across a huge rectangular pit made space for twenty people to sit next to and back-to-back from each other. Another elevated board, running down the center of the pit, prevented one from falling backwards into the mess.

The stove in my room had been lit and the warmth made things slightly more comfortable. Since I was the youngest, I was assigned an upper berth; this actually gave me more air and a bit of privacy. I stored my suitcase under the bunk, folded my garments into a cube on my chair, and crawled into my corner for a night's sleep after three exhausting days. At nine o'clock, a guard entered the barracks, sounded his whistle and yelled, "Licht aus" (Lights out). Like me, others were also in need of rest, but I think that most of us spent our time reliving the past days, wondering what was to happen to us next.

We were supposed to be sleeping when our guards came to check the rooms, but on our first night some of them had other ideas on how to have fun at the expense of their prisoners. During one of their inspections, they had found a tiny piece of straw on the floor in one of the rooms. As the *Stubenälteste* (room elder) explained to us later, there was no doubt that the room was spotlessly clean when the lights off command was heard. He was convinced that a guard placed the piece of straw on the floor to create a reason for terrorizing the men. The guards screamed, shoved, and chased everyone in that room outside into the frigid night. They were without shoes or protective clothing, and made to run many times around the roll call square before being allowed back in their room. The chicanery didn't stop there. The men were then ordered to spread a blanket and place the piece of straw on it. Everyone had to take hold of the blanket and, in a slow funereal procession, walk to the extreme opposite corner of the camp. There they had to dig a hole and bury that one little piece of straw. We watched this nonsense from our window and felt deep sorrow for our friends. It was hours before the excitement subsided and none of us slept much that night.

At six o'clock in the morning, the shrill sound of the whistle startled us. Dazed and disoriented after our restless night, I almost fell out of my upper berth. A few orthodox men in our room were already wearing their tallith and tefillin (prayer shawl and phylactics) and reciting the morning prayers. It was dark outside as I went to the wash barracks to clean my teeth, wash my face, and shave. This was no easy task, as the washroom was filled to capacity. Eventually I managed to get near one of the faucets, which had to serve more than three hundred men. After rushing back to my room, I was given some awful-tasting *Ersatz Kaffe* (coffee substitute) and then the next whistle signaled our roll call, a military rush-rush and wait routine. We raced to our assigned places, stood at attention to be counted, and then watched the guard on duty report to the commander that we were all accounted for. Lots of heel clicking and raised arm salutes followed, and then we were ready to march to the construction site. Passing through the gate, the appointed *Kolonnenälteste* (group leader) gave the command, "Mützen ab" and again, "Mützen auf" (caps off, caps on), and we were on our way to work.

We walked through a forest seeing little in the darkness which surrounded us. Like cattle, one man following the footsteps of the other, we arrived at the construction site as the new day dawned. Our job, we found out, was to build a section of the autobahn connecting Breslau and Oppeln, two cities in Upper Silesia. We were given shovels and lined up along the train of lorries waiting on the railroad tracks. After shoveling two cubic meters of sand into every lorry for half a day, I was randomly selected to join fourteen others installing railroad tracks throughout the construction site. I was glad to get away from the boring and backbreaking job of shoveling sand, but carrying iron rails and heavy wooden ties was no picnic either. This narrow spur track system was used for small locomotives to move lorries, filled with sand, from one place to another. I soon found out that my new work detail had an added benefit. Since there weren't enough guards to watch us as we moved all over the site, we did not have an SA man watching us constantly. Our German foreman had to assume that responsibility, and that made for easier working conditions.

Returning from our first day at work, we met the fifteen girls who arrived from the newly organized assembly camp in Sosnowitz. All except two were assigned kitchen work; the others helped with paperwork in the office. Records with every name, date, and company for whom the individual worked that day had to be kept. At the end of every week these forms were forwarded to "Der Stellvertreter des Reichsführers SS für den Fremdvölkischen Arbeitseinsatz in Oberschlesien," the SS organization, located in Breslau O/S. Detailed records were very important because the construction companies paid hourly wages to this SS administration. This money supposedly paid for our room and board plus one and a half reichsmark per day for every worker. We were told that the money earned would be given to us when our work was completed. The entire project was under the command of Reichsführer SS Himmler, with second in command being SS Sturmbannführer (Colonel) Lindner. It was Lindner who had full authority over all the forced labor camps and Jewish communities in the annexed territories of Upper Silesia.

Moniek and Herman worked in a group controlled by a foreman named Przybila. This man, a Volksdeutscher, was forever drunk and always looking to show that he was as good a Nazi as any of the uniformed SA guards. He constantly yelled, pushed, and beat the people in his group to force them to work faster. At times he would even use a shovel or other tool to beat a man badly if he couldn't keep up with the rest of the group. Such commotion usually attracted a nearby guard who would join Przybila in beating the poor fellow. To work in Przybila's group was the worst assignment in our camp. Mr. Winskowitz, our Judenälteste, was told about the problem and he approached the Lagerführer for help. The Lagerführer said that people could not be transferred from one group to another and the unfortunate men had to continue under Przybila's ruthless command.

Both my uncles were nearly the only ones working for this maniac who didn't run into serious problems. Having grown up on a farm in Spytkowice, they were familiar with and adept at using a shovel. Seeing that, Przybila engaged Moniek in a conversation and was absolutely surprised when Uncle told him that he grew up on a farm, then studied law in Krakow, and graduated as an attorney. He could hardly believe that any Jew had lived on a farm or worked the land. Przybila took a liking to Moniek and in time my Uncle was able to reason with him. He told this drunkard that when you give people a chance to work without interference, they will do their best to fill their quota and that would make him look good in the eyes of his superiors. Moniek became Przybila's right-hand man and eventually work was organized in a way that made it much easier for our men. This was quite an accomplishment, and people were grateful to my uncle.

Mr. Novack, a local railroad track engineer, was our foreman. Giving us instructions, he used words and terms which were meaningless to us. Even though most of our men spoke German, we could not understand what he wanted us to do. Our confusion made him think that we were either stupid or deliberately sabotaging work. He yelled and cursed but was not vicious. As the days wore on, we began to understand him better, and his attitude seemed to change toward us. Our work required some skill, but more than that we needed the full cooperation of everyone. We weren't interested in doing a "fine job," but we didn't want to get hurt either. It was essential that all eight of us who carried a section of iron rail distribute the weight equally on our shoulders. To do this, we positioned ourselves according to height. If anyone didn't carry his share of the load, it became too much for the others to bear. We would collapse under the added weight and the iron would slide off our shoulders injuring many of the workers. Mr. Novack was amazed at how quickly we had learned the techniques of building track and commented that he had never been with a crew who had learned so rapidly. We soon were able to meet our deadlines and Mr. Novack became friendlier toward us. When no one was watching, he even allowed us to rest for a little while.

We were constantly told how important it was that all rails be installed properly. Spikes holding the rails in place had to be hammered straight into wooden ties, and latches, connecting two pieces of rail, had to be bolted tightly. Sloppy work would cause a train of lorries to derail and thus interrupt the flow of work. But looking at it from our point of view, such an interruption provided a welcome break for our men. Our comrades could relax while the lorries, or at times even the locomotive, were placed back on track. Natural wear and tear on such a temporary network of railroad tracks caused bolts and spikes to come loose by themselves, but we did our best to help it along. However, we had to always be careful that the derailments didn't occur too frequently.

Our work took us from one end of the construction site to the other, and at times we met those from our transport who were separated from us at the Golgolin station. When we would exchange a few words, we found out that their situation was similar to ours. Sometimes we were even able to help relatives and friends send greetings to each other.

Winter, with its freezing temperatures, made life still more difficult for us. We needed heavy gloves to handle iron rails, as touching them with bare hands caused freezer burns. The gloves I owned were elegant and made of fine leather, but totally inadequate for the work I had to do. Not having time to wait for a package from home, I improvised by taking a heavy piece of clothing and fashioning my own gloves. My socks were also not heavy enough to keep me warm, even when I wore two pairs at a time. Others in my group used rags to wrap their feet the way they had done when they served in the Polish army. This seemed to work better than my socks so I, too, began wearing rags on my feet. Unfortunately, my shoes were snug, and the rags made them still more uncomfortable. Yet it prevented my toes from frostbite, and that was the most important thing.

The ground we worked on froze solidly in the intense cold and we hoped that the snows would follow soon. With a combination of ice and snow, we thought that work would be halted and give us a few days of rest. But this was not to be. The men shoveling the sand into lorries now had to use a pickaxe first and still keep an acceptable pace filling the lorries. The foremen and guards were constantly on top of us yelling, shoving, and using their rifle butts to push the men along. My work, laying down tracks, was just as troublesome in this weather, but with clenched teeth and determination I got through those awful days. A severe snowstorm finally closed the entire construction site and we thought that would allow us to remain in our barracks until the storm subsided. Regrettably, this was only wishful thinking. The winter of 1940–1941 measured some of the heaviest snowfalls and freezing temperatures in that region. There was so much snow that the heavy mechanized snowplows were unable to keep the roads open. With traffic at a complete standstill, we were handed shovels and ordered to remove the snow and clear the thoroughfares. So much for our long-awaited days of rest. My clothing was totally inadequate and the brutally cold winds penetrated my garments right to the skin. Every time I threw a shovel of snow to the side of the road, the wind blew it right back into my face. It was sheer torture, but to keep from freezing I had to keep moving continuously. Standing around and doing nothing was even worse than hard labor. In fact, sometimes even our guards took a shovel into their hands to keep their blood circulating, and they were warmly dressed.

We finally cleared the main roads after many torturous days, but instead of getting some time off, we were ordered to clear the local city streets, too. We were admonished not to speak to residents as they rushed past us into their enviably warm homes. Anyway, our yellow Stars of David with the inscription *Jude* (Jew) was clearly visible to everyone and left no doubt that we were to be despised and ignored. Most Germans had an expression of satisfaction on their faces, but some people seemed actually to be disturbed by the situation. I remember overhearing two ladies saying that they hoped German soldiers received more humane treatment in their captivity. I saw these same women emerging from their doorway a short while later carrying a few neatly wrapped sandwiches in their hands. They looked around, and when they were sure the guards couldn't see them, they placed the sandwiches on top of the snow pile and motioned for us to take them. Obviously, there were still a few decent people left in this part of the world.

The snowstorm eventually passed and work resumed at the construction site. The miserable weather had taken its toll on everyone's health. People had slipped on the ice and had gotten hurt. Nearly all of us suffered frostbitten fingers, feet and noses, and almost everyone had a cold. Our infirmary became the busiest place in camp, with so many people needing medical help, but only one Mr. Tischauer to take care of us all. He needed help badly and I volunteered to work with him in the evenings.

Since he had all kinds of medical books for me to read, I soon became very proficient in administering first aid. It was a little rough on me because after a day at work I had to devour my meal and rush to the infirmary. After being there a few weeks, Mr. Winskowitz had an idea and asked the Lagerführer to speak to management about having a first aid station at the construction site. He thought that many infections and possible complications could be prevented if first aid could be rendered immediately on location. Management agreed and gave permission for such a station. As I was somewhat experienced, I was happy to exchange my difficult physical labor for a medical kit. I was on my own, but the guards watched me carefully as I criss-crossed the construction site helping anyone I could.

Writing with small lettering, I squeezed as much as I could onto a simple postcard. My new position would be welcome news for my family. On every card I wrote, I told them that I was in good health and managing quite well. I didn't want to discuss my daily hardships because there was nothing they could do to improve my situation and I didn't want to add to their problems. They in turn told me that things were fine, too, even though they had to move out of their apartment to make room for Germans to live there. I knew money was scarce and food even more so. To survive, they had to purchase essentials on the black market and risked serious trouble for themselves. Yet, like clockwork, every other week I received a package filled with goodies Mutti had baked for me. I pleaded with her not to send anything because the Nazis would realize that the ingredients for her baking must have been bought on the black market. Mutti refused to listen to me and packages of love continued to arrive. They told me about happenings at home and about the many girls who had been rounded up and taken to work in Czechoslovakian knitting mills. This was the second time such a large transport of people had been assembled and sent away. Many of my friends and cousins were part of that new transport. There was more disturbing news coming out of Warsaw as walls had been erected and the Jewish population forced to move into a closed ghetto. It was the Middle Ages all over again. Mutti also told me of the persistent rumors that transports of Jewish people had disappeared and apparently been killed in eastern Poland. There was no definite proof, but such news did little to make us feel safe.

On the lighter side, one day Papa had met a German business acquaintance from Berlin. This man, so she wrote, was happy to meet Papa and told him of the labor shortage existing in Berlin. Following the suggestions of government officials, he was going to move his plant producing army uniforms to Krenau. He had authorization to employ Jewish people and now that he had met Papa, he hoped that Papa would manage the plant for him. At first Papa was hesitant, but changed his mind when given assurance that, because of the need for uniforms, his plant would be fully protected. People employed by him would receive reasonable payment and food rations. He treated Papa as a friendly business associate and hinted that once the war was won, they would continue their association in Berlin. Mutti hoped that this meeting might offer them some degree of safety.

Except for accidents, most of my comrades were in reasonably good health. However, if someone didn't feel well and was in need of a day's rest, he went to see Mr. Tischauer, who had authority to keep injured or ill people in the infirmary for a day. He was instructed to be very careful with this authority and never accept more than five sick men on any given day. But even the infirmary offered no guarantee of rest, as the camp commander regularly took people from there to clean walks or do similar chores inside the camp.

On his first inspection trip to our camp, Sturmbannführer Lindner saw two men doing cleanup work inside our compound and immediately went into a wild tirade. He threatened Mr. Tischauer, who was really the innocent party; it was the commander who had ordered these men to work. Lindner yelled, "If these Jews, these malingerers, could walk, then they should be at the construction site." Without another word, he ordered his assistant to take the two men and deliver them to Auschwitz. He and his entourage of SS officers stayed in camp all day and waited for all of us to return from work. As we stood at attention for the usual evening roll call, he came out of the commander's office, chased his dog into our midst, and terrorized the entire camp. Swinging his bullwhip, his constant companion, he charged into us, cursing and yelling. He was going to teach us to do what was expected of us. If he found a similar situation again, he threatened that the entire camp would be sent to Auschwitz. Like all the other men around me, I was shaking like a leaf after my first encounter with Lindner. As always, I went to the infirmary after roll call and saw Mr. Tischauer, still ashen white, telling me that he had seen the Angel of Death. Even though it was the camp commander who took those men out of the infirmary, he felt responsible for giving the men their day of rest.

The day after Lindner's visit, we exchanged information with our neighboring camps at the construction site and heard similar tales of woe. The Angel of Death, as we began to refer to him, visited their camps, too, and terrorized them just the way he had done to us. Auschwitz, Auschwitz, Auschwitz was the one word he used constantly. We didn't know much about Auschwitz, but whatever we had heard was enough to put fear into all of us. A few days later, our Lagerführer told us that the two unfortunate men from our camp died in Auschwitz. No further details!

Willingly or not, we had settled into a routine and gradually adjusted to our situation. In the early spring of 1941, the initial construction site was ready for expansion. All of us working for Ernst Rösner und Söhne construction company were supposed to move to a new camp in Gogolin O/S. This camp, so we were told, was closer to our work site and would save us time getting there in the morning and returning at night. We didn't expect any great changes in our comforts or lack of them, however getting away from the miserable smell of the paper mill in Ottmuth was something we all looked forward to. On a Saturday afternoon, after we returned from work, we were told to get our things together. It didn't take much time to put my few belongings into the suitcase and await further instructions. Mr. Tischauer came into my room and asked me to come with him and see Mr. Winskowitz in his office. Our Judenälteste told me that I was appointed "resident medic" at the new camp in Gogolin and my responsibilities would be the same as Mr. Tischauer had in camp Ottmuth. Surprised at this sudden change, I was pleased yet somewhat hesitant. My responsibility would be great and I wasn't sure whether I was up to this promotion. It wasn't taking care of the sick that bothered me, but remembering Lindner's camp inspection and the loss of our comrades to Auschwitz that made me nervous.

Not being at the construction site day after day would be wonderful, but the work expected of me inside camp would not be easy either. I could only hope that my efforts would be satisfactory and please my comrades. Mr. Winskowitz told me that an additional one hundred and fifty men, taken from our communities, would be added to each of our two camps and were due to arrive shortly. Roman Feiler, a friend of mine from Krenau and assistant chef at Ottmuth, was appointed chef for the new kitchen and Motek Joschkowitz, due to arrive with the new group, was appointed Judenälteste by the Judenrat in Sosnowitz. In a fatherly manner, Mr. Winskowitz placed his hand on my shoulder and assured me that I would be able to handle the assignment. To ease my worries, he told me that Dr. Landes had been chosen to be the physician for our camps. He would be stationed in Gogolin but would visit all other camps in our area from there. We said good-bye to each other and promised to keep in touch. I couldn't wait to share my news with Uncles Herman and Moniek as I knew they were concerned about my meeting with Winskowitz. They were extremely happy to hear about the outcome and delighted that we would still be together at the new camp. We got in line for the inevitable roll call, and then took our suitcases and boarded the trucks that were waiting for us.

8

Camp Life

We arrived at camp Gogolin and were surprised to see regular uniformed police replacing our SA guards. As soon as the head count and accompanying heel-clicking formalities were finished, the Lagerführer came out of his office, introduced himself, and told us that we would be well housed and fed while under his direction. In turn, he expected us to be obedient and do the work expected of us. Next, Police Sergeant Zinnecker introduced himself as our commander and told us about the rules we had to obey. He, too, spoke in a civil manner, something we weren't used to anymore. Standing at ease, he gave us instructions which suggested that discipline in Gogolin would be less rigid. The guards, who stood quietly nearby, seemed to be middle-aged, and almost all wore wedding bands on their fingers. There was a sign at the gate announcing that this was the Reichsautobahn Lager Gogolin O/S, and except for the barbed-wire fence, local townspeople would have no inkling that this was a forced labor or concentration camp. Our fears of the unknown slowly disappeared as we began our new life in camp Gogolin. We were told to pick up blankets, linens, and straw to fill our mattresses and get to our assigned rooms. We were to share our rooms with the same men as we had in Ottmuth, even though some of my comrades would have preferred different arrangements because of personality clashes. The flare-ups in camp eventually became less frequent as all of us realized that we had to help rather than hurt each other. We had to accept things the way they were and make the best of it. The lessons we had learned in Ottmuth most definitely made it easier for us to settle into our new surroundings.

With friends (I am wearing the Red Cross armband), standing in back of the display we had to create at the camp entrance.

Our camp consisted of eight barracks arranged in a great rectangle facing a center court. All rooms had windows and doorways facing this courtyard. Two small rooms were at the end of each barracks; the one most centrally located became the infirmary, and the other was to be mine and shared with Dr. Landes whenever he was in residence. This was a great improvement for me as I would have almost total privacy, something unthinkable only a few days earlier. As it was the weekend, our men had time to talk and exchange our first impressions of the camp and speculate about our future. We tried to find a reason why police units were replacing our SA guards. What we surmised was that the younger SA men must have been drafted into the army and the old time soldiers had been called up to guard prisoners. Anyway, it was a change for the better. The following day, on the construction site, we heard that all other camps in our area had a similar change of guards.

Trucks bringing the expected one hundred and fifty people arrived in camp a few days later and included some of my friends from Krenau. The strain and anxiety of the last few days was visible on their faces, and those

104

who recognized me stared at me with quizzical expressions. Following the predictable roll call and headcount, Zinnecker proceeded to give the new men the same instructions we were given. As soon as they were dismissed, the men from Krenau came to me for more information. Unlike my first camp, where no one was there to calm my fears, these new arrivals had us to ease their apprehension. I told them that work at the construction site was strenuous, but they would adjust as our group had done. Our food rations, I continued, were not generous, but enough to survive. It would take them time to get used to being prisoners, but they could do it. Imprisonment was painful and humiliating, but we all had to ignore the hurt and follow the orders we were given. Some day, hopefully soon, we would return to a normal life.

They asked me to describe a typical day at camp and this I proceeded to do. I told them that our day began at 6:00 A.M. when we got dressed, washed, cleaned our room, and had a warm drink. We then waited until the whistle to report for roll call sounded at 7:15. At 7:30, everyone, except camp personnel, would march to the construction site for a day's work. At noontime there was a thirty-minute break, and those who had saved a slice of bread from the previous evening meal could relax and eat their bread. At five o'clock, the locomotives signaled the end of a hard day and we would scramble into formation, be counted, and march back to camp for evening roll call. It was usually 6:00 by the time we had gotten washed and in line for the sparse daily food ration. Of course, a little package from home was always a welcome supplement, I added. Now it was their turn to be surprised at my ignorance as they began telling me about the changes at home. Food rations had been sharply reduced, and buying on the black market was expensive and extremely risky. They told me about the raids which took place in the early morning hours, about people taken from their homes and herded into the marketplace to be sent away. Some were assigned to work in factories and able to contact their families, while others were never heard from again. The stories they told me were grim and painted a much less rosy picture than what Mutti had written about in her letters. I was shocked to hear the extent to which their lifestyle had deteriorated. It seemed that we, the imprisoned, had a more manageable existence than our families at home. Our days would follow a set plan, while their days were filled with fear and uncertainty.

The administration of Jewish communities in the annexed territories of

Upper Silesia had undergone drastic changes. The Nazis had selected the Judenrat in Sosnowitz, the community with the largest Jewish population, to be in charge of all other Jewish communities in Upper Silesia. Two brothers, named Marin, both of questionable background, headed this Judenrat. It was their job to organize transports of people to be sent into forced labor camps and resettle families into Jewish neighborhoods — ghettos. These men became the handmaidens of the Nazis and did all the dirty work for them.

Motek Joschkowitz, our new Judenälteste, finished talking with Sergeant Zinnecker and as he passed our group, I introduced myself. Together, we walked to his office where I met his wife Lotte, one of the fifteen girls in the transport. I was surprised to find a wife accompanying her husband into a forced labor camp, as that was a most unusual situation. I wondered who or what was the reason for this very special privilege.

By the time the new arrivals had settled into their rooms, our men had returned from their day at work. We witnessed some tearful moments as

Motek Joschkowitz (left) and Uncle Moniek looking out the window from the camp office.

relatives and friends found each other after a long separation. The excitement and exchange of stories lasted well into the night, and "Licht aus" (lights off), a command never strictly observed at Gogolin, was totally ignored that evening. Our guards were understanding and did not interfere with the reunions. A few of the men came from Wadowitz and told Uncle Moniek that Aunt Mania and children were well and managing under the circumstances. This helped Moniek's mental anxiety but, of course, suffering from the separation and longing to be with his family was always there.

The following morning, after the last column of workers had left camp, the Lagerführer summoned Motek, Romek, and me to meet with him. For Motek's benefit, he told us once again what was expected of us and what we could expect from him. He explained that the construction company, Ernst Rösner & Söhne, paid for our maintenance and wanted us to be in good physical condition. They were interested in completing their contract swiftly and satisfactorily and that he would have an open ear to any problem brought to his attention. In addition to my responsibilities in the infirmary, he assigned me to go to the city every afternoon, accompanied by a guard, and pick up the mail and packages addressed to our camp.

As we walked along after our meeting, Motek asked me to describe life in Gogolin as I saw it. Among other things, I told him how Uncle Moniek had earned the respect of everyone in our camp because he had such a calming effect on Przybila's attitude toward the men. Much to my surprise, Motek had already heard about Moniek from others in camp, and when the two men met they liked each other immediately. The Joschkowitzes were only a few years older than I, and a few years younger than my uncle. They had grown up in Katowitz, spoke German fluently, and we had many common interests. Moniek, Motek, Lotte, and I became the best of friends.

The Judenrat in Sosnowitz provided guidelines which, when followed closely, were supposed to avoid problems with the SS administration. I was supposed to restrict the number of people in sick bay to 1.5 percent of the camp population. Since our camp had close to three hundred workers, we were allowed four, maximum five people in sickbay at any given time. My guidelines were also very specific regarding the nature of an injury or illness. A man had to have a severe injury or extremely high fever to remain in camp for the day. Those were the only acceptable reasons and I was the one responsible for making that decision. If I were to withhold workers for less serious causes, I would be accused of sabotage and open to punishment. Thankfully, the great majority of my comrades were young and strong and had little need for medical attention. There were some fellows who had served in the Polish army who had learned ways to fake an ailment, and if one came to the infirmary with a sudden high temperature, I was happy to go along with the ruse that they were really ill. I just had to be careful that the camp director or our guards didn't get wise to this little charade.

Whenever there was a great deal of mail at the post office, I was ordered to take someone from sickbay with me to help with the large load. Everyone wanted to go into town, although seeing Germans going about their usual business was a depressing sight for us. The townspeople, mostly women, children, and elderly men, walked the streets freely while as a prisoner I was watched over by a guard, simply because I was born to Jewish parents. Everything I saw in town was so neat and clean, just as if there was no war. The only visible signs of conflict were windows criss-crossed with tape to protect them from splintering in case of a bomb attack. I saw posters plastered all over town reading, "Sh- sh- sh! Der Feind hört zu" (The enemy is listening). This was a reminder to the Germans not to exchange information they may have innocently received from family members in the armed forces. Once back in camp, our newly arrived mail was delivered to the guardhouse where it was censored and handed to us a few days later.

Dr. Landes was supposed to share a room with me, but since other small rooms were available, he was given a place for himself, and now I had a private room, too. The doctor was a pleasant, elderly gentleman who was forced out of his practice, and like all others, taken from his family during a raid. Having Dr. Landes so close made me more at ease, and I hoped that with his knowledge and our modest supply of medication we could meet any emergencies that might arise. I learned a great deal from the doctor and was comfortable handling matters when he was away at other camps.

Work at the construction site was in high gear and our men were pushed to the limit of their strength. The increased pressure on them was clearly visible when the number of people needing medical attention rose drastically. The infirmary became so busy that Dr. Landes and I were overwhelmed by the need for our services. At the beginning of each month, I had to request medical supplies from the Judenrat in Sosnowitz. At first we received the items and quantities we had ordered, but as time went on, we received less and less, while our needs continued to grow. We were so short of every kind of medication, even aspirin was a scarce commodity. Bandages had to be reused and our girls volunteered to boil and wash them. This was helpful, but still no solution. We needed help badly, so I asked the Lagerführer to come to the infirmary and see for himself the problems we were facing. We were in dire need of medication, bandages, and someone to provide first aid at the construction site. We told him that immediate care at the construction site would reduce the chances of infections and complications. Amazingly he actually listened to our requests. He could not aid us with supplies, but he agreed to approach management for permission to allow a medic at the workplace, and a few days later our request was granted. Herman Kornhauser, one of the recent arrivals, a medic in the Polish army, was glad to offer his services. After dinner, the busiest time in the infirmary, he also worked with us helping reduce the waiting time for our patients.

On my daily trip to the post office, I would pass the apothecary in town. With envy I watched people going in and coming out with packages in their hands. I kept wondering whether I should try my luck and ask the Lagerführer for permission to buy whatever medication they would sell me. I mentioned my idea to Motek and he said we had nothing to lose. Dr. Landes also was in favor of the plan and joined us in making our presentation. At first the Lagerführer didn't want to hear of it, telling us that all medical supplies went to the army first, where they were needed most. Next in line was the German population at home. He said we'd be wasting our time, but reluctantly gave me permission to try my idea on the next opportunity. The following day, the guard and I entered the apothecary and, as required, I wore the yellow Star of David with the imprint "Jude" on my chest and my red cross armband on my sleeve. The lady behind the counter, after some hesitation, managed a faint smile on her face, and greeted me asking, "Was möchten Sie?" (What would you like?). I told her the reason for my visit and she was surprised to hear me speak to her in my Berliner German. She, like everyone in town, believed that prisoners in our camp were Polish, and not German, Jews. The owner, an elderly pharmacist, heard my request and came from behind his counter to look me over. He stared straight into my eyes for a few seconds, and then asked for my list of things we needed. I was pleasantly surprised when I was soon handed a package with most of the items I had asked for. I thanked him and paid my bill with the money we had all pooled together just in case my plan succeeded. I was elated, but when I showed the package to the Lagerführer, he was shocked that I had gotten so many unavailable items. He could have caused problems for the pharmacist, but thankfully he kept quiet. I went to the apothecary many times after that day and was always treated well. They accepted prescriptions with Dr. Landes' signature, and at times, even accepted my signature on the prescription blank.

Most of the time the guard accompanying me was eager to talk with me. Away from their peers and on a one-to-one basis, many a guard would tell me how sorry he felt for us as prisoners of war. These comments, I was sure, were based on their own experiences during World War I. One guard in particular never failed to give me courage and hope. "Once the war is won," he said, "all our lives will be normal again." He told me that Hitler and his Nazis weren't really bad. "You, the Jews from Germany or Poland," he said, "are the poor people who got caught in the middle. Hitler just wanted to punish the wealthy Jews of France, England, and the United States. They were the ones who manipulated the rest of the world and were the root of Germany's problems." I listened to him silently and nodded my head every now and then in disbelief at such stupidity. There was no use asking him why our people at home were being terrorized, or why transports of our people disappeared and were never heard from again. I knew that getting involved in a discussion like that could only cause problems and wouldn't accomplish a thing. I had more immediate issues to worry about.

The number of men with injuries and illnesses kept increasing. Still, my orders to keep the number in sickbay remained the same. How could I risk sending injured or sick comrades to the construction site when I knew they were not fit for work? At times I had as many as twelve men in bed, three times the quota I was given. I was flirting with danger and I knew it. Surely someone at SS headquarters would notice the large numbers recorded and another visit from Lindner was always on my mind. Our Lagerführer, aware of the problem, said little, but summoned Motek and me to his office one day. He told us that we absolutely must cut the number of patients at once. He was given notice that SS Sturmbannführer Lindner was on his way to inspect camps in our area and the last thing he was looking for was to get into trouble with "that man."

Having worked at the construction site myself, I knew about supply depots and the work that was done there. Leaving the Lagerführer, I had a thought which might help our men and discussed my idea with Motek. He liked what I had to say and we immediately returned to the Lagerführer's office. We asked him to speak to management and have them find some light work inside the shed for some of our injured men. That, we reasoned, would give us a chance to reduce the numbers in sickbay. He thought for a moment and promised to see what he could do. Unexpectedly, he told me that same afternoon to select six men for inside work at the supply depot. I had many patients volunteering for this work, as they were all afraid of Lindner, our Angel of Death.

His inspection came as anticipated. Lindner spent a few minutes with the Commander and, joined by the Lagerführer, toured the guards' quarters. To avoid possible problems, Motek, Lotte, and I took it upon ourselves to check the barracks every morning after the men left for work and added that extra touch wherever needed. We did all we could to forestall disaster. With bated breath, we watched every move from behind our windows. We saw members of his entourage enter and leave a few of our barracks without creating a disturbance. His visit was a short one this time and, with a sigh of relief, we watched the caravan of cars leave our camp. Later in the day, Commander Zinnecker came to Motek's office and told him that Lindner had wreaked havoc at camp Annaberg that morning and that their medic and fifteen sick people were sent to Auschwitz.

The summer season made life easier for us. Saturdays, we worked only half a day and the afternoons were used for personal hygiene. Sunday morning was the special roll call and inspection of living quarters. Everything had to be scrubbed and cleaned and, if things were not exactly as the Commander desired, he and his men ripped the room apart. Nothing would be left standing, and putting the room back together again would deprive us of our day of leisure. But if all went well, we had a day to rest, sit, talk, and dream about our loved ones at home, or even play a game of poker. We would visit friends in other rooms or even stroll the campgrounds. It was our time to socialize and sometimes even visit the ladies' barracks. Sunday was the only time we were permitted to have contact with women, other than seeing each other at meal time when they ladled out our food.

Ann Strauss, a dear friend from Krenau, worked in the kitchen and had made it her priority to supply additional food for our sick. She used whatever excuse she could think of to leave the kitchen and secretly bring us the guards' leftovers. Superior in quality, this additional food for our patients added strength to their weakened bodies. At times, that food was even more important than any medication we could have give them.

Our food rations were just enough to exist, and most of our men walked around continually hungry. At home, we were told by the new arrivals, food rations were even more scarce, but food was always available on the black market. But such purchases were very dangerous for our families as the Germans had standing orders to execute anyone who possessed items which had come from the black market. In fact, they sometimes held public hangings where the entire community was ordered into the marketplace

The kitchen staff, a few comrades, and me (I am at far left).

to witness the execution. Still, in spite of the danger, my mother continued to send me packages with baked goods from home. No matter how much I pleaded, Mutti kept sending me cookies, cakes, candies and other tokens of love.

One day I had the greatest thrill ever when I received a package from my grandparents in Amsterdam. It was obvious that it had gone through the hands of numerous censors along the way, as the package was torn and held together with string. It must have been filled with lots of goodies, but by the time the parcel came to me, there were only a few stale cookies and some of my favorite "Hopjes" candies. I had lost communication with my grandparents at the start of the war and only once did we receive an International Red Cross letter from them at home, but that was a long time ago. Mutti reestablished contact with them in Nazi-occupied Holland and gave them my address. This package was the well-intentioned result. It was a very emotional moment for me and I wrote to them immediately. I thanked them heartily but pleaded with them not to send me any more packages. After they must have denied themselves many necessities, I didn't have the heart to tell them the condition of the package I received. Little did I know that this would be the last time I communicated with them.

We were totally isolated from the outside world and, if not for the girls who cleaned the guards' quarters and sometimes overheard news broadcasts, we would have known nothing at all. Whenever there was anything of importance, they shared their news with us. The German advance and occupation of Yugoslavia and Greece came as a surprise, and on my way to the post office, my guard was proud to tell me what he knew. The news was not what we had hoped to hear. More than two years had gone by since the war had started and there was no light at the end of the tunnel. Everything we heard was about the great accomplishments of the German army as they occupied country after country. It was all discouraging, but deep in my heart, I still had faith that Hitler's Germany could not and would not succeed.

In June 1941, we heard the news that Russia had attacked Germany. We didn't believe the story and had good reason to suspect that it must have been the other way around. Our camp was located next to the main east-west railroad line where night after night we saw trains filled with soldiers and camouflaged cannons, tanks, and other equipment traveling east. Why?

The only warfare at that time was in the west. If there was an exchange of divisions or armies, transports would have to come back west, too. Since we didn't see anything like that, we knew that Germany was the one who attacked Russia. But this knowledge of who attacked whom didn't really matter. Now that fighting had begun, everyone prayed that the Russian winter would be too severe for the Nazi army to endure. If only history would repeat itself and let the Nazis suffer defeat the way Napoleon did earlier. For us, the hope that such a defeat would end our misery a little sooner lightened our spirits.

One day we received a note from the Judenrat in Sosnowitz advising us of an impending inspection by a *Stabsartzt* (regional SS staff physician). I was directed to present to him people who suffered chronic ailments and were in constant need of medical attention. In conversation with our Lagerführer, Motek and I were told that this doctor had been to camp Annaberg, where a number of men were sent home to rest and recuperate for a few weeks. We were able to confirm this from our friends working at the adjacent construction site but still felt this was a strange development. What were they up to now? At home, Lindner and his organization kept terrorizing our people, and the very same organization was now sending men back home for rest and recuperation, it didn't make sense. Willing to take a chance to get away from camp, many of my friends, including my uncles Moniek and Herman, wanted me to present their files to this SS physician.

The SS Stabsartzt arrived early one evening and, as luck would have it, Dr. Landes was at another camp. I was extremely nervous, but with my files and paperwork in order, I was ready to face the SS officer. Led by our Lagerführer, he and his entourage came into the infirmary and seemed rather pleasant, if such a thing could be said of an SS officer. I had to present every man and give the reason for his being there. It was "Jawohl Herr Stabsartzt" here, and "Jawohl Herr Stabsartzt" there. Answering his questions, he recognized my Berliner accent and was amazed to find someone from Berlin in this camp.

When Uncle Herman was a young man, he had an accident on the family farm. While cutting firewood, his hand had slipped and he chopped off a small section of his forefinger. It was simple enough to create an infection around the stub which looked rather nasty and the Stabsartzt agreed to send him home for surgery. Uncle Moniek's records indicated his many visits to the infirmary and his need for medication to relieve abdominal and gallbladder pains. Unfortunately, the doctor didn't think that he required time at home, but made a note that if Uncle's condition did not improve by his next visit to our camp, he would consider the case again. After all examinations were completed, twenty people were permitted to leave for rest and recuperation. The following day, two guards took these men by train to the Judenrat in Sosnowitz, where they were dismissed and allowed to go home. A smaller number of our patients were transferred to Annaberg. Why camp Annaberg we asked suspiciously? Wasn't Annaberg the first camp the Stabsartzt had visited and furloughed some men? The Lagerführer explained to us that Annaberg was to become a camp for the weak and chronically ill, but this information raised more questions than it answered. Was the camp in Annaberg about to become another Auschwitz?

Replacements for the men on leave arrived at our camp a few days later. Ruth Joschkowitz, Motek's cousin, was one of them, and like Motek's wife, she too was a volunteer. Ruth joined Lotte in the office and together they handled the mountains of paperwork that existed. Another addition to our staff was Manny Luftglass, a dentist from Wadowitz. He brought with him a portable old-fashioned flywheel put into motion by a foot pedal which turned the hand-held dental drill. It was a simple piece of equipment, but he was able to fill cavities and pull teeth when absolutely necessary. Manny and I shared my quarters, and since he was a pleasant fellow, we got along fine. Like Dr. Landes, he too had to visit other camps and take care of dental needs.

The newcomers brought us up-to-date on conditions at home. More streets in the city had become Judenrein, and the Jewish section became even more overcrowded. Although men and women were taken to work in camps, the incoming number was greater than those who were left. When only one or two family members remained at home, they were forced to share their living quarters with complete strangers. We heard other disturbing news — that many cities now had closed ghettos, too. It was like the Middle Ages all over again.

The news about the war on the eastern front was not encouraging. The German army was speeding toward Moscow and destroying everything in its path. Our wishful thinking that our misery would come to an end soon was not to be. Now only the involvement of America in this conflict could strengthen our resolve to continue our existence. It was inconceivable to us that the United States would watch Hitler devour Europe and not participate in the war. The time was not right for them to make their move, we reasoned, but considering the speed at which things were deteriorating, I wondered whether I would be alive to see the end of this madness.

During the summer, our work routine was manageable, but looking ahead I remembered the hardships we had suffered during the last winter and was desperately afraid. Our men's physical condition had declined and a lower resistance to colds and infections would certainly become a problem. As the cooler weather and rainy season was upon us, many men came to the infirmary with high fever, influenza, and other ailments. The number of comrades needing medical attention skyrocketed, and again we were beyond the guidelines we had to follow. There weren't enough bunks available in sickbay and I had to get special permission to keep injured people in their own rooms. It was the only thing we could do, but Lindner and his reign of terror made me shudder every time I thought of the consequences.

Lindner hadn't been to our camp since early summer as he was busy playing havoc with our families at home. But sooner or later, we knew he would visit us again. If he saw so many sick people, what would he do? We shared our concern with the Lagerführer, and again he asked the management to find light work for some of our people. As expected, Lindner arrived at our camp one day and he and his entourage spent the afternoon relaxing in the guardhouse. As soon as our men returned from work, he left the office and positioned himself on the elevated platform overlooking the entrance gate. Like an animal waiting for his prey, he stood there, feet spread apart, the ever-present bullwhip in one hand, while his other hand was rolled into a fist resting on his hip. He was ready to show us his power. The men filing through the gate followed the command of the *Kolonnenälteste,* "Mützen ab!" (Caps off!) The guard then thought it proper to recognize the superior officer by adding the command, "Augen rechts" (Eyes to the right.). That was the moment when all hell broke loose. "You God-forsaken stinky dirty Jews," Lindner yelled, "I don't want to see you ever looking at me again. I should send all of you to Auschwitz!" He then charged into the group, swinging his bullwhip, while his assistants chased their dogs into our men to bite and wound them. What a horrific scene!

We were petrified by what we saw and didn't calm down until Lindner and his cohorts left the camp.

A few weeks after this episode, during a morning roll call, the commander asked for volunteers to join the German army. At first I thought I didn't hear him correctly and turned to my friend Motek, who was at my side. Did you hear what I heard, or was I daydreaming? He was just as shocked as I was. We listened to Zinnecker explain that these volunteers would have army uniforms and rations and be part of the army engineers corps, stationed near the German-Russian front lines. Even those among us who were usually half asleep during the early morning hours were suddenly wide awake. They needed us for cannon fodder. That must have been the real reason for this announcement. Soon after everyone left for work, Motek and I went to see the Lagerführer. We told him that we needed more information because our men would surely ask us questions when they returned from work. He explained that Germany wanted to finish the action in Russia before the onset of real winter. To accomplish this, they needed every available soldier. Civilians, and others like us, would be needed for construction of roads and shelters near the front lines. Once the war was won, he continued, it would be to our advantage if Jews were part of this successful campaign. He ended by telling us that the Stabsartzt would soon be visiting our camp to examine all those who volunteered. The clever Germans — they wanted us to work in ice and snow and be exposed to Russian fire, while the German troops would remain safely in the background. Motek and I explained our views to the men, but astonishingly more than a dozen men still volunteered. They seemed unafraid to be at the front lines in the midst of a Russian winter. Most of them were former Communists, spoke Russian, and were convinced that they could escape somehow and slip across the lines into Russia.

The Stabsartzt arrived as scheduled and examined the volunteers and also those men who had chronic ailments. Seemingly satisfied with our medical efficiency, he furloughed another small group for R & R. This time, Uncle Moniek was one of the fifteen lucky ones. He was so happy with this development and told me of his plan to take Aunt Mania and the children into hiding. Moniek was confident that one of his Polish clients would surely be able to help him. Unfortunately, it didn't work the way he had planned — he couldn't find anyone willing to help. It was a bitter disappointment to him because he had defended his clients so brilliantly, yet when the tables were turned, nobody was there to help him.

Winter came early and covered the construction site with ice and snow. Using pickaxes we had to open the frozen ground, but as conditions got worse by the day, the site eventually had to be closed. We remained in our barracks for a few days and had time to rest our weary bodies. Of course, they reduced our food rations because we were not working. Still, rest was important to us and with food saved from packages received from home, we managed. To prevent us from "getting lazy," quoting our Lagerführer, he ordered Sergeant Zinnecker to have additional roll calls and make us exercise by marching around the outside of camp in the snow. During one of these exercises, Isi Zucker, a senior comrade, complained about feeling dizzy and weak. Zinnecker, who personally directed the exercise, refused to hear of his complaint. Zucker had problems catching his breath and collapsed. By the time Dr. Landes and I could reach him, it was too late. We tried mouth-to-mouth resuscitation and even an injection of camphor, the only medication we had, but unfortunately we couldn't revive him. Isi Zucker died surrounded by friends but away from his family and loved ones. Being involved with death for the first time in my life, I took this experience very hard. Little did I know then that Isi would be the first of many to die in camp. The Lagerführer must have felt a sense of guilt over the incident and gave his permission to bury Isi in an orthodox manner. With the entire camp in attendance, Isi Zucker was laid to rest at a place outside the fence. Both the Lagerführer and Zinnecker seemed ill at ease and assured us again that we were there to work and not to die. Those words didn't help much as the wintry weather, tedious work, and discouraging news from home kept us in a dejected mood all the time.

We needed something, anything at all, to lift our spirits. One day, Bronia, the girl assigned to clean the guards' quarters, brought us encouraging news. She could barely contain her excitement as she came through the door yelling, "The United States of America declared war against Germany." For so long now, this was the news we had all wished for. At once there were smiles on everyone's faces and all night long our barracks were buzzing with conversations about our future. At last, we thought, there might be an end to our nightmare.

On one of our trips to the post office, the guard who went with me mentioned a conference in Wannsee near Berlin, called especially to address the Jewish issue. Nothing specific was known to him, but he knew that Germany needed more soldiers and he believed that we would be taken out of camp and rehabilitated. I wondered how he had gotten such information because our news from home was not at all encouraging. All we heard was that there were more *Ausiedlungen* (resettlements) of Jewish people, not just from Poland, but from Holland, Belgium and France.

The work on our section of the Reichsautobahn was now nearing completion. All that was left to do was grading the roadbeds in preparation

Left to right: Me, Ruth Joskowitz, Dr. Landes.

for pouring concrete. This phase of construction required special equipment which had to be operated by skilled workers. Since none of us would be involved in this project, we began to speculate about what plans the Germans had for us. Would we be sent home as we were told originally, or would we be sent to another camp?

The answer to our question came one morning after everyone had marched out to work. Motek was called into the Lagerführer's office and was told that camp Gogolin would be closed on the following day. This, he said, would be our last day at work. Construction workers would be moved to the camp in Markstadt, and Motek and his wife were to be transferred to a new camp to continue his position as Judenältester. All the girls, his cousin Ruth among them, would be divided into two groups. One was to go to the camp in Sakrau and the others, including the chef and I as medic, would return to camp Ottmuth to wait for further assignments. Dr. Landes and the dentist, Manny Luftglass, would be moved to the camp in Annaberg.

The closing of our camp was swift and well planned. Our group had gotten used to each other and would have liked to continue to be together. There must have been some reason for Motek to start in a new camp as Judenältester while all others went to Markstadt, a place with an unfavorable reputation. We couldn't figure out why Romek, our chef, along with the girls and I, were being sent back to Ottmuth to wait for assignments. Surely none of us was that highly qualified or outstanding that we couldn't be replaced by many others. Anyway, I was glad I was not being sent to Markstadt. Dr. Landes, who visited Markstadt on his regular rounds, told us of the extremely harsh conditions that he saw there. Motek also shared the news with us that as of now, all camps in the area would no longer be known as *Reichs-Auto-Bahn Lager*, but would be known as *Zwangsarbeits Lager* (forced labor camp). This change of names made little difference to us because we considered ourselves in a forced labor camp from day one. Because our mail privileges had been cut to just one single postcard per month, I had to wait some time before I could inform my parents about my transfer back to Ottmuth.

As my friends and I parted, we promised to keep in touch with each other, while Motek promised he would try to use his influence to get us back together again.

9

Where Are Our Loved Ones?

The summer of 1942 was coming to an end and I was in camp Ottmuth once again. Nothing had changed since I had left there a little more than a year ago, except that my mentors had been sent home for rehabilitation and were replaced by Mr. Haubenstock as Judenälteste and Isi Michnik as the new resident medic. Following protocol, our guards presented us to the officer in charge, and with the usual Nazi salutes, we were officially transferred. Mr. Haubenstock greeted us and confirmed that we would only be in this camp temporarily, and then transferred to a new camp shortly thereafter. In the meantime, Romek Feiler and the girls would work in the kitchen and I had to join the workforce on the construction site.

I still had friends in Ottmuth, and given a choice I joined Herbert Böhm and Werner Neumark in their room. We compared news from home, but since communication was reduced to only one postcard a month, their knowledge was as sketchy as mine. One thing we knew for sure, nothing good was happening to our loved ones.

The following morning I was assigned to a crew shoveling sand into lorries. I hadn't done such physical work for a long time and my body wasn't used to this heavy labor. The foreman, a Volksdeutscher, stood nearby and didn't let me, the newcomer, out of his sight. Afraid of getting beaten, I put all my efforts into keeping pace with others along the train of lorries. I knew how to use a shovel, but knowing how to use my eyes was even more important if I were to survive. If the foreman wasn't looking in my direction, I used that moment to lean on the shovel and catch my breath.

The work was strenuous, but the boredom of throwing one shovel of sand after the other was what I found unbearable.

A few weeks had passed when Mr. Haubenstock handed me an envelope from Dr. Landes. Inside was a note from Motek Joschkowitz telling me that he still hoped we'd be together again. Be patient, he wrote, and he would be contacting us soon. Weeks went by without any further news from him so the girls and I mailed a postcard to his cousin Ruth in camp Sakrau, thinking she might have heard from him. Regrettably, we never received an answer from her because our mail privileges were soon taken away completely. More tragically, the card I had sent home informing my parents that I was back in Ottmuth was the last I was ever to mail to them. Their final card to me was especially devastating. Mutti told me that my uncles were forced back into camps and that the news from Amsterdam was even more painful. She heard from Aunt

Top and opposite: Ruth Joskowitz survived the Holocaust and miraculously saved this postcard and a few pictures from Gogolin. Oxidized through the years, this card and the photographs were Ruth's gift to me when we met in Israel fifty years later.

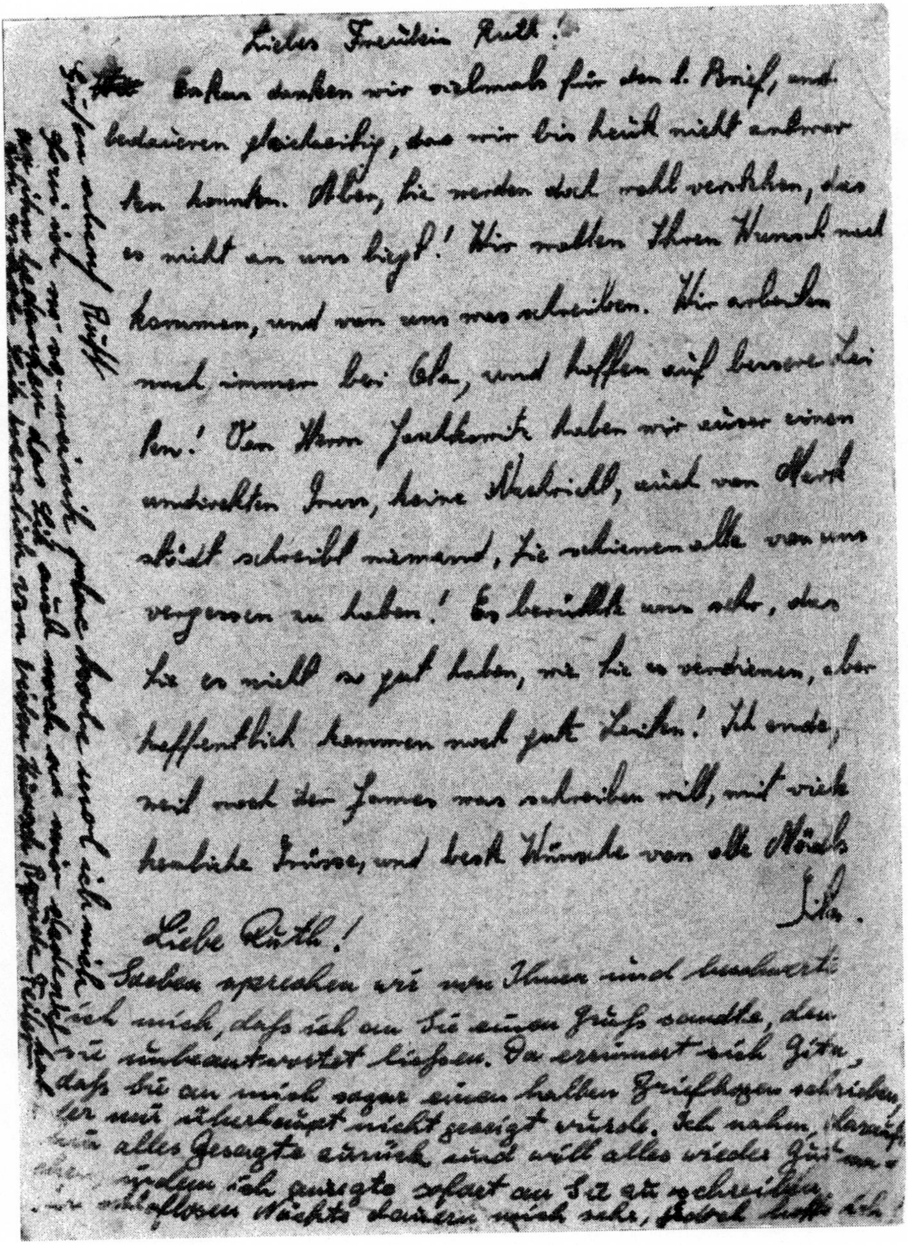

Mia that Opa, Oma, Uncle Alfred and the entire family had been taken from their homes and sent away. The only ones who were still free were my Aunt Mia and Uncle who had gone into hiding. There was no return address on the card.

The camps in Ottmuth and Sakrau were about to complete their sections of the Reichsautobahn, and as Gogolin had been liquidated before, we thought the same thing would happen here. I no longer had thoughts about being reunited with my old friends when one day Mr. Haubenstock called for Romek, the girls from Gogolin, and me to report to his office. "Get your things together," he said, "you're going back to Gogolin." What was this all about? Why were we going back to a place that had been closed down earlier, and why were we the only ones selected to prepare that camp for new arrivals? He had no answers. Something was very strange!

We arrived at the empty camp Gogolin, now looking like a ghost town. Along with the official transfer process came a gentle smile of recognition from Commander Zinnecker and a few old guards who were still on duty there. We were told to move into the rooms we had occupied previously, and ordered to prepare the camp for a transport of people arriving the next day. I asked the Lagerführer whether Motek and the others would be joining us again, but his reply was disappointing. Our new camp was only a transit camp, he said, and a full staff was not required.

One of the old guards remembered me from the days when he escorted me to the post office, and as he was always friendly I hoped he would agree to mail a letter to my parents. I wasn't even sure that my mother and father would be in Krenau to receive this mail, but I had to try and contact them. With the letter hidden inside my shirt, I approached the guard as he stood near the gate, and when no one was watching I made my request. Without hesitation, he took the letter and even refused the money I had offered him for postage. He couldn't understand why we were not allowed to stay in touch with our families, and as a former prisoner of war he objected to such unreasonable treatment.

The following day three hundred new men arrived, and as I stood watching, I saw them drag themselves and their suitcases down the road. It was a pitiful sight. Even from a distance they looked dazed and disheveled. All wore the yellow Star of David, but as they came closer, I could read the word *Juif* on some of the stars and *Jood* on others. Western Europeans were the last thing I expected to see. Why would the Nazis take Jewish people from France, Belgium, and Holland and bring them all across Germany into Polish territory? Could it be that my grandfather or Uncle Alfred were among the new arrivals? I kept my eyes wide open, hoping to find them in this large new group.

The guards pushed the people into formation for the counting process and Zinnecker told them the rules they had to obey. Many of the men didn't understand German and were confused by all that was happening. Eventually they got the gist of the instructions, including the order to unlock their suitcases and leave them in place. They were told that their luggage would be inspected and then returned to them when they were ready. In groups of twenty, guards led the new people to their rooms while the last group had to bring the suitcases to the commander's office.

Soon after their dismissal, I went to speak with a group from Holland, hoping to find a clue about the fate of my grandparents or other family members. Perhaps they had seen them or knew where they had been taken. Instead of answering my questions, they overwhelmed me with questions of their own. They had been separated from their families at the railroad station and were anxious to know where their wives and children could be. There was little I could say to put their minds at ease; I could only tell them that some women from Krenau were sent to work in Slovakian knitting mills. They wanted more details, but I couldn't provide any, and some even mistrusted what I said to them. They had seen me speaking German with the guards, so even my yellow Star of David meant little to them, as they thought it could be phony. Their mistrust of me softened in time and soon we even compared our terrible experiences with each other. Communicating with them was not difficult since many of these men could speak German or Yiddish. They told me how they were taken from their homes under the pretense of an *Umsiedlung* (resettlement) action, similar to the raids in the Polish communities. For days they were kept at an *Umschlag Platz* (assembly place), much like the camp in Sosnowitz. Having gone through a selection process, women and children were separated and taken to the rear of a train, while men boarded the front cars. The train ride was stop and go for days, but never during all those stops were they permitted to contact their families. In Gogolin, the men were ordered to get off, and their families continued on their journey.

By the evening, things had calmed down and people came to the infirmary in need of medication or replacement of medicine left in their suitcases. They came for help, but I had little to offer. Some needed their drugs urgently and were terribly concerned. Waldemar (Wally) Hirschel, the appointed Judenälteste, came to me in the infirmary to see what could be done. As the medic again, I approached commander Zinnecker and explained the problem he had created. In reply, he pointed to the pile of suitcases that would take him and his guards the whole night or more to check. The suitcases would be returned when he was done, he said, and that was final. He had instructions to search for weapons, chemicals, and other contraband and couldn't care less about medicine. He was not the man I remembered from earlier days; his attitude had changed completely. I pleaded with him and eventually was promised that he would give me whatever drugs he could find on the following morning. It was the best I could do. Being without medication for one day was not good, but hopefully not critical. I was more concerned about the future, the day after the current supply was used up.

The next day in Zinnecker's office I received a large carton filled with drugs and bandages for use in the infirmary. As he handed me the package, he saw my puzzled look as I spotted bottles of perfume, aftershave lotion, candies, wine, chocolates, watches, cans of sardines, neckties, sweaters, and a host of other things spread on the table. For a moment he seemed embarrassed, but he recovered quickly and told me to take the package and get out of his office.

As soon as the first suitcases were returned to their owners, people ran to our Judenälteste, complaining about things which were missing. Wally had no experience dealing with our commander and came to me for help. The missing medications, I realized, were alcohol-based liquids which the guards obviously wanted for their own use. I told Wally what I had seen in the commander's office and it would be up to him to ask for the items to be returned. But would it be a sound move to make this into an issue? I, for one, thought it would be counterproductive and Wally agreed with me. We had to concentrate on getting medication back to the people who needed it, and not make a fuss about missing items. Wally and I went to the Lagerführer and pleaded for the drugs to be returned. Though I angered some of the guards, we finally left with most of the drugs we had come for.

Over and over, people came to question me, "the old timer," asking whether I could give them a clue about the whereabouts of their loved ones. As I had once mentioned that women from Krenau were taken to Slovakian knitting mills, this innocent remark started a rumor that their families were definitely at the knitting mills not far from camp. Their wishful thinking had a calming effect on the men, and for all I knew it could have been true.

Wally asked me for information about "Der Stellvertreter des Sonderbeauftragten des Reichsführers SS, für den Fremdvölkischen Arbeitseinsatz in Oberschlesien," the organization which maintained labor camps in the area, terrorized our homes, and controlled the concentration camp in Auschwitz. I told him what I knew and what I believed about our uncertain future. As we got to know each other better, Wally shared his background with me. He was the director of Salamander Shoes, a well-known shoe-manufacturing business with stores throughout Europe. His business was taken over by a German trustee, and he and his family had fled to Paris. They had planned to get back to Berlin as soon as the Nazis had met their defeat. He showed me pictures of his wife and daughter and told me how proud he was of being Jewish. He was ashamed of being German, even though he was awarded the *Eiserne Kreuz, Erste Klasse* (Iron cross, first class) during World War I. He asked me, "Why these deportations? Why the forceful separation of families? What do the Nazis have in mind? Was there a connection to the stories heard earlier that high-ranking party members had met near Berlin to find a solution to the Jewish question?" He knew the answers to his questions before they crossed his lips, and with tears in his eyes he said he was convinced that he would never see his family again. Though there were years separating us in age, Wally and I became close friends, a friendship that lasted until his very last breath.

One by one I got to know my new comrades, and interestingly enough, quite a few of them were decorated German officers who had earned honors during World War I. Without exception, they were ashamed and angry that their fatherland was now mistreating them so badly. They had moved to Western European countries after the Nazis had taken control and were anxiously awaiting the day when Germany once again became the country they loved. They had traveled West, while I had escaped to Poland, in the east. Now, in this camp, we were all together sharing our misery and despair. Looking at Horst Herschel and his sons, and other fathers with sons by their side, I realized that if my parents had been able to move to Amsterdam, then in all likelihood, Papa, Fred and I would be standing here side by side with all the other fathers and sons.

I kept asking myself, why did they reopen camp Gogolin even though there was no further work to do? Why were these new arrivals here from France, Belgium, and Holland? Why were they moved all across Germany into Poland at a time when the railroads were taxed to the limit bringing supplies to the German forces? Why didn't they know where their families were sent? Why such secrecy? How could I make sense out of any of the strange things that were happening all around me? Some of our men were allowed to go home for recuperation while others were taken away and never heard from again. Volunteers were asked to work in the German army near the Russian front, and at the same time mail privileges were taken from us. What were the ultimate plans that the Nazis had for the Jewish people of Europe?

One morning, after roll call, Wally was called to our Lagerführer's office and told that Gogolin had been made a transit camp for Jewish people from Western Europe to be resettled in Poland. Two additional groups were expected to arrive during the next few days, and when the transport was complete, everyone except chef Romek and girls in the kitchen would be leaving for the new camp. Wally asked once again whether there was any information about their families. The Lagerführer told him that he had no idea where the others were now, but not to worry. He had information that we were going to a camp in Trebenau to expand the railroad station and freight terminal. Trebenau was the German name given to the Polish city of Trzebinia during the German annexation. When Wally shared this news with me, I couldn't control my excitement, and when I explained that my parents were only six kilometers from Trebenau, he understood my delight. It meant that I would be near my parents, and as medic of the camp I might be able to find a way to get to Krenau, and possibly see my parents. The prospect of going to Trebenau was thrilling, yet I wondered why I was joining this transport, while the chef and kitchen staff were remaining at camp Gogolin. The only explanation I could think of was that Zinnecker wanted me away from there. Ever since I saw what the guards had done with the contents of the "inspected" suitcases, I got nasty looks from him whenever our paths crossed. No doubt, he didn't know how happy I was at the prospect of being so close to my family.

The two additional transports arrived, and as before men were forced to leave their families on the train at the Gogolin station. Using the same pretext of looking for weapons, the guards removed everything valuable from their luggage. The people complained bitterly to Wally but were told that there was nothing he could do beyond retrieving medication. He emphasized that all of us had more important things to be concerned about than worrying about stolen aftershave lotion.

Carrying our suitcases filled with our meager belongings, our transport marched to the railroad station and boarded the cars waiting for us. The next scheduled train from Berlin to Krakow arrived and our cars were hitched to the train. To my comrades, this train ride was very traumatic because it occurred so soon after they had left their loved ones on the same type of train. It evoked bitter memories and little conversation as everyone was occupied with his own thoughts. For me, this ride differed greatly from my travel to Ottmuth some two years ago when all the men with me were young and strong. We were all apprehensive of course, but our thoughts were positive. International agreements, we reasoned, would classify us as internees, and organizations such as the International Red Cross would look out for our safety and treatment, in accordance with the Geneva Convention. As long as our families would be safe at home, we could accept the hardships of life in a forced labor camp. Wishing that this war would soon be over, we were holding out and waiting to return to a normal life.

Now, in 1942, everything had drastically changed. Traveling with me now were men of all ages who came from Western Europe. There were single men, men with sons at their side, and others who spoke of their grandchildren. Many in our group complained about illnesses and were afraid of the heavy work they would have to do. Their physical condition was only part of the problem; their emotional health after being torn from their families was even more destructive to their ability to handle their confinement. I sympathized with their suffering and understood that their current circumstances were far worse than mine. Though I, too, had been separated from loved ones by force, I had the advantage of being younger and experienced in living behind barbed wire. Two years of a slowly decaying existence had eased me into a calm acceptance of my plight. Even the small food rations didn't bother me anymore. I didn't seem to need big portions of food; my body had learned to accept the tasteless and skimpy meals. For most of my new comrades, this rough lifestyle was difficult to accept.

Our train stopped at Trebenau and we were ordered to get off. I looked at the familiar surroundings with its station as poor and dilapidated as I had ever seen it. The only noticeable difference was the sign on the wall of the waiting room that had been changed from Trzebinia to Trebenau O/S. Routinely, we stood in formation to be counted, and as the train pulled out we had our first glimpse of our new prison. As we came closer, we saw that most of the barracks were unfinished. In fact, the only things completed were the barbed wire fences and barracks housing the kitchen, mess hall, and guardrooms.

The commander of Trebenau spoke to us briefly and told us the obvious. This camp was not fully operational and we would have to sleep on the floor of the mess hall and the two barracks that had unfinished roofs. It would be our immediate task to complete the construction and that the sooner the work was done, the sooner we would be able to sleep in our own bunks. In addition to the two unfinished barracks, there were five more that only had a few prefab wall sections standing upright. What a total disaster. As it was the beginning of the fall season the weather was already getting nasty. The few rooms without a roof had potbelly stoves, but not one of them was connected. There was no straw for our bunks, not even for those which were partially completed. We received army blankets and many of us rushed to find a spot on the floor of the mess hall. Unfortunately, those who most needed the comfort of the mess hall floor were not as quick as the younger men in finding a good spot for themselves. As a result, many men were forced to sleep out in the open, protected from the elements by only a few standing partitions. It was a terrible situation.

One of the barracks had a small room marked as the office for the Judenälteste. Wally offered to share this roofless room with Dr. Hauser and me in order to set up a temporary infirmary. While still at Gogolin, Dr. Hauser, a physician who had fled Germany earlier, came to introduce himself as the appointed camp physician. Unfortunately, the doctor himself was a diabetic and suffered from deep depression. He was hardly able to function, yet he tried very hard to help me organize the infirmary.

The Lagerführer, Herr Bergmann, came to see this open-air office and infirmary and brought with him a package he'd received from Sosnowitz containing office and medical supplies. Wearing a tailored suit with the Nazi party emblem on his lapel, he was all business. Not one to give up easily, Wally tried again to get some information about their wives and children from Herr Bergmann, but his response was evasive and totally unfriendly. He did tell us that water would be connected to the kitchen the following afternoon and we'd then have drinking water and food. It would take a while longer, he said, to complete the wash barracks, and until then we would have no chance to wash ourselves.

Dr. Hauser could hardly wait to open the package containing the medical supplies and became frantic when he couldn't find insulin, the medication he depended upon for his life. There was no substitute, he said, and without insulin, his days were numbered. I tried to calm his immediate fears by mentioning that my family lived in the town nearby and we would try to find a way to get help for him.

Polish foremen arrived at camp the next morning and Wally organized work crews to get our barracks constructed. I was amazed at the way he took control of the situation even though his experience with this line of work was nil. As soon as I could, I told him about Dr. Hauser's condition and said that something had to be done, and done quickly. I told Wally how I had gotten medication and supplies from the local pharmacy in Gogolin and suggested that we try the same thing in nearby Krenau. I had hopes that my parents were still living in Krenau and that I might meet an acquaintance in the city who could help. It was the only chance we had. Wally approached Herr Bergmann but he was not at all concerned about the health of any Jewish inmate. He said, "It was most generous of the German administration to supply us with any medical supplies at all. Let's not forget that there is a war being fought and the needs of German soldiers come first." He then quoted a letter from his wounded son, a member of the Waffen SS, who complained about shortages of medical supplies near the front line. Any drugs used for Jews in our camp would deprive German soldiers of their rightful supplies and would not be tolerated. He intimated that he was an old-time party member, a personal friend of Hermann Göring, and quickly dismissed Wally's request for assistance. Wally told me the gist of the conversation and the two of us had the grim task of telling Dr. Hauser that he was given a death sentence.

For the first few days, most men worked inside the camp to finish our barracks and provide roofs over our heads. They were unfamiliar with construction work and they got hurt constantly. They were diamond merchants, lawyers, architects, engineers, teachers, artists and other professionals, and none had ever done manual labor. Unable to communicate and give instructions to these people, the foremen became frustrated. The men in turn had little interest in doing what was asked of them. They wore fine leather shoes, silk shirts, and other clothes for life in a city. Their garments got torn quickly doing construction work, but these were the only clothes they had. They were the same garments they had worn when they arrived in camp. Annoyed at the slow progress, the foremen shouted and the guards began pushing and using their rifle butts. Some men got hurt seriously while others just tripped or fell over each other. Our infirmary became the busiest place in camp and the few medical supplies we had on hand were used up quickly. Not only did we run out of simple first-aid supplies, but we had no water, let alone warm water, to cleanse their wounds properly. The smallest laceration turned into an infection and none of the men had the strength, time, or ambition to care for themselves or their personal hygiene.

The last barracks, designated to house twenty girls, was completed on the day of their arrival. As in my previous camps, these girls came from the Krenau area via the transit camp in Sosnowitz. I was sorry for the women in Ottmuth or Gogolin, but I truly pitied the girls who came to Trebenau who would have to share the hardship and filthy conditions of this camp. The Judenälteste, doctor, and medic were the only ones permitted to enter the ladies' barracks and I took advantage of this opportunity to meet with them. I had been without mail for so long that I was anxious to learn about the months since I had lost contact with my family. They confirmed that the Jewish population of Auschwitz had been resettled, and that the former Polish army barracks and nearby Birkenau were made into a concentration camp. Still, no one had any real knowledge about the activities behind those barbed-wire fences. The only thing known was that many trains filled with Jewish people from neighboring towns and as far away as Western Europe arrived there constantly. There were rumors that thousands of people were dying in this camp, but no one could confirm it.

Dr. Hauser's condition became more critical each day and soon he entered sickbay as a patient. Dr. Jacob (Kuba) Wagschal, a young physician from Lodz, Poland, and a recent graduate of the university in Paris, joined our staff in the infirmary. With a competent physician at my side, we did whatever we could to help our comrades. Kuba and I thought alike and eventually became good friends. Without much hope of success, Wally, Kuba and I again asked to see the Lagerführer about our big problems. We begged him for permission to visit the apothecary in the city and get whatever supplies we could. I asked him to come to the infirmary and see for himself our frightful situation. Rather than expose himself to the stench, filth and squalor of our sick comrades, he reluctantly gave his permission for me to go to the apothecary in Krenau the next day. A fortunate coincidence — the guard from Gogolin who accompanied me when I went to the post office and apothecary was with me again. I told him that I used to live in Krenau and that, in fact, my parents were still living there. I hinted that I prayed to somehow see them, although I had no idea how this would come to pass. As we walked along the road into town, an army truck stopped and gave us a lift right to the marketplace.

The changes in Krenau were dramatic. Only a few stores, formerly owned by Jews and now operated by Polish citizens, were open for business. The streets of Krenau, once so very crowded, were virtually deserted. It was scary when I saw the town so empty. We started walking toward the apothecary, and as we rounded a street corner I saw a Jewish militia man. We looked at each other for a moment and I recognized him as Abe Krakauer, one of Papa's longtime friends from Berlin. At first he seemed surprised to see my guard in a German police uniform; a sight familiar in Berlin, but unusual in the annexed territories. When he recognized me, he hurriedly approached us to greet me. Was this the bit of good luck that I was dreaming of? Still hesitant, I didn't know how to handle the situation. I had been told that the reputation of the Jewish militia was not always good because they were the ones to enforce Nazi orders.

My guard didn't mind my talking with Mr. Krakauer and once he heard that I was in town trying to get medical supplies, he asked whether my parents knew that I was so near. I hardly had time to answer before he turned away saying, "Meet you at the apothecary," and with that, he ran to get my parents. There were no customers in the store when we entered and the druggist came from behind his enclosure and listened to what I had to say. I spoke Polish to him, a language I had learned in camp from my Polish-speaking friends. I showed him my shopping list and written prescriptions, but before I could hand him my papers, the door swung open and my parents, totally out of breath, came running into my arms. It was an emotional scene that I will always remember. The druggist and my guard stood there bewildered, not understanding what was happening. Mr. Krakauer was next to arrive with the president of the Judenrat at his side. While my parents and I were still hugging, kissing, and crying all at once, Mr. Krakauer explained this meeting to the guard and storekeeper.

The presence of the Judenrat president turned out to be very helpful for me. Knowing the druggist well, in no time at all I was given a package containing almost everything I had asked for, except insulin. I got some oral medication for diabetes, but was told that insulin had not been available in a long time; it was simply not to be found. The president insisted on paying for my supplies, an offer I gladly accepted. Everyone in camp had chipped in whatever German marks we had left, and now I could return the money to our men.

As one policeman to the other, Mr. Krakauer chatted with my guard and casually mentioned that he might want to relax and spend time as a guest at the militia guardhouse when we completed our business here. He even suggested that he allow me to spend some time with my parents. The entire militia, and he personally, would guarantee that I would return. He also indicated that the guard would be well compensated for his cooperation. The guard then glanced at me and remarked, "There really isn't a time limit for us to get back to camp, so I guess there would be no harm in relaxing for a while."

The president of the Judenrat told me that a group of women traveled each day to work at a textile mill in Trebenau. They had seen our men working on the tracks, and as they recognized the words *Juif* or *Jood* on their yellow stars, they assumed that the camp was filled with people from France and Holland. Thus, he was stunned to find me there among the Westerners. I explained to him and my parents how circumstances and luck brought me to Trebenau and how I had managed to make my way to Krenau that day. Now that we had made contact, he promised to do all he could to assist us.

I was anxious to know if there was any information about the transports arriving from the West, in particular, the trains filled with women and children. I wanted to bring some positive news back to my comrades if I could and give them a bit of encouragement. There were no real answers, just a suspicion that the trainloads of people had been taken to Auschwitz or places even deeper into Poland. They told me of confirmed reports where whole communities were taken into the woods, forced to dig ditches, climb into them, and were then shot on the spot. Bulldozers were then used to level the ground and push earth over the dead bodies. This was the first time that such gruesome rumors had been confirmed.

Mutti and Papa had been given time off from work and I went with them to the room that was now called home. I was shocked at what I saw. They had a small, dingy room with a stove in the corner, three beds, a table, and three chairs. It was on the second floor of a very old building on a street reserved for Jews only. I couldn't believe my eyes. My parents looked at me and I looked at them. No longer able to control our emotions, we cried with bitter tears, and hugged each other again and again. When was this nightmare going to end, ... would it ever?

My brother Fred was not home and there was no way to reach him. He was on the road making deliveries for friends of our family, the Grajowers, who had given him a job delivering beer and carbonated water to German army posts in the vicinity. It was the only bottling plant in the area and the only business operated by Jews that still had a horse and wagon. Their business was considered safe for the moment because the German military and civilians had to have their drinks and beer.

Mutti was quick to make some food for me, while Papa filled me in on the latest happenings. They felt reasonably secure in their jobs and trusted Papa's acquaintance, who was now their boss. They were promised, and believed, that they would not be "resettled." In fact, Papa told me that on one of the more recent raids, a man who carried a document showing employment at Papa's factory was released and sent back home. No matter how distasteful it was for them to make German uniforms, they had to hold on to their jobs as long as possible. My parents tried to give me courage and hope. "Change was coming soon," Papa told me. The German army had met stiff opposition in their fight for Stalingrad and the long-awaited turnaround may have started. Our time together flew by quickly, and soon Abe Krakauer returned to pick me up. We couldn't thank him enough for what he had done for us. He and his militia colleagues had paid off my German guard well, and Abe promised to do what he could to have me return to town again.

Back in camp, I managed to hide most of my supplies from our Lagerführer because I didn't want to get the apothecary into trouble. Even the small amount that I showed Herr Bergmann gave rise to the remark that, "This kind of black market is the reason why our boys at the front lines don't have enough medical supplies." My guard kept quiet, and to the best of my knowledge he never mentioned the experience to anyone.

Dr. Hauser couldn't wait to open the packages, but when he saw what I had, he turned away and started crying like a baby. He needed insulin and nothing else but insulin; the substitute I had gotten was totally inadequate for him. His last hope had faded away. He knew that his days were numbered, and indeed they were. He died a few days later.

The death of our doctor added to the despair and gloom in camp. It was up to Wally and me to see that he received a proper burial and was not just dropped in a hole as the Lagerführer had ordered. I had an idea which I hoped would work. Wally, Kuba, and I went to see Herr Bergmann and, after much discussion, we convinced him that it would be much easier to contact the Jewish community in Krenau and let them come and take the body for burial at their local cemetery. All he would have to do was contact the militia in Krenau and his work would be done.

Two militiamen arrived at our camp the following morning and brought a casket on a horse-drawn cart. A guard led them to the infirmary and I could hardly believe that my brother was the driver of the cart. But with guards nearby, Fred and I couldn't even gesture that we knew each other, let alone embrace. As I led the cart to the barracks where the body was stored, one of the militiamen whispered to me, "Do what you have to, but make sure that the guard is not here when we place the body into the coffin. The coffin is filled with bread!" Quickly I alerted Kuba to run ahead and gather blankets in which the bread could be hidden. To give him time to make arrangements, my brother had the horse become unruly so that Kuba could get a head start and also alert Wally to what was happening. As Wally engaged the guard in conversation, we carried the casket into the room. With lightening speed, we dumped the bread into a corner, covered it with blankets, and placed the body into the casket. We put the casket back on the cart, and I had a moment to hold my brother's hand as he quickly told me that when the news of the death and planned burial was known, our people collected all the bread they could gather to fill the coffin. I shudder to think what could have happened if a guard had looked into the coffin as it came through the gate. In parting, on behalf of all of us, I quietly expressed gratitude to the militiamen and the people of Krenau. I also thanked them for allowing Fred to be the driver so that we could see each other again. Even though it was the unhappiest of times, it was something special to be with my brother, if only for a moment.

In the evening, after all was quiet, Wally, Kuba, and I started distributing the greatly needed nourishment. We made equal portions of bread for every room in the camp. Making sure that no guard would see us, we went from room to room and delivered our packages along with the caution for the strictest secrecy. If anyone found out how we had gotten the bread, the consequences would have been disastrous. There was enough for everyone to get a hefty slice; but it wasn't just bread that we received that night, it was knowing that people nearby were willing to help us. I was very proud of the people in Krenau, and although I wanted this episode to be kept secret, it became known that I had something to do with these "extras."

Next to the mess hall, our infirmary was still the most active place in camp. People had to wait until late at night before we could take care of everyone. This endless waiting deprived our men of badly needed sleep and rest. I told Wally and Kuba what we had done in Gogolin and Ottmuth where a medic gave first aid at the construction site. It was very effective there, and with no warm water to cleanse wounds at camp, it could be even more effective here. It would reduce the number of smaller injuries coming to us in the evening, and give us more time for people who needed serious attention.

Together, Wally, Kuba, and I went to see Herr Bergmann to make our suggestion. He listened and sat there motionless, his arms folded over his chest, without saying a single word. We didn't know whether he was even listening to us, thinking about it, or had his mind on other things. "You can go now," was all he said after we exhausted all the issues we could think of. Days went by and we had given up hope that he even remembered our conversation. Out of nowhere, one morning he told Wally to appoint a medic for the construction site. We didn't have to look very far because Peter Blank, a medical student who had assisted us during the evening rush, was anxious to help at the work site.

Two months had passed and some barracks, including sick bay, were still not completed. While construction was ongoing, our medical team shared living quarters with twenty of our comrades. This was fine with Kuba and me, but wasn't fair to the others who were inconvenienced when we came into the room after most men had gone to sleep. Worse than that, sometimes patients needed to find us in the middle of the night, and that disturbed our roommates' rest. This was not a good situation because sleep and rest were so very important for the men's well-being.

Relationships were stiff and formal in Trebenau, not like in the other camps I had been where everyone was on a first-name basis. In Trebenau, we even addressed each other with *Herr* or other appropriate titles like doctor, or even *Herr Professor*. The atmosphere was stiff, strained, and selfish; everyone seemed to be interested only in themselves. Except for the men I saw in the infirmary, I had little time to get to know my new roommates. When I did become acquainted, I found them to be a most interesting mix of people. There was a jurist, a member of the famous Warburg family, and a rabbi who at one time led a large congregation in the Rhineland. Others were talented artists, lecturers, or businessmen who had left Germany a few years earlier. In their other lives, they had the respect of their German neighbors and friends. Now it was most difficult for them to reconcile their previous lifestyle with this confinement. I often recall the man in the bunk next to mine, one Herman Spitz, the former concertmaster of the Hamburg Philharmonic Orchestra. The one and only treasure he still possessed was the wedding picture of himself and his wife Erna Sack, one of the most outstanding sopranos of the time. She was not Jewish, and to continue her career in the music world, she was forced to divorce him. Spitz moved to Paris where at first she was able to visit him frequently. Even though they were divorced, he confided in me that they were still very much in love.

Living in primitive conditions and suffering from the emotional stress of being separated from family, our men lost their will to live. No one was ever beaten fatally, but my comrades were deteriorating. From the moment our infirmary first opened, sick bay was overcrowded. Earlier rules about quotas had not changed and once again I was flirting with danger. Even though our camp population consisted of Western Europeans, the Angel of Death was still in charge. Taking into account the number of men in camp, I was permitted no more than nine people on any given day in sick bay. If I had followed this directive, many of our sick or injured would have to be sent to work. I just couldn't do it, and Kuba and Wally knew it, too. My decisions were dangerous for us and we were well aware that the day of reckoning would have to come eventually. Lindner's staff would see the daily numbers in the reports from our camp and inevitably take action against us. The Lagerführer reprimanded us time and again for the large group I kept in camp and claimed that it was sabotage. With increasing frequency he overruled Kuba's or my decision, and he had the final word. People left for work in the morning and were carried back to camp by comrades who could barely make it back themselves. The injured were dropped by their friends at the door of the infirmary and we had to work for hours to meet their needs.

One of the many casualties was Dr. Friedländer, a roommate of mine, a lawyer and lecturer, highly respected by his peers. I got to know him and admired him greatly. It had been snowing the day he was brought to the infirmary and he was in a total state of exhaustion. I put him to bed and arranged for a meal to be brought to him. While checking the patients later that evening, I saw that the doctor had not even touched his food. He removed his glasses and asked me to look into his inflamed and pussy eyes. Barely audible, he said that he was going blind from trachoma and that he now had nothing to live for. He had no more strength and was convinced that his wife and children had been killed. "There'll be a good life for all those who'll survive this war," he said to me, "you are young and must remain strong. You must do whatever you can to survive and be a witness to the world. When this madness is over, you and all the Jewish people in the world must fight and rebuild our own Jewish state so that things like this will never happen again." He pleaded with us to let him die with dignity. Kuba and I spent the night at his side, even trying to feed him forcibly, but with his last bit of strength, he refused any nourishment. He did not live to see the next day. Dr. Friedländer was the second person to die in Trebenau. Again we contacted the Jewish militia in Krenau, and as before my brother Fred brought a coffin filled with bread. Our friend received a proper burial right next to the body of Dr. Hauser at the Jewish cemetery in Krenau. The whisper of his last words, "Rebuild the Jewish state," still rings in my ears.

Party lines and policy were strictly obeyed by Herr Bergmann, but when it affected him personally, he seemed to forget the law which prohibited any German to be treated by a Jewish physician. His son, an officer in Hitler's elite Waffen SS, had been wounded during the campaign in Stalingrad, and his frozen fingers had been partially amputated. As our Lagerführer, he saw us struggle with frozen fingers and toes and suddenly became very interested in watching the way we handled these problems. He didn't offer us any help, but was impressed by how we performed and accomplished the nearly impossible with the smallest amount of instruments and medication. When his son was furloughed and visited his father, Herr Bergmann asked Kuba, the Jewish doctor, to examine his son. He was concerned about his health and wanted Kuba's opinion about the treatment that was given to him at the front lines. So much for rules and regulations.

Kuba seized the opportunity to ask for permission for me to go to Krenau again and add to our medical supplies. He proved to Herr Bergmann that we desperately needed more supplies than what we had received from the Judenrat in Sosnowitz. Kuba showed him how we used torn shirts as makeshift bandages and then had our girls wash and boil the same bandages on stoves to be reused again. This time he didn't offer any objection to Kuba's request, and again I was able to see my parents.

We were in the middle of a severe winter and there was still no hot water in our wash barracks. People began neglecting their personal hygiene as they didn't have the strength or ambition to care for themselves after a hard day of work in the wind, snow, and rain. Getting their daily food ration and stretching out in their bunks was all that interested them. The last thing they imagined doing was taking a cold shower in a place barely protected from the outside elements. Few of us had towels, so wet as we were, we would have to get back into our dirty clothes and hurry to our barracks if we wanted some warmth.

The conversations in our barracks were filled with anguish and pain. Concern for loved ones and small food rations were talked about all the time. Sometimes our discussions turned to politics and religion, and Rabbi

Eisenhard tried to console us by saying that it was God's will, and who were we to judge. His opinion was not shared by most of our men, who replied that if there was a Jewish God, how could he permit us to suffer as we did?

Our anticipated day of reckoning came on a Saturday afternoon when Lindner arrived in camp. Everyone was busy cleaning their barracks when a whistle summoned us to roll call. The snow was falling lightly as the guards chased the men out of their barracks and into formation. We still didn't know exactly what was happening until we spotted Lindner coming out of the commander's office. The feared bullwhip in hand, trailed by his dogs, he walked directly to my section of the injured and sick. Immediately, he started swinging and hitting everyone in his reach until they fell to the ground. He yelled, "You miserable Jews — you malingerers — I'll teach you what it means to avoid work. You're sabotaging our efforts." His outburst went on and on until his energy was spent, and with that he turned and entered the commander's office again.

Moments after he had disappeared, someone from the guardhouse called "Sanitäter" (medic) and the blood curdled in my veins. I knew that medics from other camps had been sent to Auschwitz after a confrontation with Lindner and as I turned to Kuba and Wally I said, "This is it — Goodbye," and they knew what I meant. Shaking like a leaf, I ran into the guardhouse. I was a bundle of nerves and whatever I did was done mechanically. I remember coming through the door, clicking my heels, and standing at attention shouting, "Jawohl Herr Sturmbannführer, Sanitäter Bachner zum Befehl" (Medic Bachner at your command). I don't think he expected to hear a Berliner dialect, and it must have taken him by surprise. I have no other explanation for what happened next as he looked at me with his steely eyes. I expected the worst and could see myself on my way to Auschwitz. Instead, he started yelling at me, "You have all these sick people because you didn't take care of them properly." Every word he uttered was accompanied by a slap on my face. I don't know what possessed me, but I dared tell him quickly that we didn't have enough medicine or warm water to even wash the wounds properly. Not expecting such audacity, he looked at me with disbelief and said to the Lagerführer, "Why is there no warm water?" The answer was a simple one: the boiler had not yet arrived. Lindner then pushed the handle of his bullwhip under my chin and threatened that if he ever found so many sick people again, he would have my hide. There was no doubt that he meant what he said. I was dismissed, and still in shock, I ran back to my roll call position with the others. After we were dismissed, Kuba and Wally came to hug and embrace me — I had survived. To this very day, I can't understand what made the Angel of Death spare my life.

As a follow up to Lindner's visit, the Lagerführer came to sick bay and took down the names of all patients, including those who were frequent visitors. On the following morning, he called the names he had listed and had them board trucks bound for camp Annaberg. I had heard that this camp had been made into a place for chronically ill and severely injured men and that only light work was given to them. No one could tell me what this "light work" was, and I feared for the lives of our transferred men.

10

From Bad to Worse

As if our existence in Trebenau wasn't hellish enough, the cold wintry weather made it even worse. On one of the very few days when work was halted by snow blanketing the construction site, Wally was ordered to prepare the few unfinished rooms for one-hundred-and-fifty additional men and five women. They were scheduled to arrive the following day from camp Spytkowice. I was taken aback by this news because Spytkowice was the village where my grandmother owned her farm, and the place where my father was born. It was a rural area and completely devoid of industry. I wondered why the Nazis had placed a forced labor camp in the middle of nowhere. I looked forward to speaking with the new arrivals because I thought I might discover the fate of my Aunts Bronia and Regina who lived in Spytkowice. They had gone into hiding with Polish neighbors, people they had shared their entire lives with. No one had heard from the sisters for a long time and it was suspected that they had become victims of their neighbors' treachery. All we knew was that the farm and house, with all its contents, were now in the hands of a local Polish farmer.

With the help of everyone in camp, we prepared the empty rooms, and watched the new arrivals as they entered our camp. Huddled together, holding on to each other for warmth and protection, they stood on the open platforms of army vehicles. Seeing them get off the trucks was a sad sight; they looked even worse than we did, if that was possible. We assisted them jumping off the trucks and getting them into formation so they could be counted. After the formalities were completed, our new comrades hurried out of the cold and into the warm barracks. Ephram Kanel, their

Judenälteste, or Foya, as he was called, told us about conditions in camp Spytkowice. It made our camp look like paradise. In the three months they were there, most barracks were never completed and no kitchen was ever available for preparing any kind of warm food. Without proper sanitary facilities, the camp was finally closed. No wonder, Foya and his people were thrilled to see our primitive wash barracks and enjoyed resting on the little bit of straw in their bunks. Foya was a very congenial man and Wally, our Judenälteste, appointed him to be his assistant.

Paul Citroen, a young doctor from Paris, had served as their camp physician, and after much prodding by Wally, our Lagerführer gave permission for Paul to work with us in the infirmary. Dr. Walter Jacoby, a dentist from Berlin, was another new arrival whose skills were much needed in camp. Walter had moved to Paris some years earlier but was never certified to practice dentistry in France. Proud of his past, Walter showed us pictures of himself with Kemal Pascha Attaturk, father of modern Turkey, whom he served as personal dentist. There were pictures of other personalities he had treated, but none of this made any difference now. To get permission for Walter to be our camp dentist, Wally had to contact the Judenrat in Sosnowitz. His request was quickly granted and simple dental equipment arrived a few days later. A recently completed barracks became the new sick bay, and one room was set aside for our quarters. Kuba, Paul, Walter, and I worked well together and being housed in the room next to the infirmary was a great convenience.

The only news reports we would ever hear was when the girls who cleaned the guards' quarters heard bits of a news broadcast occasionally. Their information was sketchy, but whatever they could understand suggested that the German army was no longer moving forward as rapidly as before, or doing as well as they did earlier. The battle around Stalingrad, deep in Russia, seemed to be a fierce and prolonged one and gave us hope that the cold weather and icy conditions would be too much for the German soldiers to endure. At the same time, other promising reports suggested that the Allied forces had contained German advances in Africa. This news helped strengthen our resolve to withstand our hardships and misery.

As we all stood together during roll call, it was obvious what a pitiful mass of humanity we had become. There was hardly anyone who didn't suffer from an injury or ailment, and for many it was sheer torture to just stand, let alone drag themselves to the work site each day. What a horrible sight! My authority as medic was extremely limited, and for each man admitted to sick bay there were always many others who needed treatment just as badly. Our kitchen staff tried to be helpful to our patients, and Adele, a girl from camp Spytkowice, was especially resourceful. Almost every day she would secretly deliver the guards' leftover food to the infirmary. That extra bit of nourishment was a godsend for our patients. But unlike the situation in Gogolin, where Ann had relatively little trouble in being a good Samaritan, the kitchen in Trebenau was controlled by the Lagerführer's wife. Had Frau Bergmann, our kitchen supervisor, ever caught her, it would have been disastrous. Adele was a beautiful young lady and we were immediately attracted to each other. Whenever she delivered the food personally, we tried to find a bit of time to be together. Knowing that camp was not a place for romance, we still found moments when we were able to hug, exchange a kiss or two, dry each other's tears, and console each other.

Our sanitary conditions had deteriorated so badly that we began to see lice on those who came to the infirmary. We kept emphasizing the importance of personal hygiene, but it was like talking to a wall. All our men worked and slept in their same layered clothes, night after night, to keep themselves warm. Going into a cold wash barracks required stamina they no longer possessed. Constant itching and scratching made the men uncomfortable in the day and deprived them of rest at night. All I could do was ask for the cooperation of the Stubenälteste in every room. I told them to insist that every man cleanse himself and wash his clothes with the hottest water they could heat up on the stove. I also asked that the following Sunday be set aside for thorough cleansing of beds and clothing. The barracks needed to be scrubbed with disinfectant, which the Lagerführer provided, and everyone, and that meant everyone, had to take a shower. I knew that this action was not sufficient, but it was the best that we could do.

Rabbi Dr. Wolff, a most pleasant man who used to head a congregation in Antwerp, came to the infirmary one evening complaining of a very high fever. We immediately placed him in bed but couldn't figure out why he was so ill. His fever didn't break, regardless of what medication we tried. On the third day, I noticed some spots on his stomach and called for Kuba and Paul to examine him. They were not sure, but they suspected that he had typhus. If this was true, we had no other choice but to inform the Lagerführer. We had no idea how the SS administration would react to this news, but pretending that the danger didn't exist could only make matters worse. Prepared for trouble, we were surprised when the administration offered to help us. News that we had lice and a possible typhus epidemic spread quickly to the outside community, and comments like "those filthy Jews" were constantly heard from the German guards and personnel at the construction site. They kept their distance from our workers, but still managed to use their rifle butts to chase our people when they were so inclined. I had no doubt that our problems started with the lack of hot water, inadequate clothing, and poor facilities for proper hygiene. Fatigue, and the pitiful food rations which were given to us didn't help matters either.

As more and more people came to the infirmary with symptoms of typhus, the Lagerführer made inquiries to locate the nearest delousing station. Luckily, the German army had installed such a station in nearby Krenau for the German soldiers who were returning from the Russian front. Hearing this, I was delighted to learn that "those filthy Jews" were not the only ones needing delousing. As fast as possible, arrangements were made for the entire camp to march into town and pass through the disinfecting process. No one was exempt, not even the sick or injured. Watching the camp population drag themselves for six kilometers into Krenau on a wintry day was painful, but it was absolutely necessary. During our absence, a pest control company was hired to fumigate the barracks and try to control the epidemic.

I had no way of contacting anyone in town about our impending trip, but my intuition told me that someone in the Jewish community must have gotten this news. I didn't want to say anything or raise false hopes, but as we neared the center of town, I received silent signals from passersby who recognized me. I understood then that the Jewish community knew all about our visit. They had volunteered to handle the logistics of the day and even had permission to feed us. We were led to the public school where we remained for many hours because the delousing center could only handle fifty people at a time. The volunteers, including my parents, were permitted to be with us at the school building, but my duties kept me away most of the time. It was my assignment to take fifty men at a time to the center and supervise them there. Fortunately, my friends

Wally and Kuba were willing to help out so I could spend some precious moments with my parents.

We were kept in the same school classrooms that I was held in when I was imprisoned there in 1940 and I could recall those dreadful times vividly! Suddenly there was a commotion at the entrance to the building as several girls were being chased off a truck. Crying and screaming, they were herded into classrooms on the upper floor of the school. I was distraught when I saw my friend Werner Neumark's wife Lotte and his sister Erna among the arrivals. Overwhelmed by emotion, we tried in vain to comfort each other.

The community served us a hot meal, a treat we all welcomed. It was amazing to me how the town had managed to get all that food together even though they had their own serious problems. I was able to introduce my friend Adele to Mutti that day and she seemed very happy to meet "my friend." I left them talking with each other, and when I caught Mutti's eye, she made sure I saw her approving nod. On our way back to camp, everyone carried packages of food and clothing that the townspeople had given to them. It was an exceptional day for us, and even our guards were treated to schnapps and other goodies. I was proud of my people in Krenau, who demonstrated the true meaning of a Jewish heart. Some of the men were actually smiling on their way back to camp, grateful for a pleasant day outside the barbed-wire fence. Thankfully, no one tried to escape as we all knew that it would have been very foolish and dangerous.

In spite of all the measures we had taken, people still flocked to the infirmary with high fever. The epidemic was in full swing and we had to act with great speed. One of the empty rooms near our infirmary became a quarantine area and I volunteered to isolate myself and stay with the sick. The number of typhus patients had grown to twenty-one, and I was all alone with them, twenty-four hours a day. I watched over them, nursed them, fed them, and gave them the only medication we had available. Injections of camphor were used as a heart stimulant to keep them strong during the crisis, and injections of a sulphur product named Prontosil was given to contain the infection. Throughout the days, I kept Kuba up to date about the treatment I had given my patients and the progress I was making. He, in turn, told me about things happening in camp and the community's fear of becoming infected.

Adele and her friends made sure that the men in quarantine received added nourishment, and since Herr Bergmann and his lackeys didn't dare enter the area, I was able to keep my comrades in sick bay long enough for them to recover and regain their strength. It was a rough time for everyone, and a miracle that I, too, had not become infected. My reward was that twenty of our men came through this ordeal alive. Unfortunately, Rabbi Wolff, the first one in our camp to get the dreadful fever, died. He was our only fatality. As before, we made arrangements with the Jewish militia in Krenau to have him buried. But, because of our quarantine, they were not permitted to enter our camp and couldn't bring us a casket filled with food.

Soon after the last patient left sickbay, the SS Stabsartzt and his team came to see us and lift our quarantine. The authorities had been kept informed of the epidemic and now were anxious to learn the details of what I did and how. They were flabbergasted that we only numbered twenty-one men with typhus in a camp of nearly five hundred. They found it even more surprising that we had only one fatality. The Stabsartzt and his staff questioned me over and over again, recording every detail. To convince themselves of what they called a miracle, they took blood samples of all the patients we treated. They returned a few days later and confirmed that the tests done from the blood samples were definitely positive. Every guard and civilian worker who had contact with us was then vaccinated, and before leaving camp the Stabsartzt personally vaccinated Kuba, Wally, and me. He told us how impressed he was by what we had done, and his report would now be on record with the medical authorities in Oppeln O/S and Breslau. Compliments given to Jews by this Stabsartzt were most unusual, and we found it hard to believe that words of praise could possibly come from the mouth of an SS officer.

Spring was approaching and the weather had turned milder and more comfortable. It was astonishing how a little bit of warmth and sunshine could lift the morale of our people. On Sunday afternoons we would gather outside our barracks to talk and encourage our talented artists to entertain us. Understandably, they were in no mood to perform. "You can't expect me to sing while my mind is preoccupied and my stomach is empty," most replied. Yet, there were moments of nostalgia when someone felt like singing, and once he got started, others followed along. Peter Dinhoff, a coffeehouse musician, played his violin for us and then shared his instrument with Harry Spitz, the classical musician. Excellent voices and superb violin music helped even the most depressed men forget their problems for a little while.

It was Purim, 1943, but in camp, this day was no different from all the rest. At noon, Adele rushed into the infirmary obviously troubled. She was heartsick as she quietly told me what she had heard from Polish people making deliveries to the kitchen. They spoke of a raid on Jews in Krenau and how everybody was held captive in the schools until they were taken to the transit camp in Sosnowitz. She had heard that not one single Jew remained in the city. As my parents were promised safety by working on German uniforms, I hoped with all my heart that they were not included in the raid. I also prayed that my brother might have been spared if he was out of the city making deliveries. I was devastated and in a daze as I tried to tell myself that my parents and brother were safe, but deep inside, I knew this wasn't so. Adele kept visiting the infirmary to be with me whenever she could. Many others, too, came to offer their sympathy. Most had met my family on that delousing day in Krenau and understood my pain and trauma. I tried to be calm, but when I got to my room that evening, my emotions got the better of me. Kuba, Paul and Walter did their best to comfort me, but it was useless.

The next morning I tried to find the guard who had gone with me to Krenau and had met my parents. I begged him to visit the city again and find something, anything, which would give me a glimmer of hope. Amazingly he agreed, and, using his off-duty time, he went to Krenau to find out what he could. All he could tell me that afternoon was that there wasn't a single Jewish person left in town. The Jewish area had become a ghost town, he said. In one fell swoop I had lost my parents, brother, grandmother, aunts, uncles, cousins, and friends. I was now as alone as most of the others in our camp.

The Judenrat in Sosnowitz was no longer able to send us medical supplies, and our meager reserves were almost gone. Once again I begged the Lagerführer to let me go to Krenau to replenish our empty shelves. I didn't expect to have great success, but surprisingly he was willing to let me try one more time. Visiting Krenau was a personal mission as well as necessary for our infirmary. I was anxious to see anything that might give me a clue as to my family's whereabouts. With the same guard at my side, I wandered through the desolate town. It was eerie looking into open doors, empty houses, and vacant apartments. Other than stray cats and dogs running wild, there was no sign of life anywhere in the Jewish ghetto. Occasionally I saw a Polish man dragging a piece of furniture from one of the open apartments, but there were no police stopping him from taking whatever he wanted. I detoured to see the apartment where my parents had lived and felt nothing but emptiness. I tried to control my emotions as I entered the apothecary, but it was difficult. I got an understanding look from the pharmacist, a few friendly words, and a small package containing bandages and aspirins.

The lack of medical supplies was only part of our everyday problems. Our bigger concern was that our Lagerführer insisted on sending sick people out to work and threatened that he would have to send another transport of sick people to camp Annaberg. One morning he did just that. After roll call, he had all the sick men stand on one side of the square, while the rest of the camp was sent out to work. When the last detail of men were outside the gate, the sick were told to take their belongings and board the army trucks stationed outside the camp. There, guards from Annaberg had arrived to make the transfer of prisoners. One of the guards, seeing my armband with the red cross insignia on it, approached me and asked for my name. He looked around to be sure that no one saw him give me an envelope and then walked away quickly. Before I could even say a word, he returned to his transport and continued his duties.

I was shocked at having received a message from anyone in the outside world. Other than my parents or brother, I didn't think anyone could possibly know where I was. It turned out that the writer of this note was Halinka, a girl who shared the apartment with my parents and whom I had met when I visited Mutti and Papa. In this note she explained that while cleaning the guardhouse she heard someone say that he was assigned to bring a transport from Trebenau to camp Annaberg. Remembering that I was in Trebenau, she asked the guard to do her a favor and deliver this message to me. Writing in Polish, a language she knew the guard did not understand, she described how the entire Jewish population in Krenau had been taken to the staging camp in Sosnowitz. Some, including her, were selected to be moved to Annaberg, while others were sent to Gross Rosen, Funfteichen, and most to Auschwitz. In Sosnowitz, she had seen my mother, grandmother, and others of my family locked up and guarded. They were part of the group marked for Auschwitz. My father was also headed for Auschwitz, but suddenly someone she didn't recognize pulled him out of the group and pushed him into a transport assigned to the labor camp at Funfteichen. My brother Fred, she wrote, had left the house early that morning to make his deliveries and she didn't know what had happened to him after that. I never had an opportunity to thank her, or even let her know that I had received her note. But for now I still had hope that Papa and Fred might be alive. However, Papa, never physically strong, had a problem with his right leg and I knew he would suffer greatly in a labor camp. The news about Mutti, my grandmother, and all my other relatives was chilling. I thought of Mutti's smiling face and the words of courage she had given me only a few weeks earlier and I felt completely destroyed. Kuba, Wally and Adele found me crying in my room as I showed them the note. Adele translated it for me in detail so that I could understand every Polish word. They were my good friends, and I never needed them more.

Monsieur Klein, as he was known to us, was one of the men sent so abruptly to camp Annaberg. He had two sons in our camp who had gone to work that morning expecting to see their father again that night. They were totally crushed when they were told what had happened to him. Unable to cope with the situation, the older brother tried to escape from work the following day, but the guard on duty caught him and brought him back to camp. After reading the report, our Lagerführer was furious at the guard for not shooting the escapee on the spot. Klein was kept in camp the next morning, but at midday he was ordered to go outside the gate and keep on walking. Men in camp alerted Wally, Kuba and me as to what was about to take place. The commander and Lagerführer stood at the gate motioning Klein to keep on walking. We ran to the fence and urged him to stop and turn around at once. But Klein was in a trance, he didn't seem to hear us, or just didn't care any more. He was still walking when the guard took aim and shot him in the back. He fell to the ground and Kuba and I were ordered to pick up his body. The guards thought that he was dead, but miraculously he was still alive. The bullet had entered his back and exited through his chest without causing damage to his vital organs. We brought him to the infirmary to see what we could do for him, but having no X-ray or other equipment we just cleansed his wounds, closed them, and hoped for the best. Later that evening, Herr Bergmann came to the infirmary expecting to find a dead body ready for burial and became furious when he found that Klein had survived. He ordered us not to change his dressing or give him any kind of medication to relieve his pain. To make sure that we obeyed, he took a pen and made several cross marks on the bandage, which he came to check each day. Regardless of the consequences, Kuba, Paul, and I changed his dressing every night and replaced his bandage, always careful that the pen marks were back in place. When Klein did not succumb by the fourth day, Herr Bergmann angrily ordered him out of the infirmary and back to work.

The Lagerführer suspected that I was involved in Klein's recovery and punished me by making me work again at the construction site. I received the brunt of his anger, but Kuba was on his blacklist, too. I believe that Kuba's treatment of Bergmann's son earlier that year may have avoided even harsher punishment for both of us. I know I had given Bergmann many reasons to be angry at me before because I was the one who, in German, had to convince him to go along with Kuba and me on medical decisions. He didn't appreciate my constant pleading, and this incident with Klein must have been the last straw.

I was assigned to work with German railroad engineers installing signals along the newly laid tracks. We were five inmates doing the physical labor, and four German mechanics completing the connections. Their main topic of conversation was always about the brave soldiers who had accomplished so much during the war. One day I heard them speak about an insurrection in the Warsaw ghetto. It seemed that the German soldiers were facing great difficulties in subduing "those Jews." They also talked about how unhappy they were to hear about the German losses suffered when they met strong resistance deep inside Russia. I loved hearing this kind of dialogue as it lifted my spirits and made a great difference in my friends' morale when I brought news back to camp.

Because so many people had been sent to Annaberg, our camp population was much smaller now and we needed less help in the kitchen. To keep the proportion of kitchen staff in line, Herr Bergmann sent four girls to a knitting mill in Sudetenland. Adele was first on his list because he knew of our friendship and wanted to punish me still further. I was at the construction site when this move took place, and by the time I came back to camp Adele was gone. We never even had a chance to say good-bye to each other.

Even with fewer people in camp, our infirmary was always busy. Kuba, Paul, and our dentist had an extremely rough time keeping up with all the work to be done. Both Kuba and Wally constantly urged the Lagerführer to let me come back to the infirmary, but it took months before he finally gave in. He obviously knew that changes in camp were imminent anyway, and he now didn't care where I would work.

It was the middle of September, 1943. Routinely we started our day with roll call. Coming out of my barracks, I was shocked to see our entire camp surrounded by SS men with sidearms mounted, ready to storm the camp. Including those in sick bay, we were all ordered to join in the formation. When the counting was completed, the commander announced, "You are going to another camp, and to make it easier for you, leave your personal belongings in your rooms. We will transfer everything by truck and your things will be waiting for you at the new camp." This scene made little sense to us unless our destination was Auschwitz. Marching through the gate, Kuba, Paul, Wally, and I were at the end of the column. As I passed the Lagerführer, he turned to one of the SS men, and pointing to me said, "Gib besondere Aufsicht auf diesen Burschen! " (pay special attention to this fellow). Addressing me directly, he said, "Du wirst nun deinen Verdienst erhalten" (Now, you'll get what you deserve).

As we turned the corner outside the gate and marched down the road, we passed a road sign pointing to Auschwitz, thirty kilometers away. There was no further need to ask for the name of the camp we were headed to.

Having been singled out to an SS man for special attention, I was frightened beyond belief. I knew I had to lose myself among the others near the front of the column if I had any chance of surviving. Since our people were not walking in strict formation, I was easily able to move halfway up the column, where I joined my friend Foya. Out of sight of the guard, I removed my Red Cross armband, changed caps with Foya, and prayed that the SS man would not recognize me.

Normally we walked with one guard at the head of the column and another at the end. Sometimes we would have two or three additional guards who would be spread throughout the group, but this time the guards were at the side of every third row with rifles pointing at us as if we were the most dangerous of criminals. Two comrades near me on the dusty road were kind enough to offer me a drink from their canteens, and when I took a sip I had quite a surprise. Instead of water, I was drinking vodka! These men, who spoke Polish fluently, were rather resourceful. They had diamonds hidden on their bodies, and whenever they had the opportunity, they sold them to Polish laborers at the construction site. From these sales, they then were able to purchase food and drink.

The vodka started to have the desired effect and many of us began to sing. Defiantly, we sang the "Marseillaise," other French marching songs, Hatikvah, the Belgian national anthem, and any Hebrew or Yiddish songs that came to our minds. The guards were smirking and jokingly remarked to each other, "Come tomorrow, they won't be singing." At sunset we arrived at the infamous iron gate that proclaimed in bold letters, "Arbeit Macht Frei" (Work makes you free). Recognizing the sarcasm in this sign, my friends and I walked quietly through the gate into the unknown. The reputation of Auschwitz-Birkenau was known to us. We had heard about the murders and crematoriums, and that no one ever left Auschwitz alive.... Would I?

11

Auschwitz

That long and harrowing day was behind us. Inside the gate, capos, instantly recognizable by the armband on their sleeves, shouted commands at us flavored with repulsive pornographic words in German, French, Polish and Yiddish. Capos were trusted prisoners who, as the name implies, were leaders. A majority of them were German career criminals taken from prisons and moved into concentration camps to assist the SS. They had special privileges and lorded it over us. Their backgrounds and lifelong experiences in prison had made them as ruthless as the SS guards. The difference between the two were the uniforms, and the fact that capos had no guns. They were permitted to carry sticks and used them excessively to enforce their rule. In time, a few Jewish inmates attained the rank of capo as well. It was their reward for ruthless behavior toward fellow prisoners. Privileged prisoners were easily distinguishable by their armbands, well-fed looks and clean prisoner uniforms.

Hitting us with sticks, the capos herded us through a narrow door into an empty barracks. The bedlam and confusion they caused left no doubt what we might expect in this camp. The kitchen was closed for the night we were told, and though we had nothing to eat all day, food was the last thing on our minds. Inside the cold and unfinished building we were ordered to be quiet, lie down on the floor, and await registration in the morning.

Hardly an hour had passed when the doors to our barracks opened and another transport of the unfortunates joined us. I recognized Motek Joschkowitz, Lotte, and my friend Erna Neumark as they were pushed into our barracks. The last time I had seen Erna was in Krenau on the day of our delousing and seeing her again in Auschwitz was a sad reunion for both of us. The capo, noticing our meeting and embrace, immediately shouted threats and vulgarities, making it clear that this was Auschwitz, and, unlike labor camps, contact with the opposite sex was reason enough to get killed and cremated! Almost immediately, Lotte, Erna, and the other girls were led to the farthest corner of the building where the women were being kept.

Motek and I managed to exchange what news we had and briefed each other about our experiences during the year that we had been separated. Concerned about his wife, he started walking toward the rear of the barracks where Lotte and the others were segregated. When the capos saw him moving in the forbidden direction, they hit him mercilessly, even before he got close to Lotte. No one dared help him. We had already learned that keeping our mouths shut was the only way we might have a chance, any chance at all, of surviving this hellish place.

I was shivering badly as I lay on the cold damp ground, fearing what the next day would bring. I couldn't calm myself, and like the others, found sleep impossible. Slowly, and without alarming the capos, Foya crawled next to me to whisper that our lawyer friend Benno Mendelsohn had recognized the capo who had made such a fuss when Erna and I embraced. He was a man from Paris whom Benno had defended many times in court. For old times' sake, the capo told Benno what to expect when we went through the selection process in the morning. He said that everyone would be stripped naked and their clothing and possessions confiscated. The capo was willing to take any of his valuables for safekeeping, but Benno didn't really trust him. Foya still had some diamonds and U.S. dollar bills hidden on himself which he hoped would buy his freedom some day. Now he knew he could no longer hold onto his stash. He offered to share his wealth with his friends and gave each of us a few loose diamonds. We were cautioned to hide our little packet deep inside our rectum to try and pass the extremely thorough search. If a capo or SS man were to find anything concealed in our mouth or rectum, our punishment would be death. Cautiously, in the quiet of the night, I tore a piece from my shirt, wrapped the three small diamonds into the dollar bills, rolled it into the piece of cloth, and inserted it as deep as I could into myself.

The shrill sound of a whistle signaled the start of my first day in

Auschwitz. Everyone received a warm drink, a piece of bread, and ordered to get into formation outside the barracks. Standing five abreast, facing an open square, one row after the other was ordered to run across the square, a distance of perhaps twenty-five yards. On our left side an SS officer stood in the company of an attractive woman. Talking and laughing together, he never even gave us a glance. As we ran past him, he motioned with his finger to the left, or to the right — to the left, or to the right — on and on. Some of us ran the distance quickly, while others just managed to limp past the officer. We soon learned that our speed or lack of it didn't matter at all. Waiting for us at the end were a few capos who, under the watchful eye of SS guards, pushed us to our assigned direction, left or right. Those headed to the left boarded a waiting truck, while the others were steered to a nearby barracks. When it was my turn to run, I remember seeing the SS officer laughing heartily and embracing his female companion with his left arm, while giving signals with his right hand. When I completed my run, a capo immediately pushed me toward the barracks on the right and my immediate fate was determined. As I came through the door, confused and bewildered, an inmate grabbed my left forearm, pushed up my sleeve, and whispered into my ear, "You're a lucky one, you've just passed Dr. Mengele's inspection." Still holding my arm, he told me to look at the scene outside the window. "Look at your friends on the truck, look at them well — it will be the last time you'll ever see them. All those on the trucks," he said, "are being taken to the gas chambers." As I looked in horror, I recognized Leo Hirschel and his sons, Benno Mendelsohn, the Klein brothers, Hermann Blumenreich, a former captain in the German army, Felix Gompert and Abram Herschkowitz, and Leon Blumenthal, well-known actors of the Yiddish stage in Paris, among this group. Why was I spared from the gas chambers? Why was I selected to be in camp? My friends, now on the truck, didn't look any different than I did, or the others who stood at my side.

I was distraught and unable to grasp the enormity of what had happened during the past few minutes. I didn't even feel the slightest sensation when the tattoo needle burned the number 159942 into my skin. I was so affected by the scene outside the window that I could hardly speak when someone asked for my name and place of birth. I was oblivious to everything as I was shoved into an adjoining room, ordered to undress and leave everything on the floor in front of me. SS guards chased me, naked and confused, into a corner where inmates shaved and clipped every single hair on my body. A quarter inch of hair was left on my head, enough to cut a pathway with their clippers from my forehead to the back of my scalp. This pathway, the barber explained, would make us recognizable in case we ever escaped. Nicknamed "lice alley," it turned out to be a most appropriate description.

With my feet spread apart and my hands behind my head, a guard looked into my mouth, pushing his finger under my tongue. He then made me bend forward to examine my rectum and I frantically saw my death in sight. By some stroke of luck, I passed his inspection and was then ordered into the showers.

As I exited the shower room, I was given a set of cotton underpants, shirt, blue and gray striped prisoner uniform, and matching coat. A cap, wooden shoes, blanket, and metal dish and spoon for food completed my outfit. After this "registration," we waited anxiously for the remainder of our transport to come through the exit doors of the shower. I searched for Motek but he never came. My friends Wally, Foya, Kuba, Walter, and Paul were among the last to come through the shower door. Dazed and unable to speak, we were encouraged by seeing each other, but horrified at not seeing the others. This was my induction into Auschwitz. The motion of Dr. Mengele's finger had made the difference between life and death.

Dressed in my ill-fitting prisoner uniform, and carrying the few items I was given, I joined others already standing in formation. We were counted and led to the section of the camp that was to house us. Walking on the main road, we passed many subdivisions of the camp, all of them enclosed by an electrified barbed-wire fence. I saw guard towers with mounted machine guns and large spotlights controlling the entire length of the fence.

As if this wasn't secure enough, there was another fence about three yards inside each enclosure. We then entered a section named "quarantine camp" where we were counted once again. I guess they absolutely had to make sure that no one disappeared while walking from one area to another. Standing at attention, waiting for my block assignment, as these barracks were called, I looked around and saw the chimney emitting smoke and the noxious sweet smell of burned flesh. As if struck by lightening, I suddenly realized that this was the place where my mother and all my family had been murdered. My mind raced and my heart beat out of control as I pictured the countless atrocities which must have and were still taking place here. Hours had passed since the selection process was completed and I wondered if the smoke now rising into the sky was the last remains of my friends and comrades. Horrified and in a daze, I couldn't even shed a tear.

How could I exist in this place? Would I become one of the many walking skeletons I had seen as we moved along the main road? How long could I hold out and what would it take to survive? Would I live to see the end of this war, or would I be part of the smoke one day? The number tattooed on my arm, 159942, indicated that many thousands of our people had been registered in Auschwitz before me. In fact, I had heard from a fellow inmate that ours was actually the second series of recorded numbers. Judging by the number of barracks I had passed, there couldn't be that many people living here. Where were they?

As we walked through the muddy campgrounds, my wooden soled shoes with stiff and unyielding leather tops made every step painful. There was no flexibility and every step I took added another layer of clay to the wooden sole. After a while, it felt like I was walking on stilts. It was sheer torture. Adding to my misery, the hidden packet in my rectum became more irritating by the minute and I couldn't wait to get into my bunk so I could find relief. At long last, the *Blockälteste* (a fellow inmate with authority similar to a capo) ordered us to occupy an empty spot on the three-tiered bunks. A bunk was really only a platform covered by an inch of straw with space for six to barely stretch out. There was just enough room between each platform to crawl in, although small men could manage to sit up in-between the tiers. A little sack filled with straw was to become my pillow and completed my new "home." As one of the younger inmates, I was ordered to take a spot on the uppermost tier, which others found too difficult to reach. For me, it was actually a better location because I could sit up straight between the platform and the roof and have better ventilation as well.

I spread my blanket, hoping to rest for a moment before moving my valuables to a place less painful, but the inevitable whistle ordered us to get outside "on the double" for the evening roll call. Though I had not realized it, selecting my bunk near the door was a lucky choice. Those whose bunks were in the rear of the block had a problem reaching the exit, as the narrow aisles were always crowded with men trying to get out quickly.

Adding to the pandemonium were the capos, who used their sticks to hit and chase us. It was all so well designed to harass, beat, and torture us. The very last ones coming through the door were the men who had come to Auschwitz–Birkenau at an earlier time. Eyes, void of any expression, and emaciated bodies were proof of the starvation and inhumane treatment that was routine in Auschwitz. With their strength and speed gone, they were the ones who suffered the most. The SS guards at the door ordered them to get down on the floor and do ten pushups. The men tried to obey as best they could, but too weak to lift their bodies off the ground, they were trampled and hit with rifle butts. It was simply awful to see. Many of my comrades were injured and bleeding badly by the time they joined us in formation. No one dared make a sound or help anyone because we knew that we, too, would then be subjected to the same punishment.

Counting and more counting seemed to be a favorite activity in Auschwitz. Either our guards were unable to count the rows of people standing and multiply that number by five, or they had trouble finding those who were missing. While standing at attention during the whole procedure, we were not permitted to even move a muscle. This position was difficult to maintain for the stronger men among us, but absolute torture for those who could barely stand up at all. Many of the missing men were in the toilet barracks suffering from diarrhea, a result of malnutrition. Capos took pleasure in chasing these poor fellows from the toilets and forcing them to their place in roll call. Shoved and beaten, they fell to the ground in pain and were pummeled some more. I was told that this, my first roll call, was an easy one in comparison to some, which could last for many hours until everyone in camp was accounted for.

Finally, after being dismissed, we received our meal for the day. It consisted of a bowl of warm water with a few pieces of potato or vegetable swimming around in it. Occasionally, one of us found a bit of horse meat mixed in, too. A small piece of bread completed our ration, which I ate with my soup, and put the rest of my slice into my pocket to eat the next morning.

Speaking with a few old-timers in my block, I was informed about more of the miseries of life in Auschwitz–Birkenau. Words were not really necessary because their appearance said it all. Some of the men could hardly climb into their bunks on the upper tier and required assistance to lie down and rest. Washing themselves was also a problem as it required strength that they no longer possessed. Personal hygiene was almost non-existent, and aiding a friend was something only a few of us could manage. Everyone was simply concerned about their own survival.

As anxious as I was to remove the valuables I had hidden, I knew I had to be patient. For safety reasons, I decided to wait until everyone was asleep. What a relief it was when I finally retrieved my packet and hid it inside my shirt. Totally exhausted, at long last I fell asleep. The wash barracks was far from my block, so as soon as I heard the wake-up whistle, I hurried to be one of the first on line. It was cold and dark as I rushed along with my wooden shoes ripping into my feet. With hundreds of men pushing and shoving for a bit of water from the few available faucets, washing myself was difficult. I managed to rinse my mouth, wash the sleep from my eyes, and use my shirt as my makeshift towel. After this experience on that second morning in camp, I understood why so many men didn't even bother trying to clean themselves.

Back in the block, I went to my bunk for the piece of bread I had saved from the night before. It was gone. Obviously, one of the men must have seen me hiding it and stolen it from me. I was furious, but could understand how this would happen. Only someone who has ever suffered hunger pains can realize how a man can lose his self control and do anything to satisfy his emptiness. Still, stealing food from another inmate was despicable and deprived a fellow comrade of his chance to survive. No one had seen the theft and I had no one to accuse. I learned an important lesson that morning and was extremely careful in my actions from then on. I drank the warm liquid that was given to me and was now ready for roll call.

Morning roll call varied little from that of the evening before, except that in the morning capos, joined by the *Stubendiensts* (block orderlies), had the job of inspecting the bunks, and bringing out the corpses of those who had expired during the night. It was a picture out of Dante's *Inferno*. Without respect for the dead, the corpses were dragged along the ground and piled up at the end of our column. You see, everyone had to be counted: the living, the wounded, the sick, and even the dead. The old-timers, I realized, were so hardened to the scene that they never took notice or shed a tear, even if the dead person was a friend of theirs. Like a pile of junk, the corpses were left on the ground to be hauled away by a special squad. Pushing a four-wheeled wagon from block to block, two men heaved one corpse on top of the other and delivered their load to the crematorium. They repeated their rounds as many times as necessary until all the corpses were removed and the area was ready for the next roll call.

Counting completed, I was assigned again to work carrying sand from one side of the camp to the other. Joining three other men, I had to load a wooden box with handles and move heavy sand across the campground. We tried to keep our balance but couldn't help stumbling under the weight of the sand. With glee, the SS guards used their rifle butts liberally to keep us moving swiftly. This job lasted for days and I began to wonder how long I could endure such tedious and boring work. I asked myself what I had done to deserve such punishment. If there was a God in heaven, how could he allow such a disaster to take place? The small portions of food and the strain of our labor started to take its toll on me and my friends. People who went to the infirmary were considered malingerers, and sick bay was actually a dangerous place to stay. It was from the infirmary that many selections for the gas chambers were made and I vowed never to go there under any circumstances.

Being shoved or getting hit was common in Auschwitz, and I, too, had my share of beatings. Still, I managed to get through many months of their fiendish tortures without being seriously injured. I tried to be especially careful to avoid the ire of the guards or capos, and that became my most important task. Punishment often meant being whipped; five or ten lashes was the smallest amount I had seen, and twenty-five was not unusual. All too often we were made to witness the scene where a man was stretched across a table and pummeled into unconsciousness. It was a horrible experience to stand at attention and watch the agonizing procedure. Making it even worse, many times a friend was made to administer the punishment. If the blows were not forceful enough, the friend was tortured, too. As weak as our men were, I don't believe any of them ever survived these powerful beatings. Besides the extreme pain the men must have felt, their open skin quickly became infected and they had little chance of recovering. This unimaginable brutality was the norm in Auschwitz. I began to think that those sent to the gas chambers when they first arrived were actually better off than us because they were no longer suffering.

It seemed to me that we were existing in a well-planned holding pattern. We were made to do whatever work we were still capable of, but in time, we would die anyway. On days when the gas chambers were not fully utilized I would see the SS select those among us who were the weakest and lead them to their final shower of death.

In the evenings I managed to see some of my friends and we would commiserate with each other. My physician friends, Kuba and Paul, had gone to the infirmary to see if they could be of any assistance. They were told that there was no need for their services as there were many doctors, but no medicine available. Kuba described to me the scene in the infirmary where emaciated bodies, infected wounds, and filth and stench were everywhere. Kuba said he heard the moaning and groaning of our comrades and was glad that he was not accepted to work there; he didn't think he could handle that experience. The infirmary was a place where the skeletons waited to die; even if they could still walk, their destination was the gas chamber.

Every language on the European continent could be heard in camp because people had come to Auschwitz from all the places Nazi Germany had conquered. I thought of the Roman empire and the adage "All roads lead to Rome." Now it seemed that all roads led to Auschwitz. Rome and the Catholic Church were the cradle of anti–Semitism, and with the crusades, inquisitions, ghettos, and pogroms, the Jews from within the European communities were nearly eliminated. Now, the Nazis were finishing the job with the unprecedented slaughter taking place in camps like Auschwitz.

I knew when it was morning or evening even without a watch, but it really didn't matter what time of day it was. Every day was the same for me. We were told when to get up and when to go to sleep. The time in-between was filled with hard but unimportant work. Only the evening brought some relief as we looked forward to our daily food rations. Like caged animals, we anxiously awaited the moment when we could put some food into our mouths. Unlike criminals, who used a calendar to mark the days bringing them closer to their release, we had no calendar, and we had no sentence.

The Nazis had destroyed my home and family, taken all I possessed, and reduced my identity to a mere number. Still, I was fairly young and refused to let them break my spirit or take away my dignity. I was not yet willing to give up on my life. Only by struggling along and arbitrary luck was survival possible and I continued to hope for a miracle.

The thought of escaping from camp had crossed my mind, but it was never more than a fleeting thought. There were electrified double fences with guard towers surrounding every section, plus fences and guard towers surrounding the entire complex. Adding to this were the vicious dogs who were trained to jump and tear apart anything at a moment's notice. Even if one succeeded against such impossible odds, the Polish communities outside of camp would be only too happy to help the SS in tracking down any escapees. The Polish people, never fond of Jews throughout the years, would surely enjoy helping Germans capture Jewish prisoners. It would definitely be a highlight of their day. Still, some of our men were desperate enough to take a chance at freedom or a quick death. Every day there were a few who found it easier to end their wretched existence by touching the electric fence or getting shot by a guard in the tower. This was not for me — not yet. I was a seasoned prisoner, and if anyone could survive, I was determined that it would be me.

I remember vividly the day that an escape was attempted by three of our men. Their absence was discovered during the evening roll call. The entire camp, thousands of us, had to stand at attention way into the night until the three were captured and brought back. It was horrible seeing their bloodied bodies being dragged before us. Those of us who were not yet hardened to view such a despicable scene, cried along with the recaptured men. After endless pummeling, the men were then stretched over tables and tied down for another fifty lashes from the SS guards. The bullwhips tore the flesh from their bodies, and their screams reached the core of my very being. When the men lost consciousness from the excruciating pain, capos were ordered to pour cold water over their bodies and leave them alone in their misery. The rest of the camp was dismissed and warned not to approach, speak, or touch them.

All too often during roll call or witnessing the barbarism around me, I couldn't help but question the Almighty. "God, where are you hiding? What happened to the love you have for us? Are not the ones who are killing us also your children? Don't you have any control over them? Don't they live by the same commandments that we do? Are their beliefs so different from ours? God, if you are real how can you let this happen?" Thoughts like these constantly swirled around in my head.

The camp was always full of rumors and one of them was that we were to be visited by representatives of the International Red Cross. Most of us were encouraged by the prospect, but our comrades who had experienced a previous visit didn't expect anything in camp to change. When a delegation from the Red Cross came to Auschwitz earlier, they were shown blocks especially prepared for them to see. Women and children were displayed in clean and tranquil scenes including playground activities. The delegates were not permitted to walk around freely and never saw what was happening in the rest of the camp. They were either gullible and blind, or just chose to ignore the smokestacks or the smell of burning flesh. Would this visit be any different? We just couldn't believe that the Western countries were unaware of the constant trainloads of people being brought to Auschwitz. Intelligence services must have known that people were disappearing at an alarming rate and literally disappearing into thin air. Why didn't the Allies come to destroy the gas chambers and railroad tracks leading to them? We had no answers for any of our questions.

In spite of the cold, wet, winter, which drained every bit of strength from my body, I was alert enough to avoid a serious infraction of SS rules. I saw my comrades, one after the other, becoming *Muselmen* (a term used to describe a man barely alive whose skin loosely covered his bones), men too weak from diarrhea to keep themselves clean. These pitiful comrades were the ones who suffered the most and I was determined not to become one of them. Death or thoughts of dying were constant companions of everyone in Auschwitz. Many a time when I was squeezed in-between two people in my bunk for the night, I found that one of them had not awakened in the morning. I was ashamed by how much I had gotten used to the scene around me as I struggled against the downward pull of death. I started wondering how much more I could really take of this living hell.

Lice were again crawling over everyone, and no matter how we tried to keep ourselves clean, it was useless. Our blankets were covered with insects and the constant itching and scratching kept us up all night. Eventually, typhus was reported in our section of the camp. The SS men made arrangements for us to be vaccinated against the epidemic but Foya, Wally and I weren't sure what their plans for us really were. Would this injection help us or be a lethal one? I didn't trust any of the Germans, but I had no way of avoiding my shot. No one wanted to hear that I had been immunized earlier in Trebenau, so like the others I stood in line and watched the medic vaccinate everyone with whatever medication he had in the syringe. Using a twenty-five cc syringe, without changing or sterilizing the needle, he injected one person after the other. Out of the arm of one and into the arm of the next man in line. I counted those standing ahead of me, and by the time it was my turn, twenty-three others had been injected with the same needle. Amazingly, neither I nor my friends became infected or had any adverse reaction.

There was talk about a major selection that would soon take place. Selections were routine, but they were usually looking for sick and weak people from the infirmary, or others who just didn't pass inspection. Now, so the rumor had it, only stronger people would be chosen to do work at another location. I had little faith in rumors, and anyway, I had never heard of a transport leaving Auschwitz. My friends and I watched the proceedings and when we saw that the sick were not selected, we thought there might be some truth behind this newest rumor. Remaining in Auschwitz offered little chance of surviving, so I decided to try and become part of this group. Anything would be better than staying in Auschwitz, I thought. If the transport was headed for the gas chambers, well, I had gambled and lost. But if it was really leaving camp for a work detail, there was hope. Kuba and Paul were my only friends who decided to stay where they were.

I didn't push myself to the front of the group, but I did nothing to avoid being selected either. As expected, the SS officer ordered me to board the waiting truck, which took a road to the main camp of Auschwitz and away from the gas chambers. This was a very good sign. My friends and I breathed a sigh of relief as we were moved to the disinfection facility. As before, I cautiously placed my valuable packet into my rectum and was ordered to strip, get shaved, and then pushed into the showers. I could hardly believe it when real water poured from the shower heads above us. It was a wonderful feeling as the warm water poured over my body. It was most luxurious being able to wash myself thoroughly. After all I had been through, this experience was truly fantastic. A clean prisoner uniform was then given to me and my transformation was complete.

Food rations were then doled out, followed by orders to board the freight cars standing at the railroad siding. Our cars even had potbellied stoves for warmth and room for everyone to sit on the floor. We had no clue about our destination, but nothing could be worse than Auschwitz.

12

Warsaw Ghetto

SS guards walked along the outside of the train and locked the doors before the train started moving. Inside the car, each of us picked his place on the floor and was fairly comfortable with the potbellied stove providing a bit of warmth on this wintry evening. Our mood soon began to change, from utter despair to having a slight bit of hope for our future. Not only were we alive, but we were clean, deloused, and in fresh uniforms and leather shoes. This was almost too good to be true. The leather shoes on my feet made me feel almost human again, but I couldn't help wondering who had worn those shoes before. They didn't fit me well, but that was unimportant. They weren't like those I had worn in Auschwitz that had caused me so much pain.

While traveling through the night, we tried to see through the small barbed-wire-covered window, but couldn't figure out in which direction we were headed. The click-a-dee-clack of the wheels along the rails had a soothing effect on me and I fell asleep easily. The next thing I remember was when the train came to a sudden halt. One of the men who stood near the opening told us that he saw silhouettes of city buildings in the early morning mist. He was sure that we were in a large city somewhere in Poland. We heard the guards walking and talking outside the cars as they came to unlatch the doors. Their vicious dogs barked loudly and the SS guards shouted orders for us to get off the train at once. It was their usual type of welcome, but we had gotten used to this scenario. There was no platform to make our exit easier, so we had to jump from the train to the ground below and get back on our feet quickly. We had to be fast because the German shepherds were trained to attack if we weren't fast enough to suit the guards. My friend Foya was standing next to me, and as he looked around, he exclaimed, "My God, this is Warsaw! I remember this area from my childhood."

We were steered to the waiting army trucks and our entire transport, some two thousand of us, were driven through Warsaw into a totally destroyed area. Mountains of rubble and facades of burnt-out buildings were everywhere. I originally thought that these were the remains of the first days of war when the Polish army tried defending Warsaw against the German invaders. But when I saw walls with Hebrew lettering still visible, I knew that I was looking at the ruins of the Warsaw ghetto. This was the site of the heroic uprising by the remnants of the Jewish community who had fought the Nazis bravely for nearly a month.

Our camp was inside the former ghetto walls and near the old cemetery grounds. There, one thousand fellow Auschwitz prisoners who had arrived in Warsaw earlier had started construction of the barracks which would become our living quarters. Everything in our block was new and clean. What a difference from what we had left behind. Rather than six or seven people sharing a platform, we had individual bunks. They were three-tiered and stood two together with space in-between for easy access. We even had sacks filled with straw to sleep on and clean blankets to cover ourselves. The washrooms were located conveniently and there were windows allowing daylight into the barracks, something unheard of in our previous camp. I couldn't understand the reason for such luxury, but gladly accepted the change from hellish Auschwitz. We were registered and given new prisoner numbers all over again. My name, which had been changed to number 159942 in Auschwitz, was no longer of value. Now I became *Häftling* (prisoner) number 4279. By the time we had settled in our barracks, the earlier prisoners had returned from work and told us what to expect in the Warsaw camp. It became our assignment to remove the evidence of the massacre in the Jewish ghetto that had taken place just a few months earlier.

After roll call on the next morning we were led to various streets to begin our work. Brick by brick we had to remove facades of buildings which were destroyed by heavy bombardment. The bricks then had to be cleaned and neatly stacked for Polish men to haul away. It was an eerie feeling to walk past burnt-out buildings that used to be the homes of our

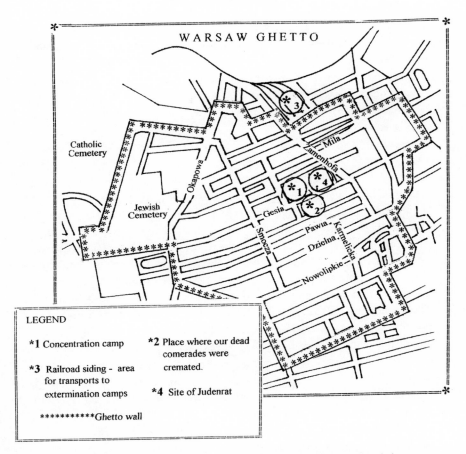

LEGEND

*1 Concentration camp

*3 Railroad siding - area
for transports to
extermination camps

*2 Place where our dead
comerades were
cremated.

*4 Site of Judenrat

**********Ghetto wall

Jewish brethren. Dried blood, a silent witness to the fighting and destruction that had raged there, was still visible on the ground.

One of our men was made to climb up the slippery facade and tie a rope around the wall between two windows. This was dangerous to do because sometimes it was impossible to find a safe foothold. Once the rope was secured, our men had to pull it in unison until the wall gave way and collapsed. Hitting and pushing us, SS guards and capos made sure that everyone pulled on the rope with all their strength. Those closest to the wall had to be extremely fast and lucky not to get hurt, or sometimes killed, by the collapsing wall.

Brick by brick, using pickaxes, the walls were taken apart. The work was backbreaking and risky, especially when we stood on ice or slippery ground. Also, unprotected from the cold wind and freezing conditions, men then had to remove the mortar with a hammer before stacking the bricks near the curb. We had no gloves to protect our hands from freezing, while our guards would stand around an open fire keeping themselves warm. Their only job was to prod us into doing more work and doing it with greater speed.

The guards were older than the ones we had in Auschwitz and most of them did not speak German fluently. They were Volksdeutsche from Romania, Czechoslovakia, and Yugoslavia and recruited to replace the young SS elite who were transferred to the front lines. Wanting to show their German superiors that they were good Nazis, they eagerly pummeled us and encouraged the capos to do the same. These capos, a group of career criminals transferred to Warsaw from the infamous camp Buchenwald, took pleasure in humiliating and hurting us. In contrast, our Blockälteste were political prisoners, incarcerated when the Nazis first came to power. They were much more lenient toward us than the capos ever were.

Occasionally we found usable items hidden in the dirt. Although it was prohibited to talk to the Polish drivers who came to haul the bricks, there were times when something of value was exchanged for a sandwich. The drivers were as interested in getting dishes, clocks, watches, or anything of value as we were in getting something extra to eat. Hiding behind stacks of bricks, out of sight of our guards, exchanges were handled quickly and efficiently. My friends and I stayed near each other as much as possible and shared our occasional windfall. Foya's main interest, however, was to work stacking bricks and be near the Polish men he hoped would help him communicate with his family. He thought that his wife might have reached safety with friends in Switzerland and even had an address for her there. Fluent in Polish, he tried to find someone willing to help him in exchange for one of his diamonds. Eventually, Foya was able to bribe our capo to let him load bricks into the carts and thus was able to concentrate on his mission.

Daily roll calls were relatively short and simple when compared to those in Auschwitz. Since our food rations were a bit more generous, we didn't have many people suffering from malnutrition and diarrhea, which could cause delays in the counting routine. As soon as we were dismissed, I would hurry to the wash barracks to clean myself and return to my block. Heinz

Karliner, our Stubendienst, stood ready to dish out our food for the day and sometimes asked me to help him. I was grateful for this opportunity because, after the food was distributed, I had the job of cleaning the barrels. It was like getting another portion for myself as I could easily fill my dish again by scraping the bottom and sides of the barrel.

Heinz and I had much in common since we both grew up in Berlin. He was just two years my senior and had gotten married a few weeks prior to *Kristallnacht*. In the aftermath of that infamous night, he was one of the twenty-six thousand Jewish men who were taken to concentration camps. His hair was now snow-white, something strange for people our age. I remarked about it one day and he told me how this had happened to him in camp Sachsenhausen. One day everyone in his barrack was ordered to place their straw mattresses into the middle of the room and lie down on them. People from other rooms were then made to pile their mattresses on top of the others and lie down, too. Another layer of mattresses and people were then ordered on top of that, and on and on. This sadistic exercise lasted forever, or so it seemed to him, and many of the men suffocated. Heinz survived, but his hair turned snow-white a few days later. From Sachsenhausen he was sent to Auschwitz, and from there he was sent to Warsaw.

As an old timer from Sachsenhausen, he knew a few of the capos and Blockälteste in our camp, and our Lagerälteste appointed him to be a Stubendienst. Having a friend with good connections was helpful in my meeting Lazar Hoffman, the foreman of a crew painting the guard's quarters. With Heinz's recommendation, I became part of his crew. This assignment had excellent advantages. It kept me out of the cold and nasty weather, and many times the guards gave me their leftover food. Their rations were so much more edible than the slop we received that I could hardly believe my good fortune. In turn, I was able to share my regular food portions with my friends.

Another plus to my new job was that I sometimes heard radio newscasts which occasionally contained encouraging information. Reports indicating that the Russian army was in pursuit of the retreating Germans was like music to my ears. I could hardly wait to share such news with my friends in the evening. It renewed our determination to hold out a little longer. Since Warsaw was now so close to the eastern front, we might be liberated fairly soon. Our thoughts and discussions were full of, "What if? ... What would we do if the Nazis tried to kill us prior to their surrender? What would happen if they took us away or moved us deeper into Germany?" Though we would have preferred being liberated by the Allies, just being liberated was all that mattered.

My housepainting assignment didn't last very long, but it got me through the worst of the winter months. Again, through Heinz, I made contact with another capo who was willing to take me on in his crew in exchange for the last of my little diamonds. My new job involved working in a group of sixteen men pushing a large wagon to gather beams and other lumber needed for firewood in the kitchen. Moving the wagon along the uneven cobblestoned streets was strenuous and especially difficult when the wagon was filled with heavy lumber. Still, my job was never monotonous, and working with the same men and guards every day was less stressful than other jobs I could have had. Our guards were of Romanian background and making money was always on their minds. They had a contact waiting for them on the Polish side of the wall, and whatever we found in the course of the day was moved across the wall with ease. They made lots of money from these transactions, but we benefitted, too. We were never severely beaten, and at times they shared their good fortune with us by treating us to some extra bread.

One day our guards led us to an area that we had never searched before. Our wagon was nearly filled when they directed us to a sealed basement marked, "Off limits, by order of the German commander of Warsaw." Our guards paid no attention to the sign and forced the door open anyway. They must have known that the basement was filled with copper wire and bicycles, items of great value. We were ordered to load a few of the bicycles into the wagon, cover them with wood, and proceed to the ghetto wall. As always, their contact was waiting, and a few minutes later, the bicycles were on the other side. The guards then told their contact to return in the afternoon for a second delivery of bicycles and to bring with him sixteen portions of bread, kielbasa, and small bottles of vodka for everyone in our group. It was a wonderful feeling having a full stomach, especially when the vodka took its effect on us. Holding on to our wagon, we steadied ourselves as we walked through the gate of the camp. The slightest suspicion by the guard on duty would have had dire consequences for everyone. This routine lasted a few weeks and my extra food was by far the best meals I had eaten in many years. The guards made a fortune, and our capo Otto, the career criminal from Hamburg, also got a large share of the loot. I shudder to think what could have happened if the German commander had decided to come by and liquidate his private holdings!

Filled with excitement, Foya told us one evening that his hardships during the winter months were worth his effort because he had finally made contact with Polish partisans. We told him to use extreme caution because partisans, we had been warned, were not particularly interested in saving Jews. He knew that, too, he explained, but he was sure that this contact could be trusted. As a test, Foya asked the man to send a messenger to his wife in Switzerland and bring back information only she could supply. To cover expenses, he gave the man a small diamond as a show of good faith. Foya thought that an escape from camp was possible if we planned properly and had dependable help from the outside. He was sure that his contacts would provide the help we needed, but Wally, Walter and I were skeptical. Still, the possibility of a successful escape was enticing. A few weeks passed before Foya heard from his contact. His news was all bad. The message he received was phony and could not have come from his wife. It would now have been suicide to use any escape plan offered by his contact. Foya's disappointment was overwhelming and he never really recovered from his failed efforts. We all tried to lift him out of his despair but we made little headway.

Roaming through the rubble of the ghetto in search of lumber, one day I walked into a large courtyard. Standing behind a pillar and facing the open plaza, I recognized the Paviak, a feared Polish prison. I stopped short when I saw five men handcuffed to each other, blindfolded, and led away from the building by German soldiers. The men were taken to stand against a wall and were promptly shot. As soon as I could move without being seen, I gathered some lumber and quickly disappeared. The following day, Polish men who were hauling bricks told us about newspaper reports stating that five hostages, intellectuals of the city, were executed. They said that this action was in retribution for the activities of Polish partisans against German authorities.

Another painful incident which I will always remember occurred one afternoon when we were pushing a heavy load of lumber toward the kitchen. Crossing our path was a guard escorting a young girl in her teens, holding on to what could have been her little brother. Judging from their ragged appearance, they must have been hiding someplace inside the ghetto and were found by the Germans. It didn't take long before I heard gunshots coming from the area to which the two children had been led. In the evening, we learned how these children, ghetto survivors, were found. They had made a home for themselves on a piece of flooring left attached to the facade of a corner building. As our men had climbed upward to attach a rope, the youngsters fled, but unfortunately they were caught by SS guards. People working in the guardrooms learned that they had been interrogated for hours because the SS officers wanted to know how they had managed to get food, and if there were still others in hiding. The heinous slaughter of two courageous children demonstrated again that Nazis had no mercy or compassion for anyone. From that day on, our men were even more careful when working near the walls, as there still might be a survivor hiding within the ghetto.

Keeping ourselves clean was much easier for us in Warsaw than in the other camps. However, hard work, tired bodies, and cold weather caused many men to neglect their personal hygiene. It came as no surprise to us that lice became a problem once again and typhus soon appeared in epidemic proportion. Nearly half the camp became infected and three large blocks had to be cleared to house the sick. My friends, Walter and Foya, were among those who were stricken. Our barracks had to be disinfected so we were taken to Paviak, the Polish prison. They had a delousing station in the jail, similar to the one in Krenau, but that's where the similarity ended. One had to see the interior of this prison to believe it. It was the most dilapidated, dingy, and smelly building imaginable. It looked like the dungeons I remembered seeing when I visited ancient castles in my childhood.

Many of my comrades became ill, and only a small number recovered from this epidemic. Somehow, the vaccination Wally and I received in Trebenau was still effective, and neither of us came down with typhus. Every evening after work, Wally, Peter, and I visited our friends and tried to make them as comfortable as we could. Walter recovered and was dismissed from sick bay, but was so weak that he soon had to return to bed. The food we brought him did little to help and he soon died. Within a short period of time Foya did get better but never regained his physical strength and was constantly in and out of sick bay.

When some of the men in my own work crew came down with the

fever, I was able to use my influence in getting Wally and Peter reassigned to work at my side. With the loss of life from the epidemic so tremendous, disposing of the dead became a gruesome ordeal. A special detail of inmates had the unpleasant job of collecting the corpses and bringing them to a courtyard across from the entrance to our camp for cremation. At one point the number of dead was so huge that my group was ordered to assist the special detail by delivering a load of lumber for the pyre. There, behind the remnants of a building facade, we saw the most ghastly scene imaginable. Bodies were piled one on top of the other and covered with firewood. Another layer of corpses and more lumber was then placed on top of that. Arms, legs, heads, and torsos all lay twisted in front of me. I will never forget that sight. I was sickened beyond belief.

To replace those who had died, fifteen-hundred additional men were sent from Auschwitz, most of them recent arrivals from Hungary. Much to my surprise, very few of them spoke Yiddish and it was rather difficult communicating with them. The only Yiddish-speaking group was the Hasidim, faithful to their Klausenburger Rebbe. As was their tradition, they kept very much to themselves and had little contact with the rest of the camp population. On one occasion, I did converse with the rebbe and some of his closest followers. From them I learned that my friends Kuba and Paul eventually did work in the infirmary at Auschwitz–Birkenau after all, and I was deeply saddened when I heard that Kuba had attempted to escape from camp. The horrendous conditions in the infirmary must have been too much for him and, out of desperation, he tried the impossible. He and two other prisoners were recaptured and then quickly executed by hanging. Kuba was such a caring man whose knowledge had saved so many lives. I was proud to have been his friend and heartbroken that his life had ended as it did.

Early on the morning of June 6, 1944, word spread that someone had heard a radio broadcast reporting that Allied troops had landed in France. If that was true, it was the news that we had waited for years to hear. Hopefully, the Allied invasion would hasten the end of our suffering. The Russian army coming from the east was not far from Warsaw, and now the Allied forces were closing in from the south, reestablishing a front in the west. My day's work proceeded like all others, except that one of our guards approached me when no one was nearby and said, "The Americans have landed in France this morning. You're a smart fellow. What do you think will happen next?" I was surprised by his question and the manner in which he addressed me. Ever since the day when we liquidated the hidden bicycles and copper wire, casual conversation with our guards was not uncommon, but this kind of remark was unexpected. He must have given thought to what his future might now be like and obviously needed a sounding board, which he hoped to find in me. My reply was a risky one, but I took pleasure in giving him my answer. I told him that I believed the days of the Third Reich were coming to an end and, as a Romanian, he would have a special problem. He would be considered a traitor by his own people, and as a German SS man, he would share in the responsibility for the atrocities committed. I had never seen him shoot anyone, but just wearing his uniform would be reason enough for someone to take revenge against him. I told him that my advice would be to get rid of his gun and uniform and disappear as fast and as far as possible. He stood there and nodded his head in silent agreement. Somehow, pushing my heavy load of lumber felt much lighter for the rest of that day. A week later, we had two new guards with us. I never saw my two Romanian guards again.

Gathering lumber became a more difficult task for us as our supply was dwindling and our new guards enjoyed using their rifle butts to speed along the loading detail. One day, a rifle butt struck my face and broke my nose. In excruciating pain and with constant bleeding, I had to continue working and wait until evening for some help in the camp infirmary. Our medic, Raymond, gave me some aspirin tablets to ease my pain and applied cold-water compresses to reduce my swelling. After a few hours of rest that night I again had to face a full day's work if I wanted to live.

We usually kept our windows open during the spring and summer nights, and faintly at first, but louder as the weeks passed, we heard the sounds of exploding bombs and saw searchlights scanning the sky. The Russian army was definitely coming closer to Warsaw and their bombing raids were music to our ears. We prayed for a quick liberation, but we had this uneasy feeling that the Nazis might have other plans to preempt our freedom.

On July 28, 1944, a hot summer morning, we were ordered to remain in formation after roll call, something very different from our regular routine. The day before, we had been told by Polish drivers that the Russian Army was a mere thirty kilometers outside of Warsaw, so we believed that something was about to happen, but what? The Klausenburger Rebbe was standing near me and I heard him say that this was the day prior to Tish'a-B'av, an important day of sorrow and fasting in our Jewish calendar, not a good omen. We stood in formation for what seemed like forever and could see the commander's office busy as a beehive with guards going in and out. Hours passed and the hot sun baked us in the plaza. Suddenly, one hundred men from the first block were ordered to move out of camp. A while later, another group of one hundred was ordered out, too. When a third and fourth group were also marched out, we really became frightened. The entire camp always went to work at one time and all together, so why were they now taking us out in small groups? Also, normally, we could see our people working from inside the camp, but not this time. Were the Nazis killing us a hundred at a time?

Alphonso, a young attorney from Salonika, was a respected leader of our Greek friends. He thought that we should take the knives we kept in our bunks, strap them to our forearms, and hide them under our sleeves. If they were going to kill us, we would be ready to attack them and kill as many Nazis as we could. Alphonso would be the one who would give a signal when we were to charge the guards as they prepared to shoot us. One by one, we sneaked into our block and fastened the knives to our arms. We were ready, but most of us were shivering in spite of the heat on that July day.

Eventually the gate opened and the hundreds sent out to work earlier came back into camp. We were relieved to see them, but this action made no sense to any of us. After standing in formation all day long, we were finally told that our commander had received orders to close the camp the following morning. Those unable to make a two-day march must report to the infirmary and, if accepted after examination, they would be transported by truck along with the people from sick bay. The instructions sounded innocent enough, but with the Nazis, one never knew. Immediately, we were concerned about Foya. He had gone to the infirmary again a few days earlier, but now no one was permitted to leave the sick bay. We, the old-timers, had seen enough to smell foul play, but many recent arrivals didn't heed our warnings and volunteered to be examined so they could ride on the trucks. All this feverish activity was fertile breeding ground for rumors, and the camp buzzed with all kinds of stories. They ranged from a rumor that the Russians would catch up with us outside Warsaw, to a more realistic one that we would be marching all the way back to Auschwitz or even farther west to Dachau.

All through the night we watched searchlights scanning the sky and listened to the heavy sound of artillery fire. The fighting seemed to be very close now and we all prayed that the Russians would enter our camp before the Nazis could execute their plans for us.

Hardly anyone slept that night, and as we stood for roll call the next morning, we were certain that difficult days were still ahead of us. As soon as all men were accounted for, we started our march out of camp. When we passed the barracks filled with our sick, we saw no trucks waiting for them — but instead heard the chilling sound of machine-gun fire coming from inside the barracks.

13

Death March and Dachau

Guards walked on both sides of our column in line with every fourth row of men, sidearms mounted and pointing at us. They led us out of Warsaw no differently than the day they brought us into Auschwitz, but this time we were so much weaker that we could barely drag ourselves along the narrow dirt road. Our assignment to level the remnants of the former ghetto remained unfinished and rubble and facades were still visible everywhere. This didn't matter to us, and with the Russian army closing in on Warsaw, there certainly would be even more destruction. Our route took us through the outskirts of the city in a westerly direction and as we looked back toward the camp, all we could see was black smoke rising into the sky. With the sounds of machine-gun fire from sick bay still ringing in our ears, we had little doubt that the source of the black smoke was the burning down of the barracks and corpses of our comrades by the Nazis. Wally, Peter, and I had tears in our eyes as we thought of Foya and this terrible tragedy.

Rural Poland had very few paved roads, so the twenty-five hundred of us raised a huge amount of dust as we shuffled along the country roads. It was bearable when walking at the head of the column, but the dust made breathing very difficult for those farther back. There was no water, not even a drop to rinse our parched throats. We had no food nor time to rest or catch our breath. Soon people started falling behind as many comrades found it difficult to keep going at even a slow pace. Those at the rear of the column were egged on by guards and as they fell to the ground they were immediately shot. The trucks following us then collected the corpses, leaving no shred of evidence of what had occurred.

Late afternoon on the second day of our march, we crossed a bridge over the river Lowicz near the town of the same name. There was a meadow along the side of the river and we were finally given a period to rest. As some of us were close to the riverbank and desperate for water, a few of us dared to step into the river to fill our dishes with water and satisfy our thirst. The dirt and other things floating around were unimportant to me; quenching my thirst was the only thing that mattered. Others began entering the water, too, but every step they took raised more silt and dirt from the bottom of the river. Soon the men had to go deeper into the river to get anything that was drinkable. Suddenly, machine-gun fire from the other side of the river and from the bridge we had crossed earlier filled the air, killing all the unfortunate men still in the water. The river turned red as the dead corpses floated downstream. To make sure that no one could possibly escape, they even shot at the dead bodies floating in the water.

When we continued our march, almost mechanically I placed one foot in front of the other, inching along, hour after hour and day after day. A small piece of bread and a warm nondescript liquid called soup, served to us at night, was all the nourishment we received for the entire day. Wally began to complain that he couldn't keep up with us any longer and, even with support from Peter and me, he tripped and fell often. The more our little group fell behind, the more dust we were forced to swallow. Finally, Wally could no longer hang onto us. He pushed us away, lowered himself to the ground, and refused to listen to us any longer. Weakened as we were, and blocking the road for others, there was nothing we could do to save him as we were being pushed forward. I turned and waved to him one more time, and with his last bit of strength, he lifted his arm for a final good-bye. There was no time for us to shed tears for our friend; we simply had to continue along the road with the others. Peter and I were now the only ones left from our Trebenau circle of friends and we wondered how much longer we, too, would be able to last.

One night as we rested near a lake, the lush grass gave us the idea that by digging into the soft earth we might find water. Sitting in groups and camouflaging our activities, we used our hands, spoons, and metal dishes to dig. At arms' depth, we actually did find water. It wasn't clean, it wasn't pure, but no one seemed to care. It was something that would quench our constant thirst. When we awoke in the morning, the meadow looked like a moonscape full of tremendous holes. Lazar Hoffman, my housepainting foreman, along with a few others, planned to use the meadow as a way to escape. They buried themselves deep into the holes they had dug, hoping to crawl out after everyone had left. It was an act of desperation which I believed had little chance of success. But just maybe they were correct in trying the impossible.

As we dragged ourselves along the next day, we were ordered to get into ditches and clear the road for German army units moving eastward. A general in his staff car drove past us, stopped, turned around, and asked to see the officer in charge. The SS lieutenant approached him, and the general, in an angry voice, complained that this was no way to treat prisoners. He asked for the officer's name and promised to file a complaint. The lieutenant calmly replied that this was none of the general's business and threatened to arrest him if he did not move on quickly. The general was furious, but drove away just the same. It was obvious how powerful the SS really was.

The day after the encounter with the general, we arrived at a railroad siding near the city of Posen. After so many days of marching, we were all fully exhausted. As we rested near a railroad siding, waiting for the train which would take us to our destination, we were finally given some cooked food from an army canteen. Summoned to roll call, the first since leaving Warsaw, we were divided into groups of one hundred and herded into the boxcars now standing on the track in front of us. Those World War I vintage railroad cars were designed and marked to carry eight horses and twelve men. Now, one hundred of us were crowded together without an inch of room to spare as we waited for more of our comrades to arrive.

Who were these men who were to join us, we wondered? We were sure that all the men in sick bay had been shot and cremated. Could we have been wrong about the machine-gun blasts we had heard when leaving Warsaw? The answer came soon enough. A truck driven by Polish militia arrived bringing Lazar and the others who had buried themselves in the meadow the day before. Polish peasants had found them and turned them over to their militia. Immediately and without hesitation, our commanding officer ordered them to stand against a wall, and had two guards with automatic rifles kill them in front of our eyes.

Our car doors were locked from the outside and the train started its journey into the unknown. Through our little window, we saw that we were in Germany, traveling west. If we were headed back to Auschwitz, we would have been going south. So where were they taking us? Our destination was important to us, but our immediate problem was more serious than that. Crammed in like sardines, we had no room to sit and little air to breathe. Adding to our misery, the hot sun turned our car into an inferno. We had no water to drink, just a pail in the corner to be used as a comfort station. The smell that permeated the car was unbearable. The train stopped a few times during our journey, and when it was convenient for our guards, the doors were opened and we were given permission to empty the pails. Only once through the entire trip did we get a pail of drinking water. But since everyone was overcome by thirst, fights for a drop of the precious liquid caused much of our water to be spilled. Some of our men became so desperate for fluid that they actually used their own urine, if not for drinking, then for wetting their lips. Hunger pains are bad, but only someone who has suffered both hunger and thirst knows that thirst is far more painful and debilitating.

Days of walking, followed by this torturous train ride, made our men behave more like animals than human beings. We were suffocating, dehydrating, starving, and dying of exhaustion. As our friends expired, we piled one body one top of the other against the wall to provide space for those still living. Totally dehumanized, we had lost all sense of self-respect or compassion. Every man was for himself; surviving the present moment was all that counted. Will I be next? was the only thought on everyone's mind. I crawled into a corner of the car and sat staring into the semi-darkness. The rhythm of the wheels along the rails must have put me into a half-sleep and I can't remember much of that day and night. All I remember was reliving another lifetime filled with happiness. All the beautiful things from my earlier life came back to me — my childhood, my parents, Fred, my grandparents, and the wonderful times we had cherished together. I don't know how long I was so mesmerized, but when the door banged open and the sudden bright sunshine came into the car, I was shocked back into reality. We had no time to adjust to the daylight as the barking dogs and screaming SS men chased us out of the boxcars. Those who could jumped from the car to the ground, but once there, we had problems getting back on our feet. My muscles were cramped, but afraid of getting hit by sticks or rifle butts, I forced myself to stand on legs that no longer wanted to support my frail body. Our guards, who normally would hit and beat us, stayed away because the stench coming from the train and from us was overpowering. We were ordered to remove the dead from the train and place them in front of our boxcar. By sheer willpower, we dragged ourselves through the gate of the infamous concentration camp, Dachau.

There were no additional roll calls for us that day as we were led to our assigned blocks and given food even before we were registered. After a refreshing shower, and getting a clean uniform, I felt as if I could become human again after all. Of the nearly fifty-five hundred men who had left Warsaw on July 29, less than thirty-five hundred of us entered Dachau on August 6, 1944. Nine days in hell were behind us, but what was to come next? My identity was changed once more and I became *Häftling* No. 87888.

The commander of Dachau had seen us as we entered camp, and with what must have been a first in concentration camp history, we were actually allowed to rest. Isolated from the other Dachau inmates, our roll calls were simple and didn't take much time. With the exception of occasional marching exercises, we had time off. At the end of the week, we were selected to work on a "special project" at a small site only two hours away from the main camp. In comparison with our journey to Dachau, the short trip felt like a pleasure ride. Two guards sat in the center of the car and twenty-five of us were seated on either side with the doors remaining open for our added comfort. The train stopped at the little town of Mühldorf, and to our surprise there were no dogs or rifle butts to greet us when we left the cars. Half the men in our transport were taken to a camp near the railroad station and the other half, including Peter, Heinz, and I, boarded trucks which took us to the newly erected *Waldlager*.

Located in the midst of a pine-tree forest, surrounded by a double row of electrified barbed-wire fences, there were tents, arranged in blocks, to house us. Each tent was large enough to accommodate twenty men. We were given straw and blankets and told that the tents were merely temporary quarters until our permanent bunkers would be ready. What was happening? Overnight, everything seemed more civilized. Even our guards were no longer nasty and rough. They were all just elderly retired World War I soldiers dressed in SS uniforms. With our food rations better than before, the whole atmosphere seemed less frightening to us.

On the following morning we marched to a construction site deep in the heart of the forest. There we were joined by our comrades who had been taken to the camp near the railroad station. The construction site was a huge complex where thousands of Russian prisoners were already at work. Separated from them, and working in small groups, our job was to fill lorries with sand as I had done years before in camp Ottmuth. Our supervisors were all German and wore the Nazi uniform of Organization Todt. (Todt, an architect and early follower of Hitler, organized and led construction battalions to build infrastructure and defense projects throughout Germany before and during World War II. Many of these OT men were unacceptable as party members because of former union or Communist Party affiliations. Having them in OT construction battalions gave the Nazis a way to keep these workers under control.)

Seeing the size and location of this complex, we began to understand the reason for the sudden change in our treatment. The Nazis needed laborers desperately to complete the project that they were working on. The V-I and V-II flying bombs which terrorized London had not succeeded in "wiping London off the face of the earth," as Hitler had claimed. Now, persistent news reports told of newer weapons, soon to be available, which had greater accuracy and destructive force to replace the flying bombs. This complex could have been the site selected for making such promised weapons. However, based on what we saw, I didn't think that this place would ever produce anything at all. There was just too much work to be done. With Allied forces bombing and destroying the entire area, Allied armies would surely reach us long before this building would ever be completed. My friends and I believed that perhaps atomic energy might actually have been the core of this project.

Caution, usually associated with construction, was nonexistent at the work site. Assignments had to be done quickly and every shortcut was used to speed things along. Lives, especially the lives of prisoners, were meaningless to our captors. One day I worked with a crew installing heavy wooden braces to support a form for pouring concrete. A brace was lifted by a crane and manipulated into position by men holding ropes. The rope I held suddenly snapped and I lost my balance, falling about ten meters into a large cavity. Miraculously, I survived the fall, and when someone tossed me a rope I was able to successfully climb out of the hole. In great pain, I had to ignore my injuries and continue working. The alternative was not a pleasant one to consider.

Not long after this incident, I was assigned to a cement-mixing detail. All day long I had to carry cement bags, each weighing fifty kilos, and dump them at the concrete-mixing machine. Luckily, our supervising OT man was considerate of us as we did this backbreaking job, and that was a blessing. He spoke to us in his Berliner slang, and at one time I replied to his remark in my own hometown jargon. He looked at me in surprise, never expecting to find a *Landsman* (compatriot) in our group. I soon found myself getting easier assignments, and whenever possible he would come to chat and share his sandwich with me. In time, Fritz started bringing cooked food and leaving it in the storage shed. At lunch time, he would order me to get some tools from the shed and that gave me a few minutes to eat the food that he had brought. He confided in me that he was an old-time Communist, and for his own protection from the Nazis, he had decided to join Organization Todt.

Every day Fritz would bring me up-to-date on current events. He said it was quite clear that the end of the war was near. Even if the stories heard on the radio about miracle weapons were true, the German army could not stop the Allied advances. The complex we were building must have been of enormous importance to their efforts, but even with people working around the clock, with unlimited materials, it could never be completed in time. It seemed that the Nazi dream for world supremacy would fail at last. "We must just make sure that all of us come out of this mess alive," Fritz would say. He took me to a place where he had hidden some clothing and an ID card for me and warned me again and again that I must not be taken back to the main camp in Dachau. He had heard rumors that those returning there would be liquidated. He gave me his address in Berlin and hoped that I would get to him in the near future. It was a wonderful feeling to know that I had someone ready to help me when the right moment came my way.

Next, Fritz gave me the job of directing lorries filled with concrete to a newly constructed platform, built by Russian POWs, to facilitate dropping the load. A guard stood at the edge of the platform to have a better view of the site, while an OT foreman supervised two Polish workers who did the actual dumping. Suddenly, the plank I was standing on gave way and I jumped up, trying to hold onto a nearby rail. The entire structure made of wooden planks and iron rails completely collapsed. The lorry and everyone standing on the platform fell into the pit. My foot was wedged between planks and rails and I was in excruciating pain. Cranes were brought into position to lift the debris and to rescue us. Still, of the four people near me when the structure collapsed, the guard and one Polish worker were killed. The OT foreman and the other Polish worker were badly injured, and so was I. Holding onto that rail for the extra fraction of a second was enough to delay my fall and I landed on top of the rails instead of being crushed by them. When I was finally pulled out of the pit, I couldn't walk or place any pressure on my foot. I was sure that I must have torn a ligament, fractured my ankle, or both. Fritz ordered me to do some work in the shed so I could get off my feet and, once inside, I found some wood to use as a makeshift splint. By tearing a strip of cloth from the bottom of my shirt, I bandaged my ankle as best I could and was grateful for the help I had received. Walking back into camp was absolute torture, but supported by my friends and hopping on one leg, I somehow made it all the way. As I approached the gate, I clenched my teeth, and walked as straight as everyone else through the entrance. If I hadn't walked normally, I could have been pushed or shoved and aggravated my injury even more. My comrades took me to the infirmary where Raymond, our medic and friend, did what he could to help me. He had a few aspirins which made my pain more bearable and the cold compresses he applied eventually reduced the swelling.

Raymond, Heinz, Peter, and I, all of similar age, became good friends during our final days in Warsaw. This friendship grew even stronger on our arduous trip to Dachau. We became a support system for each other, and whenever possible we tried to find better jobs for all of us. With Raymond in charge of sick bay, I felt comfortable being treated there; still, the disturbing news he brought me the next day was frightening. He reported that many of the sick people were scheduled to be taken back to Dachau. To avoid my being chosen, we improved my splint, and with a strong bandage supporting my leg, I limped to work with the other men that next morning. Fritz rescued me once again by finding work for me in the shed so I could get off my feet. A few weeks later, my ankle had improved enough so that I could move around with much less discomfort. There was no doubt in my mind that, had this accident occurred in Warsaw or Auschwitz, or without Fritz's help, I would not have come through this episode alive.

The winter season was upon us and our permanent quarters, actually bunkers, were finally ready to be occupied. They were simple squares dug into the ground with a thatched roof placed above. Each bunker provided room for twenty of us to rest, and a wood-burning stove in the center gave us some warmth. Twelve of these units formed a block, and my friend Heinz was appointed Blockälteste for one of the sections. At first Heinz was leery about his assignment because in Auschwitz the position of Block-älteste was something frowned upon. At Mühldorf, however, his job was different. He was just required to see that all tents were kept in order, keep count of the people in his block, and distribute our daily rations.

Thankfully, Allied forces were making steady progress in Italy and France. Their bombers flew over our area more frequently, and the wailing sound of sirens, signaling us to take cover, was a sound we loved to hear. These sirens became an almost daily routine and gave us time to rest. Midmorning, we would look for vapor trails of approaching Allied aircraft and, when the alert was sounded, we would run quickly to find cover deep in the forest. We tried not to show our emotions, but we were thrilled by the sound of the exploding bombs. Interestingly enough, no bomb ever hit our construction site. I often wondered whether the Allies knew that our work would never be completed and therefore saw no need to waste bombs. However, the damage caused to neighboring communities was extensive. No sooner was the "all clear" signal given than a number of our men were taken away to remove road obstructions, repair railroad tracks, and douse fires in nearby communities.

Only once did a bomb land near our camp. I had worked the night shift and was in camp that morning. The sound of approaching bombers aroused my curiosity and I went outside of my bunker to look around. Standing at the entrance, a piece of shrapnel whizzed by my right ear and missed my head by a fraction of an inch. One fragment, ever so small, hit my left forearm, but without proper instruments to remove it, the piece of metal had to remain in my arm. Luckily the shrapnel never traveled and never bothered me. In fact, it is still there.

In tandem with allied advances in the south and west, the Russian army moved into Germany from the east. Fritz told me that Auschwitz had been evacuated and its many inmates were walking all the way to Buchenwald and other camps in southern and western Germany. This news was confirmed a few days later when we were told to prepare bunks for five hundred people arriving from Auschwitz. I was due to work the night shift again and was in camp the afternoon that this group of men arrived. What we saw was simply tragic. In a state of total exhaustion, the newcomers dragged themselves through the gate and onto the roll call square. Everyone in camp that afternoon came out to see if they could find a familiar face, someone who might have information about a relative or friend. I stood on the side of the road when suddenly I saw the unbelievable. Was I hallucinating, or was it really my brother Fred? I looked again to be sure before I called his name. When he glanced my way, he recognized me, too. Fred had gotten so much taller since I had last seen him in Trebenau some two years before. He was also much skinnier, as we all were.

I could hardly wait until the new men were dismissed so I could take Fred into my bunker, give him food, and make him comfortable. We just sat there in shock and looked at each other in total disbelief. Finding each other like this was as if we had found a needle in a huge haystack. From all the thousands and thousands of inmates and the many camps that he could have been sent to, he was here with me in this small, out-of-the-mainstream location. He told me about his weeks of endless marching in the cold, wind, rain, and snow of winter. Receiving only the smallest food rations, thousands of people died along the way. His stories were familiar to me and very similar to my own nightmarish march from Warsaw to Dachau.

When I returned from work the next morning, Fred was rested and we had time to continue our talk. He confirmed what I knew about that awful day in 1943 when we had lost most of our family. When Fred had returned from making his deliveries, he had no idea of what had taken place in town. He was immediately arrested and taken to the staging area in Sosnowitz. There he found out that Papa had been in a transport destined for Auschwitz, but somehow became part of a group headed for a forced-labor camp. He also learned that Mutti, Grandma and all our other relatives were sent to Auschwitz and presumed killed in the gas chambers. We had little hope of seeing Papa again either, as we knew that life in a labor camp would be difficult for him in his delicate condition. His broken shoulder and slight heart problem would make his chances of survival very small. Fred and I were the envy of everyone in camp. We had actually found each other after years of separation. Our reunion gave hope to others that somewhere, someplace, a close relative of theirs might also still be alive.

My friends helped me with Fred's recovery, and after he regained some of his strength I was able to get him assigned to work in my group. I introduced him to Fritz, and he seemed genuinely happy for us both. He even promised to do all he could to find another set of clothing and ID card for him. There were some problems, he said, but he didn't elaborate. Work at the construction site was sporadic since Allied bombers had destroyed the supply routes and materials didn't get through on schedule. Instead of our usual jobs, we now worked in nearby communities clearing the damage caused by bombs. On one of the days when we worked at the construction site, I sadly learned that Fritz had been transferred to another location. I went to our hiding place, hoping that he was able to leave a package of clothing for Fred, but no such luck.

Just about that time our clothing depot had run out of striped uniforms and we were issued solid color garments instead. Stars of David were either painted on them or cut out on the jacket and above the knees of the trousers. As soon as possible, my friends and I changed into these less recognizable garments thinking that, in case we could somehow escape, it would be easier for us to camouflage these plain uniforms and blend in with other people. Luckily, I found solid color garments for Fred, too.

As much as we enjoyed hearing the sounds of Allied bombs and seeing the destruction they caused, the raids caused hardships for us, too. Destroyed roads and railroad lines made food deliveries into our camp irregular. There were days when we had nothing to eat and had to wait until roads could be cleared for food to be brought into camp. Despite our difficulties, we were encouraged knowing that the war would soon be over.

A new camp commander and assistant arrived to replace the old officers. The new commander was a Catholic school principal and army colonel during World War I. He was a reasonable man and often visited our infirmary to chat with Raymond and others in the room. Because of the need for younger soldiers at the front lines, he and those with him now had been drafted and given this assignment, for which he reluctantly had to wear the SS uniform. He wanted us to understand that he was not a Nazi, and remarked that all our guards were also old army men forced to serve in the camps. They were more concerned with their own well-being than the job they were here to do. He did not object to having this information spread around camp, and hoped that by doing so we would all feel more secure.

By then it was the early part of April and our days were spent mostly inside the camp. Work at the construction site had been suspended and we were free to rest, but we were perpetually hungry. Nobody even bothered looking at our hair anymore, and the *Lause Allee* (lice boulevard), so very important at one time, had grown in and was no longer visible. The news we heard suggested that many smaller camps in the area were closing each day and that their inmates were being returned to Dachau. Along with this frightening information there was some positive news, too. The Allied forces had crossed the Rhine and would soon reach the city of Nuremberg. What would all of this mean for us?

One day the commander called a special roll call to address us. "Three days ago," he said, "I received orders to put you on a train headed for the main camp in Dachau. Using one excuse or another, I was able to delay this departure. Now, however, there is no food left in camp and the roads are in such bad shape that, even if flour was available, it couldn't get to our bakery. I can no longer stall and must comply with my command. But," he continued, "the rail system, especially near Munich, has been totally destroyed. There is no way that you'll ever get back to Dachau. The Allies have taken Nuremberg, and are closing in on this area. The guards with you on the train are elderly men carrying no more than six rounds of ammunition. They are there to protect you, so don't do anything foolish!" After his speech, we were dismissed, led to the railroad station, and made to board the waiting train.

14

Escape

We left Mühldorf station as we had arrived. Twenty-five of us sat on the floor on either side of the open door with three guards positioned in the center of the car. Not moving an inch, our train remained at the station for hours. I nibbled on the small portion of bread each of us was given as we left camp, and drank the water from containers which our guards refilled as needed. Eventually, the train started moving forward, but after a few kilometers it came to a halt. After traveling about twenty kilometers in this stop-and-go fashion, we reached the station in Taufkirchen, where everything came to a complete stop. Dachau was only eighty kilometers from Mühldorf, but at the rate we were traveling it would take days for us to get there. Our commander seemed to know what he was talking about. The railroad system was definitely not functioning any longer.

Train after train was parked, waiting for the one in front to move. I couldn't help but think of the days, after Hitler had invaded Poland, when trains stood in Chrzanow, not going anyplace. As we sat in our cars we heard the sounds of approaching Allied bombers, and our guards cleverly asked those who wore striped uniforms to use their jackets to wave at the planes flying overhead. How things had suddenly changed. Our guards now wanted us to protect them! The planes came near but did not shoot at us. Instead, they bombed the planes standing at the little airport across the tracks, but unfortunately those targets were just cardboard dummies.

Hours had passed when the stationmaster ran out of his office waving his arms and yelling a message that nobody could understand. He raced back into his office, turned the radio to full volume, and placed the microphone for the loudspeaker near by, so that all could clearly hear the announcement coming to us from Radio Munich. Repeated over and over again, the announcement told of a revolution in Munich, and instructed all army personnel to put down their arms and cease fighting immediately. The war was lost, it said, it was all over! Hearing this, many of our guards followed those instructions and quickly disappeared. Some of the others stood there dumbfounded and didn't know what to do next. Many of our comrades jumped from the train and ran into the street heading toward the city, but Fred, Peter and I decided on a different course of action. We crawled underneath the train, crossed the tracks, and ran into the nearby woods. Our hearts were pounding as a million thoughts crossed our minds. What would happen to us next? If indeed there was a revolution, would we be able to find safety? We had made our first step toward freedom but we had to proceed with extreme caution. If this revolution was somehow crushed, we would have to use the forests to make our way toward Nuremberg and the advancing Allied forces. We pushed our way through trees and bushes and realized that no one at all had followed us. Just then, we heard gunshots coming from the direction of the city. What was this shooting all about? Whatever the reason, we had made our decision and needed to distance ourselves from the area as fast as possible.

We moved deeper into the woods and removed the prisoner numbers from our uniforms. We tore into the cutout Star of David on our jackets and pants and dirtied the other painted ones so that our garments were beyond recognition. Through the years, Fred and I had learned to speak Polish well enough to get by, and knowing that Polish and French workers from the construction site were let go earlier, we decided to pretend that we were part of their group in case anyone stopped and questioned us. I spoke some French, too, but Peter, who had lived in Paris for a long time, spoke the language like a native. We had no documents, but our plan was the most reasonable explanation we could think of.

Late that afternoon, we came to a hill on the other side of the forest. Before us was a quiet landscape of fields, trees, and a small farmhouse. Hiding behind a bush, we studied the little house, which appeared to be deserted. Slowly we moved closer, and like thieves, we entered the empty house. We found some of the farmer's clothing, put it on, and took our prisoner garments along to dispose of them in the forest. Finding some bread in the pantry, we took that, too, and made our getaway with great haste before anyone came home and caused trouble. Crossing the fields, we got back into another wooded area where we sat down and enjoyed the wonderful bread we had stolen. I couldn't help but wonder what would have happened if the farmer had returned while we were still there.

Daylight began to fade and we knew we would have to spend the night in the woods. Other than my scout training years before, I had little experience living in a forest. We didn't know what kind of animals would be prowling these woods or how dangerous they could be. But being completely exhausted, we had no other choice but to stay put. Our long and draining day was behind us and we needed rest badly. A spot behind some bushes gave us a little protection, and a layer of pine needles provided us with a surface we could rest on. We had all slept on things much worse than this, but for safety reasons we slept in shifts. One always kept guard while two of us slept restlessly.

The morning dawned and we were cold and damp after the uneventful night. It was very quiet. No shooting could be heard anywhere. Nuremberg was still a distance away and we had to be extremely alert if we hoped to get to the Allied lines. We walked along the edge of the forests and were hidden by the trees and bushes that surrounded us. We zigzagged constantly, always continuing in the direction we thought best. At one point, we observed German army units setting up defensive positions in the nearby fields. This was somewhat encouraging as it meant we were nearing the front lines. On the other hand, it showed that the Germans were not obeying the order to put down arms.

I must have walked a little too far outside the forest because suddenly a bullet swished by my head narrowly missing me. I jumped back and we all ran for cover. We hit the ground and covered ourselves with leaves and other debris that was all around us. No sooner had we hidden ourselves when two soldiers passed near the edge of the forest. I heard one of them telling the other, "Ich hab' ihm grade hier gesehen" (I saw him right here.). When they finally passed our hiding place, we breathed a sigh of relief, but still stayed motionless for quite a long while. This was truly a very close call.

Another night and day went by and we started seeing more and more civilians, alone or in pairs, moving across the fields in the same direction that we were headed. Judging by their clothes and bundles, we assumed that they were foreign laborers trying to get back to their homes. Being near these people was a source of comfort because it made our own story so much more believable. Still, there was something in that forest which made us all uneasy. After years in concentration camps, I think we had developed a sixth sense. We felt that we were being watched. I couldn't see anyone in particular, but I knew that someone had his eye on us. Finally, we spotted a man wearing a French army uniform standing between the trees in our path. We couldn't avoid passing him, so we said, "Bon jour," as we approached him. He started speaking to us, and Peter, our French linguist, replied to his questions. Peter told him that we were recruited foreign workers and in turn he revealed that he was a French prisoner of war detailed to work on a German farm. In fact, he said, there were many small farms in the area where French prisoners were working. It wasn't too long before he told us bluntly that he didn't think that we were telling him the truth. "Don't answer," he said, "but I think you have escaped from some prison camp." He must have been watching us for some time to have come to this conclusion. We were relieved when he told us that he was an officer in the Maquis (French partisans) and would be glad to help us. Peter told him that we hadn't eaten much for days and the Frenchman took some of his own bread and shared it with us. He then gave us directions to a farmhouse where a number of French prisoners were working. He gave us the name of the soldier we were to ask for and said that we were to tell him who had sent us. "You'll be given lodging for the night and food. Then someone will direct you to the next safe house along the rescue trail for French escapees. Speak only to this man and to no one else." He sounded sincere and we had no reason to mistrust him. Meeting this man turned out to be very fortunate for us.

We arrived at the farm and met the French soldier we were told to see. He was most obliging and didn't even ask us any probing questions. He provided us with food and then arranged for us to sleep in his barn. A roof over our heads and relaxing on soft hay was absolute luxury after our experiences. In the morning, we were able to wash ourselves and our host brought us bread and a warm drink. He then gave us instructions for reaching the next station on our way to liberty. The farmhouses we visited became busier night after night as we came closer to the front lines, and barns were crowded with people resting on heaps of straw and avoiding being drawn into conversation. Some mornings we would see German uniforms discarded in dark corners of the barn, obviously left by soldiers who came in during the night and walked out as civilians in the morning.

The forests, so empty when we began our escape, became heavily traveled. Foreign workers who had been dismissed or had left work for their own reasons were now moving along with us. We were pleased with the added legitimacy they gave to us. However, not everyone was walking toward the front lines. I spotted some German families moving deeper into the country and away from potential danger. We also saw German army and Waffen SS units near us positioning themselves to confront the Allied forces.

At one point all civilians were detoured, and we were not able to travel to our next destination. We needed to find shelter, but how and where? We had come so far; getting caught in crossfire had to be avoided. Afraid to rest because some soldier or SS man might stop and question us, we continued along the edge of the woods. We searched for a way to circumvent the trouble spot, but all roads were blocked. Waffen SS units were hiding in the ditches off the road, and as we passed one such unit I heard an officer yell, "Halt die drei Burschen" (Stop the three fellows). We made believe we did not hear him as he ran toward us with his revolver drawn. He shouted, "Von wo kommt ihr und wohin wollt ihr gehen?" (Where are you coming from and where are you going?) Stammering, Peter replied in French that we were foreign workers like the others near us. The officer didn't understand French, so I added in a most broken and distorted German, "gehen haus" (going home). "Wo ist dein haus?" (Where is your home?) he wanted to know. Showing him that I understood the word "haus" (home), I looked around and pointed to houses in the distance saying, "Ja, haus hier (house here), haus hier."

Convinced that we were harmless simpletons, he was ready to let us pass when a brilliant idea struck him. Using hands and body, he made us understand that we were to walk down the center of the road. "Soon," he said, "American tanks will be coming around the bend, and when you see them, raise your arms high. They will not shoot you." We had to do as we were told, but as we walked on, we were sure that we would be shot in the back. Thankfully, nothing happened. I then suspected that he was using us as a signal for his troops to ambush the oncoming American tanks. We could hardly wait for the moment when, at the turn in the road, we could jump into a ditch and disappear into the forest. The deafening sounds of artillery shells and exploding bombs left no doubt that we were in the middle of the front lines. Soldiers and civilians were all around us as we ran through the forest and up a hill. We didn't even dare to stop and catch our breath. As twilight approached, we had not yet figured out a way to get back to the road and find the next safe house.

As we walked on, we spotted a pastor leaving a farmhouse and heading in our direction. As he came closer I approached him and said, "Herr Pfarrer, glauben Sie dass der Krieg bald zu ende ist?" (Father, do you believe that the war is about to end?). Cautiously he nodded as if to say I agree with you. I continued, "Darf ich ihr Vertrauen haben?" (May I trust you?). "Vollkommen" (absolutely), he replied. I told him that there was no doubt that this area would fall into Allied hands in the next few days or even hours, and that the Nazi era would be over. "You're a man of the cloth," I said, "I'm placing our lives in your hands." He encouraged me to go on. I told him that we were Jews who had escaped from a concentration camp, and as he looked into my eyes and placed a hand on my shoulder, he said, "Wait here, you are now safe and in good hands." He turned around and went back to the house, returning a few minutes later to lead us to a small barn. "The house is overcrowded with people seeking shelter," he said. "It would be better for you to rest in the small, empty barn. No one will know your secret and soon someone will bring you blankets and food." He gave us his blessings and we thanked him for all he was doing for us.

We were so tired that even the deafening noise of exploding shells all around us didn't prevent us from falling asleep. In the middle of the night, the noise suddenly stopped and we awoke with a start. The stillness seemed so strange. We looked outside but it was pitch dark and we couldn't see a thing. We had to be patient and wait for the dawn before we could learn what was happening around us. Our excitement was too great for us to fall asleep again and our thoughts wandered wildly. Could it be true, or were we dreaming? Did we dare believe that the Allies had taken this area? Was it possible that we would be free and safe at last ? At the first signs of light, we went outside to look around. All was quiet and peaceful. As daylight became brighter we could see the bottom of the hill and white flags hanging from the houses along the road. White flags meant surrender. We were not dreaming after all!

We hurried down the mountain to look for Allied soldiers and safety. Running toward the street below, we saw soldiers in strange-looking boxes on wheels rolling down the road. They were so different from any kind of vehicle we had ever seen before. Living behind barbed wire, removed from the rest of the world, we had never seen a Jeep. At the corner of the road a soldier stood leaning against a fence. We ran toward him and he instinctively reacted by pointing his gun at us. Excitedly I yelled, "Happy to see you, are you English or American?" He put his gun down, looked at us again and replied, "American."

That magical day was Tuesday, May 1, 1945. We laughed, cried, and jumped for joy! We were free! We were alive! We had actually made it!

I explained, or tried to explain, to this soldier who we were and where we came from, but he didn't seem to understand me. We both spoke English, but mine was school-taught English, while he spoke with a deep southern accent. I was frustrated and so was he. Not knowing what to do next, he contacted his superior on the radio and was told to make us wait there until we could be picked up. A lieutenant arrived who obviously had some knowledge of death camps in Germany and Poland. After asking us a few questions, he took us in his jeep to the POW camp in Moosburg. That camp had been liberated only one day earlier and a contingency of the International Red Cross was now in charge.

As we entered the Red Cross office, the officer on duty ignored us completely as we were not POWs or registered in his camp. He didn't offer us any food or any kind of help. His actions were in line with our earlier experiences with the IRC during the war. They never really investigated the concentration camps they had visited or enforced any international human rights agreements. They were empowered, in fact obligated, to examine our camps, but they were useless in giving us any relief from our suffering. The IRC officer treated us like outcasts and had guards escort us out of the camp. There we stood, in our first hours of freedom, without a clue of what to do next.

At the gate we saw a liberated POW speaking to a comrade, but they were not speaking English. It took me a moment to realize that they were speaking Hebrew. What a surprise! I came closer to them and said, "Shalom Chaverim" (Peace my friends.). Pointing to Fred and Peter, I continued, "Aa-nach-noo ye-hoo-dim" (we are Jews) and we have escaped from Dachau concentration camp. Our conversation continued in Yiddish, and after they questioned us and were convinced that we were indeed survivors, they began to embrace and hug us. We were all family! They were members of the Palestine Brigade who had been taken prisoner during the Italian campaign and liberated only a day earlier. The Palestine Brigade was a supply unit for the British army and consisted of very dedicated and strong volunteers determined to help defeat the Nazis. They, out of necessity, had to remain a small and nondescript group because of Britain's fear of antagonizing the Palestinian Arabs. The Arabs objected to Jews having their own military force, so the Brigade, like the Mule Corps during World War I, was a compromise arrangement.

Yossi, one of the two released POWs, wanted to take us to the Red Cross office inside the camp, but we told him of our latest experience with this humanitarian organization. This hardly surprised Yossi and his friend, but it still made them furious. Yossi had grown up in Leipzig and had lived through years of Nazi brutality before moving to Palestine. He was determined to get back at the Germans and help us as much as he could. He requisitioned a jeep and all five of us made our way to the City Hall. "Wo ist der Bürgermeister?" (Where is the mayor?), Yossi yelled at the receptionist. "Upstairs in his office," she replied. Taking two steps at a time, Yossi ran up the stairs and barged into the office. The mayor stood up and automatically raised his arm in the customary Nazi salute. This was enough provocation for Yossi to scream and slap him in the face, Nazi style. Two days after the surrender, this mayor still had the audacity to wear the Nazi party emblem on the lapel of his jacket. Enraged, and speaking in German, Yossi pointed to my brother, Peter, and me, and asked the mayor, "Do you know who these people are?" The mayor stammered, "No, they look like vagrants to me." Yossi slapped the mayor again and yelled, "They are Jews and so are we. You made them look like this, we are some of the very few that you and your Nazi cohorts did not succeed in killing." The arrogant and once powerful mayor was now a frightened and cowering weakling.

We took delight in seeing the tables turned. Yossi demanded that we be given housing, food, clothing and someone to take care of our needs. The mayor clicked his heels and replied, "Jawohl!" Two women in the room started crying and one of them pleaded with us to come to her house to get clothing belonging to her sons who were in the army. She offered us the money she had in her purse and promised that we would get all the assistance we needed. We believed that her actions were a sudden acknowledgment of guilt, but it was still not what we wanted. We thought it best for us to get a residence on the main street of this little town. That way we would feel safe and close to our new friends who might visit us when they could.

We requisitioned a house in town and our new landlady pleaded with us to allow her to stay. She promised to cook and clean and generally help us recover. We knew that she was just trying to protect her home, but the new arrangement suited us well. Living in the woods and on the run had taken away all our strength. Her home was the perfect place for us to recuperate until we figured out what to do next. As we roamed through the house, we found among other things a picture of her husband, in the full uniform of a high-ranking Nazi.

Our circle of Palestinian and American friends from the Moosburg camp grew quickly. They brought us goodies from the PX such as wine, liquor, cigarettes, and delicacies we had forgotten even existed. One day a Palestine Brigade soldier brought me a rifle and a few rounds of ammunition. "It's yours for twenty-four hours. Do as you please and no one will ask any questions," he said. I knew very well what I should do, but I couldn't bring myself to kill anyone just because they were German. It was not in me to become a killer. I returned the gun the following day without a single shell missing.

Our landlady resented having so many POWs in her house. Her behavior, never really friendly toward us, now turned hostile. It exploded one morning when we requested eggs for breakfast. She replied that she had none even though we saw chickens roaming in the backyard. I called her a liar and we decided to search the entire house. Not only did we find eggs, ham, cheeses and other foods in the basement, but a hidden and locked door, too. We suspected that someone must be hiding there, but she wouldn't open the door for us. When we started to break it down, she took out her key and begged us not to hurt her teenaged daughter. Afraid of what might happen to them, they cried and held on to each other tightly. "We should do to you what your soldiers did when they forced their way into our homes," I said. "But we are Jews, and we would never stoop so low as to act the way you brutal Germans did. Now that you have lied to us, we can't trust you any longer. Take your daughter and leave the house at once."

Later that day, someone from the mayor's office came and apologized for the woman's poor judgment. She pleaded with us to accept her apology. Since we really needed rest and someone to care for us, we finally decided to allow the mother and daughter, supervised by the mayor's office, to tend to our needs.

The days passed quickly and our friends were ready to be repatriated to Palestine. They asked us to come along and start a new life on a kibbutz (agricultural community). They said it would be relatively easy for them to get us uniforms and identities of fallen Brigade members. Once in Palestine, they said, we could use our own names and live a normal life. Only a few years ago I would have given everything I had for such an offer. But now we had to get back our strength and then try to find our dear ones, if any had survived. They understood our feelings and wished us good luck. We said, "L'hit-ra-ot" (Until we see each other again), hoping to meet again in our Jewish homeland sometime in the future.

Peter registered and joined a transport of foreign workers leaving for Paris. He, too, wanted us to come along with him, but I gave him the same answer I had given our Palestinian friends. We promised to keep in touch, but that would not be an easy task. None of us even knew of an address or place that we could contact each other. We said good-bye, knowing that we would probably never see each other again.

15

Liberty at Last

Peter and our friends from the Palestine Brigade were on their way home and the celebrations of having survived the war gave way to utter loneliness. We were free, but Fred and I were all alone in a small German town surrounded by people we despised. Three weeks had gone by and we had regained much of our strength. The time had come to move on. Uppermost on our minds was the need to find any family or friends who, like us, might have survived this tragedy. But how and where should we start? There was no transportation, no telephone, no mail, not even a newspaper to help us contact anyone. Germany was in shambles and any kind of communication was unlikely to be restored in the immediate future. How would we ever find anyone else who might still be alive?

Munich was only about forty kilometers away and I thought that being in the big city would be the best place to begin our search. We were not the only homeless people in the area and I was confident that some organization would be able to give us shelter. Our landlady was only too happy to see us leave, and even gave us a hefty supply of sandwiches for our trip. On the road to Munich, we luckily hitched a ride on an army truck which took us directly to the city hall in the heart of the city. The building was damaged and closed, but an MP (Military Police) officer directed us to a nearby school which had been taken over by UNRRA (United Nations Relief and Rehabilitation Administration). This school was made into a DP (Displaced Persons) camp to take care of the many foreign workers liberated and stranded in Germany.

Fred and I began to look for others who had also been liberated in the area. On foot, or by hitching rides, we searched other local UNRRA camps and eventually found a few comrades from our camp in Mühldorf. They told us that our people who fled the train at the station in Taufkirchen were recaptured in the town by the Waffen SS men. This explained the gunshots we had heard after our escape into the woods. Back on the train, our comrades sat in cars for days without any food. All they had was the water brought to them by guards as they awaited Allied forces to liberate them. From that train they were taken to Feldafing, a recreational facility once used by German officers and now a large DP camp administered by UNRRA. The comrades we met had come to Munich very much the way we did, and for similar reasons. We received food and shelter from UNRRA, but they were still not able to assist us in finding surviving relatives. It occurred to us that making a list of survivors and publishing it in the surrounding DP camps was a logical place to start. To do this, Henry Schwimmer and I, plus a few other men, formed the Committee for Liberated Jews in Bavaria. Word about the existence of our committee spread rapidly, and in spite of the difficulties in finding and contacting people, the number of names on our list grew incredibly fast.

All nationalities, except for the Jewish people, had their government representatives in DP camps to register and repatriate them to their homeland. These representatives put pressure on the Jews to return to our countries of origin, too. Understandably, having endured so much pain from those countries, going back to live with these people again was the last thing we wanted to do. Our homeland was Palestine and that was the place we believed we must go. To organize a Jewish section in DP camps to work the way other nationalities functioned, we needed authorization from UNRRA headquarters. Henry and I decided that we must visit the officer in charge of UNRRA operations in Munich and see what we could accomplish.

Colonel Malcolm McDonald received us with a friendly smile and listened politely as we told him the purpose of our meeting. We were not interested in being repatriated. We just wanted our own division in DP camps for the time being and asked for permission to establish a Jewish National Section. Believing that we were just a couple of youngsters with foolish ideas, he obviously was not aware of the enormity of the disaster which had befallen the Jewish community in Europe. The colonel replied that our request was without foundation since no Jewish state existed.

"You are citizens of the countries you came from, and you must return there," he said. We replied that Palestine was our homeland, and even though it was now under English jurisdiction, it was the country that we belonged to.

We were terribly disappointed at having accomplished nothing, but undeterred, we decided to take a white bed sheet and some blue ribbon and sew it into a Jewish flag. We raised that flag over the entrance to the Deutsche Museum, a building that was used by the Nazis as a bomb shelter during the war. It now served as a DP camp for our Jewish comrades who had settled in Munich. Ours was a primitive flag, but it was our flag, the Jewish flag, and seeing it fly over a building in Munich was a very emotional experience for us.

Jewish GIs who had learned of our presence came to us with hopes of finding their relatives who had remained in Europe during the war. They offered us assistance and made copies of the list of names we had compiled. They brought us news that the American Joint Distribution Committee, JOINT for short, and the Hebrew Immigrant Aid Society, known as HIAS, had representatives in Paris who were ready to come and help us as soon as they got clearance to enter the newly occupied territories. In the meantime, one of these GIs introduced us to a member of the military government who gave us permission to occupy a mansion at No. 10 Möhl Strasse. This beautiful building on a quiet residential street near the English Garden became our office and headquarters.

General Eisenhower, we were told, was about to visit the camp at Dachau. With our repatriation problem ever on our minds, we hoped to get a ruling on this issue from the supreme commander. Henry and I, along with a third member of our newly organized committee, asked one of our army friends to give us a ride to Dachau, where we hoped to get a chance to speak to the general. Visiting Dachau and recalling memories of our imprisonment was not an easy task, but we needed General Eisenhower's ruling. Entering the gate was heart-wrenching, and we were even more shocked when we saw many of our sick comrades still inside the camp. The damage caused by malnutrition was so severe that even with the fine care they had received after liberation, help had come too late for many of them. Days and weeks after liberation many former inmates were still dying in the camp. The general was visibly moved by what he encountered on his visit. When he saw our emaciated comrades, he questioned why these people had not been transferred to a healthier environment. He was not satisfied with the answer he was given and immediately ordered Germans to vacate their homes in town so the sick people could be moved there at once. When he was told that we, former inmates of Dachau, had come from Munich to have him clarify a question, he graciously listened to our story. He replied that, for the time being, no one could force us to go back to our country of origin. We were thrilled with his reply and could hardly wait to get back to Munich and tell our friends what the general had said.

Through word of mouth, news about the existence of our committee, known by its Yiddish name, *Shah-rith Ha-pleh-tah* (community of the broken ones), spread. Though there was no transportation to speak of, people came to us from camps and places we had never known existed. They came to register and check for names of relatives or friends who had already signed up. The once quiet Möhl Strasse became the center of Jewish activities in Munich. By the time the social workers from JOINT and HIAS had arrived, they had a good base from which to start.

Fred and I had our fill of camp life, but getting an apartment in the nearly destroyed city of Munich was next to impossible. Using the contacts I had made, the military government issued a note instructing the German housing authority to immediately provide housing for Fred and me. The office I went to was bursting with German people who had lost their homes during the war and were looking for a place to stay. With my authorization in hand, I went directly to the front of the line and approached the clerk. At first I was yelled at, but when I showed them the official government document, the crowd turned silent. Volumes could be written about the reaction I saw in their faces. For once, I had the upper hand over the Germans. I must admit it felt great!

We were offered a room in a luxury apartment where everyone shared the kitchen and sanitary facilities. For the moment, we had no other choice but to accept this room if we wanted to leave the camp. One room in the apartment was occupied by Erich Kästner, the well-known author of books for the young. "Emil und die Detektive" and "Der 35. Mai," were some of his stories I remember having read in school. Two other rooms were occupied by Paul von Verhoeven, one of the foremost movie directors in Germany, his actress wife, and their three children.

The curfew forced everyone to spend their evenings at home, and rather than remain by ourselves we joined the other residents around the kitchen table for kaffeeklatsch and chatter. The group wanted to hear our stories, but except for Kästner, who admitted having heard about the brutality in concentration camps, the others professed ignorance about Auschwitz and German atrocities. But somehow I sensed their shame for the actions that had taken place under the Nazi regime.

Soon after JOINT and HIAS started their operation, our offices and storage facilities on Möhl Strasse became too small, and as JOINT was an affiliate of UNRRA, there was little problem in requisitioning another mansion. We were given a building around the corner on Maria-Theresia Strasse and that became the emigration division, the department where I was asked to work.

Many weeks had passed and a few streets had finally been cleared of enough rubble and debris for streetcars to pass. Now there was a limited amount of local transportation, but intercity travel by train was still non-existent. Ignoring travel hardships, people continuously arrived in Munich and Möhl Strasse began to have the appearance of a marketplace. This was the place where survivors came to meet others, always hoping to find some-one who could give them information about their loved ones.

On foot or by hitchhiking, some survivors returned to their homes in Poland soon after liberation, but once there they were very disappointed. Polish people had moved into their homes and greeted them in angry tones. "What are you doing here? You're still alive? What do you want? This is now our place!" Not only was their reception unpleasant, but some-times even life-threatening. As quickly as they could, most of them made their way back to the safety of DP camps. This situation didn't deter my brother from visiting the family hometown of Chrzanow to see things for himself. We wanted to know what was left of the city and find out whether any of our relatives had survived. If someone was alive, we wanted them to join us in the American Zone of Occupation. It was a difficult trip for Fred and it took him many days to get there. He found a city without life and totally devoid of Jews. He was told that a few survivors had returned but spent only a few days in town before leaving for places unknown. Fred was able to learn that our cousins Bertha, Sala, Lusia Fischler, and Papa's brother Herman had been seen recently and were thought to be headed to Munich. He also met someone who had seen Papa some time ago in the labor camp at Fünfteichen. When he was spotted, Papa was in poor health and the source of this information didn't believe that Papa could have survived.

Our emigration department at the JOINT was ready to go into action, but all we could do for now was register those who needed to contact relatives overseas and request immigration papers for them. We had one military phone line connecting our office to JOINT headquarters in Paris, and once contact was established we were able to quickly get documents for these people. Using army trucks, the lucky men and women were transferred to Paris where they could visit consulates, obtain visas, and be on their way to a new life.

Amsterdam had been liberated nearly six months earlier, and I had good reason to believe that a new telephone directory would have already been published. If, in fact, such a directory was available, it would be a good place to start the search for my Dutch relatives. I mentioned this thought to my contact in Paris and was pleasantly surprised when our courier from Paris brought me a copy only a few days later. Nervous, and afraid of being disappointed, I skimmed through the pages. There are no words to describe my elation when I found Aunt Mia and Uncle Bobby's telephone listing. Turning more pages, I even found a listing for my Aunt Mali.

Since I now had my own telephone extension on my desk, I called my contact in Paris, and using whatever army routes we could connect to, we reached the Amsterdam network. When I heard Aunt Mia's voice saying, "Hello," I was in tears as I answered, "Aunt Mia — this is James." There was silence at the other end of the line and I had to repeat my name again and again. She obviously needed a moment to get over the shock of hearing my voice. I could hear her sobbing. She was unable to talk to me. Uncle Bobby then picked up the phone and spoke with excitement in his voice. The joys and sorrows of this telephone call were indescribable. Uncle confirmed what I had suspected; my grandparents and Uncle Alfred's family were taken by transport to Poland and presumed dead. Aunt and Uncle were luckier because, when they had come to Amsterdam in 1938, they had to live there illegally. This, as it turned out, made it easier for them to live in hiding during the war. My Aunt Mali had used her business contacts in Holland and Belgium to escape into France, and there she had lived in hiding with her daughters Edith and Ilse. Every time I called Aunt, and I did call often, she pleaded with my brother and me to move to Amsterdam and live with them. At first I said, "We'll see," but I really had no intention of remaining in Europe. Because of my connections to influential officials, I had received some fine offers for an important future in Germany, but I wanted none of that. I wanted out of Germany, out of Europe.

More than three months had passed since the war had ended and the *Süddeutsche Zeitung* (Bavaria's largest newspaper) was ready to publish again. The first issues appeared as one-sheet tabloids publishing the most important information for the area. As I worked at my desk one day, a friend of mine brought me the latest issue. Showing me the column headed "Greetings from Relatives in Berlin to Relatives in Bavaria," he pointed to the middle of the listing, and there it was: "Abraham Bachner, Suarez Strasse 38, Berlin, sends greetings to his sons James and Fred Bachner in Munich." It took me a moment to digest what I had seen and to understand that Papa was alive and in Berlin. I grabbed the paper, rushed home, and showed it to Fred, who was also overwhelmed by this wonderful news. After much conversation it was agreed that I would travel to Berlin as Fred had already made the trip to Chrzanow earlier.

I prepared some documents to help me cross the border between the American and Russian Zones of Occupation. Since there was only one official crossing point and that was far away and difficult to get to, I thought I would use a well-known, but unofficial, crossing point closer to Munich. Going from western Germany to the east, many civilians had taken this route before and, by hitching a ride on an UNRRA truck, I had hopes of getting to Berlin much easier and faster.

The village I approached was filled with people who, like me, wanted to cross the border. Unfortunately, and unbeknownst to me, the Russians had started enforcing their no-crossing rule a day earlier. Local residents, familiar with the terrain, were charging a fee to guide groups across the border and I joined such a group. Quietly, in a single file, we moved through the territory, but when we approached an opening, our guide disappeared and Russian soldiers suddenly were there pointing guns at us. I showed them my official documents, issued in English, French and Russian and watched in disbelief how this soldier turned my papers upside down and sideways, obviously not able to read at all. I tried to speak to him in Polish, adding the few Russian words I had learned along the way, but my words fell on deaf ears. He just tore all my papers to shreds and confiscated everything I had with me — cigarettes, watch, and my wallet filled with money. He and his comrades then brought everyone to their headquarters at a nearby farm. The entire group, men, women, and children, were herded into a dark and dingy basement. What irony! After all my years of hardship, I was now sharing a prison cell with Germans who had imprisoned me for so long. My captors were the very soldiers who had come to end my oppression. Unbelievable!

A few days of confinement had passed and we were ordered to do some cleanup work on the farm. The Russian officer who gave us our orders spoke some German, mixing it with Yiddish words. I managed to get close to him and, speaking Yiddish, I said that I had been liberated from concentration camp Dachau and was on my way to find my father in Berlin. He looked at me for a moment, and without uttering a word, he walked away. The following morning I was ordered to go to his office and wait for him there. Speaking Yiddish he yelled, "You are a spy. You were carrying maps of this and other areas," he said. I had a lot of convincing to do before he believed and accepted my explanations. He returned my wallet, but of course it was emptied of all its contents, and told me to leave. I asked him to replace my documents so I could continue on to Berlin, to which he replied, "Just go to the railroad station and take the next train; all of them stop in Berlin." I did as I was told, and hoped that no one would stop me along the way. Being in Russian-controlled territory without identification papers I knew could be dangerous. I had to be very careful and lucky if I were to make it to Berlin.

My train arrived at Charlottenburg station early on a Sunday morning. The streets were deserted as I walked the distance to Suarez Strasse. I rang the doorbell and Papa opened the door. It took him a long moment to recognize me. Neither of us was able to speak; we just hugged and kissed, and hugged some more. Gusti, a lady I had met years earlier in Chrzanow, came to the door to greet me, too. Before we said another word to each other, I was ushered into the bathroom to clean and refresh myself. During all the time I had spent in the basement on the farm, I had no chance to wash or shave, much less take care of the clothes I was wearing. I looked and smelled like a homeless beggar. Papa gave me some of his own clothes; they didn't fit well, but for the moment they would do. After a good shower and shave, I actually felt like myself again.

We exchanged stories of our imprisonment and our miraculous survival. He told me that he had become so weak those last few months of incarceration that if the war had lasted a few more days, he would not have made it at all. In the final days at camp Gross Rosen, he weighed ninety-five pounds and was barely able to stand on his feet. Gusti Landerer worked in a knitting mill near Gross Rosen and when she found Papa in this near death condition, she nursed him back to health. Together, they came to Berlin a few weeks earlier, with the hope that Fred and I would also return to Berlin if we were alive.

Papa told me the story of how he learned that Fred and I were in Munich. That, he said, was truly a miracle. A few days after arriving in Berlin, he had gone to the reopened Jewish Community Office for some information. As he left the office, the man he had visited called after him, "Mr. Bachner, you forgot something." He then handed an envelope to Papa which had been left in the office. Amazingly, this exchange was witnessed by Isi Aaron, a friend of mine who was with me in Warsaw, Dachau and Mühldorf. When he heard the name Bachner, he approached Papa and asked if he had relatives named James and Fred. "Of course! They are my sons, what do you know about them?" Papa replied excitedly. Isi said that we were well, living in Munich, and that he had been to my office only a week ago. This news caused great joy at the Jewish Community Office and someone suggested that Papa visit the nearby office of the Süddeutsche Zeitung. They were planning a special edition of greetings to relatives in Bavaria, and perhaps someone who knew us might read the notice. Well, that was exactly the way it happened; a perfect example of being in the right place at the right time. Fred and I would have found Papa eventually, but our reunion could have been many months later.

There was absolutely no doubt that Mutti and all our other relatives in Chrzanow had been murdered in Auschwitz. So was Gusti's husband. Together, Gusti and Papa came to Berlin and were married shortly before I had arrived. Hearing about their marriage was painful for me but I understood their circumstances and the importance for my father to have a companion to try and rebuild his life. I believed that Fred, too, would understand the situation. There weren't many families where three out of four members survived the camps, so we were really among the fortunate ones. I explained to Papa and Gusti that neither Fred nor I had any desire to live in Germany or any place in Europe. But for now, I wished to bring them to Munich so we could live as a family. Papa needed time to take care of things he was involved in, but as soon as possible, they would definitely join us in Munich. I remained in Berlin for a few more days to see the familiar places in the city that I had called home for so many years. Most of the city was reduced to rubble and I had some sad moments when I thought about the wonderful childhood I had enjoyed in Berlin. I soon became restless to get back to my work in Munich, but afraid of repeating my border-crossing experiences, I contacted Hagganah and joined their underground route out of Berlin. (Hagganah, the underground Jewish army which defended our people in Palestine, was now busy in Europe with their "Aliyat Beth" operation. Secretly they moved fellow Jews out of Eastern European countries and into Palestine.) At the same time I made arrangements for Papa and Gusti to follow me a few weeks later.

Back in Munich, I related my entire story to Fred. When I told him about my Russian imprisonment, I first realized the tremendous danger that I had been in. No one would have known what had happened to me if this Russian officer had insisted that I was a spy. Communists were known to have made such accusations, often with dire consequences for the person involved.

In preparation for my father's arrival, I used my uniform to get housing for our family from the Housing Administration in Munich. This was payback time, and as the Germans had done to Jews in Chrzanow, I now requested a comfortable house for our family. It took a bit of time, but in the end I received papers to occupy the house of a party member in Schwabing.

The German mark was completely worthless, but with the supplemental food rations from UNRRA and packages from JOINT, we weren't lacking basic supplies. As a full-time employee, wearing the UNRRA uniform, I had entry to the officers' club and was able to make purchases at the PX. My eyes opened wide as I entered the PX for the first time. After all those years of being deprived of comforts and beautiful things, the simplest items for everyday use seemed luxurious to me. The PX was a veritable paradise! There was so much to buy, so many things that I had forgotten ever existed, and items I had never seen before. This was an entirely different world. What a contrast to the dark streets, destroyed buildings, and empty stores of the rest of Munich.

Now that I had a family and was no longer on my own, I needed to readjust my plans for the future. Papa and Gusti had physical problems and would not do well in the pioneering society of Palestine, so we now had to look for other places to make our new home. The United States, New York in particular, remained a dream that we had harbored for many years. Maybe we could revive the affidavit we had received from Opa's brother years before if he was still alive. Whatever the future had in store for me, it would never change my desire to do all I could to see our Jewish homeland rebuilt. But for the time being, I had to face reality. I was part of a family of four who needed a more normal lifestyle.

The Jewish Agency (the Jewish Government in exile) had opened an office in a building next to ours, and I was one of the few outsiders invited to attend a meeting with prominent leaders of the Zionist organization. Those attending included David Ben Gurion and Moshe Shertock who, in later years as Israel's foreign secretary, had changed his name to Sharett. They had clandestinely come to Munich because Great Britain had a warrant posted for their arrest. As leaders of the Hagganah they were suspected of being involved in recent terror attacks in Palestine. At this gathering, we were told about the work done by Aliyat Beth, the underground migration to Palestine, and the many people who were trickling out of Russia, Poland, and other countries in the east. We were asked to provide transportation, make pickups at the Czechoslovakian border near Munich, and bring these people to various DP camps in our area. Many of them were transferred to farms in Southern France and Italy where they could learn to work the land. As soon as Hagganah was able to obtain a vessel, they and others from DP camps were sent across the Mediterranean to Palestine.

Unfortunately, Great Britain's patrol boats prevented most of these ships from landing at their destination. British sailors boarded the ships as they came close to shore, confiscated them, and put our people in detention camps in Cyprus. This was a tragedy of enormous proportion. Coming out of German camps and wanting nothing more than their freedom, these unfortunate people found themselves behind barbed-wire fences once again. This time under English control. Attempts to leave camps in Cyprus under cover of night usually failed, yet occasionally a few people on a small ship did manage to outwit the British patrols and land in Palestine. Desperate behind barbed wire, a well-organized breakout from a Cyprus camp did succeed, and allowed many of our men, women, and children to board the largest freighter Aliyat Beth could afford to buy. Filled to capacity, the ship was named *Exodus*. This vessel made history when it openly defied

English policy and their blockade. The publicity about hardships suffered by those aboard forced the British government to finally let the ship and passengers reach their destination.

Life in DP camps was boring and unproductive. Their questions were always the same. What will happen to us next? When can we start to rebuild our lives? The longer our comrades languished in German DP or British detention camps in Cyprus, the more determined they became to return to our homeland in Palestine. Again and again the Jewish Agency asked Great Britain to remove the blockade and implement the mandate given to them by the League of Nations after World War I. But, disregarding the hardships the people had endured, Britain stalled as much as possible to placate their Arab friends.

The displaced persons issue became of great concern for many of the world leaders, and President Truman was the first to act to ease the problem. He asked the U.S. Congress to free more than twenty-five thousand immigration quotas not used during the war, and permit that number of DPs to enter the United States. JOINT and HIAS, representing the American Jewish community, were willing to assume responsibility that these people would not become a burden to the U.S. government. This was exciting news for all of us and turned our dream of settling in New York into reality.

At about the same time, UNRRA announced that the university in Munich would be offering classes in higher education for DPs who applied. I had a tough decision to make because I had always wanted to be a physician, and if I stayed in Munich I could realize that dream. Still, wanting to get out of Germany and out of Europe, I chose to apply for a U.S. visa and leave Europe together with my family.

The long-awaited day arrived when my office was notified that we were to register twenty-five thousand DPs to enter the United States. This news traveled quickly and people started lining up in the street, waiting to register. Sitting at the source, I was able to register my family, including our cousin Bertha who was then living with us. It took time for our documents to be cleared by the CIC (Counter Intelligence Corps), F.B.I., and all the other authorities involved, but finally the day came when we were told to report to the consulate to pick up our visas. It was one of the most beautiful moments in my life, but what a pity that this day had not come a few years earlier.

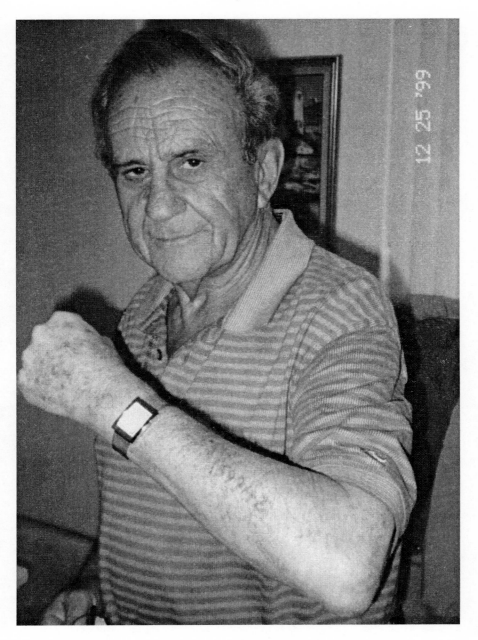

More than half a century has gone by, and just as my tattoo has not faded throughout the years, neither has my memory.

My Darkest Years

More than nine hundred of us left Bremerhaven, Germany, on January 3, 1947, aboard the troopship *Ernie Pyle*. Thirteen days later, after a stormy voyage at sea, we arrived in New York. Delirious with joy and filled with hope, I stood at the railing of the ship in the early morning hours waiting for daylight and a glimpse of the Statue of Liberty. There wasn't a dry eye among the nearly one thousand former DPs as the harbor tugboat pushed the ship past the outstretched arm of Miss Liberty. As the leader of the transport, I had been given money from JOINT which I kept in the ship purser's office. Prior to disembarking, I had the pleasure of handing twenty-five dollars pocket money to every passenger on board the *Ernie Pyle*. It wasn't much, but to us it was a fortune. As we disembarked, each of us carried a small suitcase filled with our pitiful belongings. In addition to my suitcase, I carried a violin which I had bartered on the black market in Munich in exchange for cigarettes. My other possessions consisted of the gold Swiss watch on my wrist, the twenty-five dollars from JOINT and another fifty dollars cash that I had accumulated from my days in Munich.

Volunteers from the Jewish community welcomed us to New York and the United States. With tears in our eyes and smiles on our faces we said, "Thank you," again and again. It was late in the afternoon by the time the bus took us to the Belleclaire Hotel on Broadway and 77th streets. It was a feast for our eyes as we drove along the bustling streets. We couldn't stop ooing and aahing as we marveled at all the lights and the stores crammed with merchandise. We saw happy and busy people leading their normal everyday lives. The contrast between the dark cities in Germany and life on New York's Broadway was incredible. I had literally come out of darkness to be reborn in this magnificent new land.

There were no official records, but available information proved that more than 6 million men, women, and children had perished, and that only 350,000 to 380,000 of our people survived the Holocaust.

Epilogue:
My New World

Overwhelmed by the sights and sounds of New York, I felt like the legendary Rip Van Winkle, the man, so the story goes, who fell asleep in the Adirondack Mountains and couldn't find anything familiar to him when he awoke twenty years later. Language was not my problem, but adjusting to my new surroundings required patience. Using a pay phone, going through a turnstile when entering a subway, and all the other things New Yorkers took for granted were strange to me. I remember the time when I had met someone while lounging in the hotel lobby and became involved in a most interesting conversation. Looking at his watch, the man excused himself saying, "I have to rush and see somebody. I'll see you later." After waiting there for a while, I got angry for having been stood up. Days later, I learned about the true meaning of "I'll see you later." Incidents like this happened quite often, and I soon realized the value of growing up in a place where one shared schooling, surroundings, and life in general.

I was envious of the men and women my age who passed me on the street, all with a purpose and leading busy lives. This was the land of unlimited opportunities, and I was determined to be part of it.

JOINT and other Jewish organizations were generous and helped us to get settled in our new environment. We stayed at the hotel for many weeks and even received cash to buy our food. Every two weeks I would meet with a counselor who advised and suggested what I should do next. Hoping that my art talent would give me a start, I began looking for work as

215

a commercial artist. Language was not my problem, but for the limited number of available positions I had to compete with soldiers who had come home after serving in the army and I was low man on the totem pole.

People would come to the hotel lobby in search of survivors who may have information about their relatives, and in this way Gusti met a long-lost cousin. Through his contacts, I got a job as a commercial artist in an advertising agency. Papa and Gusti found employment in the garment center, and Fred, always interested in cars, got a job as an apprentice at the local Lincoln-Mercury dealer. We pooled our incomes, found an apartment in the Bronx and furnished it as best we could. We were well on the way to fitting into the American way of life.

At my last meeting with my counselor I asked him about making arrangements for repaying our debt to JOINT. Much to my surprise he said, "You owe us nothing! There is nothing to be repaid, no loan agreement to be signed, and no commitment to be made. Remember what we've accomplished here. The day will come when you'll be able to help others, so don't forget us." We shook hands and I left his office. No one ever had to remind me that helping others is so much better than being on the receiving end.

Our clothing was old and of European style, so a portion of our first earned money went to buy American clothing. We were anxious to be American, look American, and live like Americans. Nothing less would do. In Berlin, Papa manufactured the finest men's clothing, and we still wanted to wear only the very best. Papa believed that one can recognize a successful person by the way he carries himself, and to make the right impression at this stage in our lives was very important. With that in mind, the three Bachner men proceeded to Manny Walkers on Seventh Ave., a fine men's fashion store, and purchased our first suits and topcoats.

I worked during the day and went to City College at night taking courses in advertising. As the company I was working for grew, I advanced to production manager in the art department, and eventually became its art director. I had made new friends in the local Zionist group, and between theater, concerts, operas, nightclubs, and movies, I tried to catch up on my lost years. This was also the time when Great Britain was forced to bring the Palestine issue before the United Nations. So, in addition to my other activities, I did my share of demonstrating in front of the United

Nations Assembly in Lake Success and then at Flushing Meadows when the Palestine partition plan was being debated.

Papa and I had managed to save some money, and joining a jewelry manufacturer we had met, we started a costume jewelry design and manufacturing business. We did fine for the first few years, but Japanese competition changed the scene drastically and our business began hurting.

By then my family had moved to Kew Gardens Hills in Queens and I had joined the senior alumni of our Jewish Community Center. It was there that I met Marilyn, the love of my life. We got married and I returned to the advertising field for my livelihood. My former boss was willing to employ me again and since I had developed a fine rapport with many clients earlier, he asked me to service these clients as account executive, and in time I became a junior partner. Evan, our firstborn was on the way, and I was happy to have the greater income. When our son Robert arrived to make us a family of four, we moved into our own house in Syosset, Long Island.

We were blessed with two wonderful boys who grew up in a lifestyle that was denied me, and Marilyn and I did all we could to give them the best we were able to afford. Active in our community, we were involved in PTA, Cub Scouts, Boy Scouts, and all the things most American parents participated in. As a family, we traveled to Israel and Europe, and became very active in our temple.

It was only natural that from the day I earned my first dollar, I did all I could to help others in need. We donated and chaired fundraising activities for the United Jewish Appeal and other vital causes. Our boys knew about the Holocaust, but I never burdened them with too many of my bitter memories. They grew up to become fine men, orthopedic surgeons by profession, and proud of their Jewish heritage. That heritage is now being handed down to Evan's two sons, Joshua and Stephen, and Robert's three daughters, Allison, Emily, and Jessica.

More than half a century has gone by since the days of the Holocaust and I still can't believe that I had come so close to death. The scars of this period and the tattoo on my forearm are deeply embedded and will never fade, but thankfully I was able to build a new life for myself and my family. Marilyn and I retired to Florida in 1986, and live in a country club community. We both love the sunshine, have discovered golf, and in spite of our aches and pains enjoy our golden years with friends and family. As a member of the speakers' panel for the Holocaust Studies Program at Florida Atlantic University, I speak to youngsters and educators alike about my experiences during this horrible period, and get satisfaction when I see that my message finds receptive ears.

Can another Holocaust ever happen? This is a question I am asked quite often, and I would like to respond, "Never!" But I am not sure. The years after the Holocaust have shown that genocide is still a menace in many parts of our world. Unwillingness to accept and tolerate others, regardless of background, is at the core of much of the world's suffering. Addressing younger people, I make it a point to speak of the need for understanding, acceptance, and tolerance. Those are the lessons that we must learn from the Holocaust if we are to make the world a better and safer place to live. Albert Einstein once said, "Genocide began with the rousing of historic hatreds by the Nazis, involved the cooperation of many people, and depended on the indifference of many more." This must never happen again.

Speaking about my experiences, I have been asked many times how I could have possibly survived for so many years. Honestly, I have no answer. I can only say that it was good fortune and being at the right place at the right time. I believe that inner strength and resolve gave me the courage to hold out for yet another day. Still, there were times when I envied those who were taken to the gas chambers for a quick end to their suffering.

Those twelve years of the Hitler regime were a chapter in man's inhumanity to man that has no equal. It was a time like no other!

Index

Index

Index